FANTASTIC SCIENCE FACTS

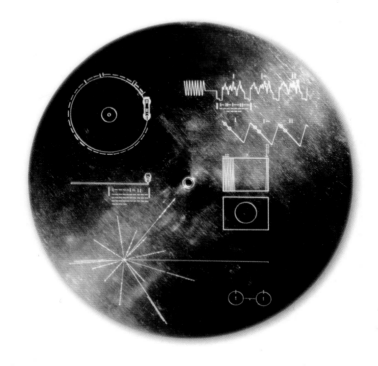

FANTASTIC SCIENCE FACTS

Miles Kelly

First published in 2017 by Miles Kelly Publishing Ltd
Harding's Barn, Bardfield End Green, Thaxted, Essex, CM6 3PX, UK

Copyright © Miles Kelly Publishing Ltd 2017

This edition printed 2019

4 6 8 10 9 7 5

Publishing Director Belinda Gallagher
Creative Director Jo Cowan
Editors Carly Blake, Fran Bromage, Rosie Neave, Sarah Parkin,
Claire Philip, Amy Johnson
Cover Designer Simon Lee
Designers Kayleigh Allen, Dave and Angela Ball at D&A,
John Christopher, Jo Cowan, Sally Lace, Andrea Slane
Image Manager Liberty Newton
Production Elizabeth Collins, Jennifer Brunwin-Jones
Reprographics Stephan Davis, Callum Ratcliffe-Bingham
Assets Lorraine King

ISBN 978-1-78617-336-2

Printed in China

British Library Cataloguing-in-Publication Data
A catalogue record for this book is available from the British Library

Made with paper from a sustainable forest

www.mileskelly.net

Contents

SCIENCE......................................12–55

GREAT SCIENTISTS...................56–89

INVENTIONS..............................90–127

SPACE 128–167

EXPLORING SPACE.................168–211

FLIGHT 212–255

SPEED...256–293

EVOLUTION 294–329

HUMAN BODY.......................... 330–371

INDEX..372

ACKNOWLEDGEMENTS..................383

SCIENCE

Why do we need science? 14

Machines big and small. 16

When science is hot! 18

Engine power 20

Science on the move 22

Noisy science 24

Look out – light's about! 26

The power of lasers. 28

Mysterious magnets 30

Electric sparks! 32

Making sounds and pictures .. 34

Compu–science............ 36

Web around the world. 38

What's it made of? 40

World of chemicals 42

Pure science 44

Small science 46

Scientists at work 48

Science in nature. 50

Body science. 52

Science in the future 54

GREAT SCIENTISTS

What is a scientist? 58

Mathematical marvels 60

Baghdad brilliance 62

Thinking again. 64

Microbes and measures 66

Motion man 68

Nature's secrets 70

It's chemistry. 72

Sparks of genius 74

Cured! 76

Dangerous rays 78

Atomic science 80

Space and time weirdness 82

Star gazers 84

Plan for life 86

Frontiers of science 88

INVENTIONS

In the beginning 92

The first inventions 94

Making fire. 96

New ways of moving 98

On the farm 100

Under attack! 102

From stone to metal 104

Boats and sails 106

Wonderful clay 108

Sailing into the unknown . . . 110

Weapons of war 112

Harvesting nature's energy . . 114

Marks on a page. 116

Making things bigger 118

Making music 120

Keeping in touch 122

Keeping a record. 124

Round the house 126

SPACE

Surrounded by space 130

Our life-giving star 132

A family of planets 134

Planet of life 136

The Earth's neighbours 138

The smallest of all 140

The biggest of all 142

So far away 144

Comets, asteroids and meteors 146

A star is born 148

Death of a star 150

Billions of galaxies 152

What is the Universe? 154

Three, two, one... lift-off! 156

Living in space 158

Home from home 160

Watching the Earth 162

Voyage to the Moon 164

Are we alone? 166

EXPLORING SPACE

To boldly go... 170

Who explores, and why? 172

Early explorers 174

Man on the Moon! 176

Plan and prepare 178

Blast-off! 180

In deep space 182

Ready to explore 184

Flyby, bye-bye 186

Into orbit 188

Landers and impactors 190

Robotic rovers 192

Close-up look 194

Exploring Mars 196

Back on Earth 198

Towards the Sun 200

Asteroids near and far 202

Comet mysteries 204

Gas giants 206

Into the future 208

Space magic and myth 210

FLIGHT

Flying machines 214

The first flights 216

Early days of flying 218

Parts of a plane 220

How planes fly 222

Powerful engines 224

Climbing, diving and turning 226

Taking off and landing 228

The flight deck 230

A passenger jet airliner 232

At the airport 234

Helicopters 236

Lighter than air 238

Taking off vertically 240

Planes for war 242

Working planes 244

Planes for fun 246

Planes at sea 248

Flying faster than sound 250

Flying in space 252

Strange planes 254

SPEED

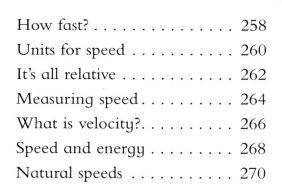

How fast? 258

Units for speed 260

It's all relative 262

Measuring speed 264

What is velocity? 266

Speed and energy 268

Natural speeds 270

Life in the fast lane 272

Breeding the best 274

Out in front 276

Designed for speed 278

Making a breakthrough 280

Modern speed machines 282

Reaching the limit 284

Speeding up, slowing down . . 286

Stop! 288

Special speeds 290

Ultimate speed 292

EVOLUTION

Life on Earth 296

Darwin's travels 298

The riddle of life 300

Classifying species 302

The struggle for survival 304

Looking for evidence 306

Fossil clues 308

Evolution through time 310

The start of life 312

Early animals 314

Moving onto land 316

Reptiles and dinosaurs 318

The first birds 320

Mammals take over 322

The human story 324

Designer evolution 326

Evolution in action 328

HUMAN BODY

Outside, inside 332

Baby body 334

The growing body 336

On the body's outside 338

Hair and nails 340

The bony body 342

The flexible body 344

When muscles pull 346

Muscle power 348

The breathing body 350

Breathing parts 352

The hungry body 354

Bite, chew, gulp 356

Food's long journey 358

Blood in the body 360

The beating body 362

Looking and listening 364

Smelling and tasting 366

The nervous body 368

The brainy body 370

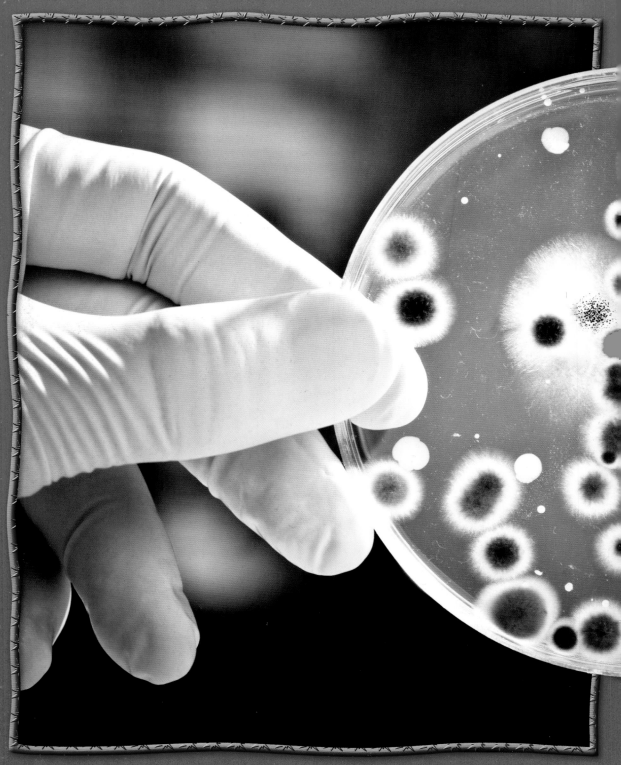

SCIENCE

- Powerful machines
- Thermal radiation
- Refraction and reflection
- Laser light
- Generating electricity
- Radio waves
- Acids and bases
- The Periodic Table
- Sub-atomic particles
- Scientific method

Why do some engines use explosions?

What does 'ultrasonic' mean?

How big is a light wave?

What is glass made from?

When is a laser good for your health?

Why do we need science?

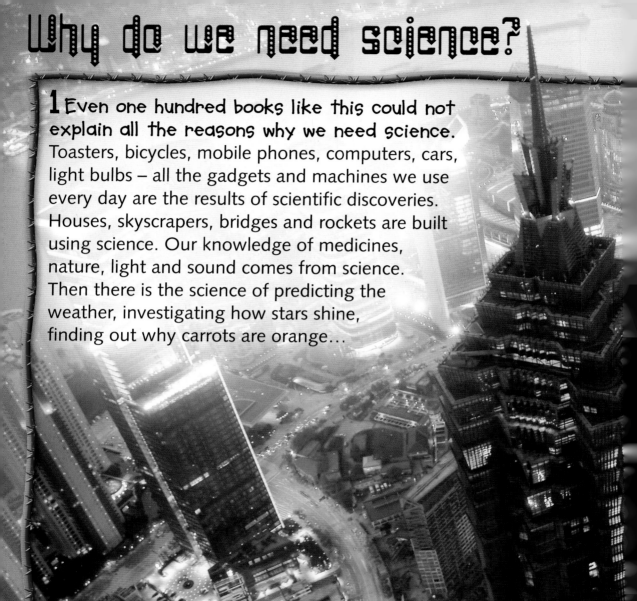

1 Even one hundred books like this could not explain all the reasons why we need science. Toasters, bicycles, mobile phones, computers, cars, light bulbs – all the gadgets and machines we use every day are the results of scientific discoveries. Houses, skyscrapers, bridges and rockets are built using science. Our knowledge of medicines, nature, light and sound comes from science. Then there is the science of predicting the weather, investigating how stars shine, finding out why carrots are orange…

▼ In a big city, science is all around you — everything from sky-scraping buildings to speedy vehicles and useful gadgets is based on science and technology.

Machines big and small

2 **Machines are everywhere!** They help us do things, or make doing them easier. Every time you play on a see-saw, you are using a machine! A lever is a stiff bar that tilts at a point called the pivot or fulcrum. The pivot of the see-saw is in the middle. Using the see-saw as a lever, a small person can lift a big person by sitting further from the pivot.

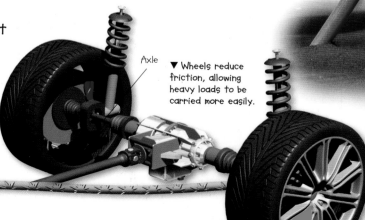

► On a see-saw lever, the pivot is in the middle. Other levers have pivots at the end.

Thread

► Turning a screw moves it along with more force than the effort used to turn it.

3 **The screw is another simple but useful scientific machine.** It is a ridge, or thread, wrapped around a bar or pole. It changes a small turning motion into a powerful pulling or lifting movement. Wood screws hold together furniture or shelves. A car jack lets you lift up a whole car.

4 **Where would you be without wheels?** Not going very far. The wheel is a simple machine, a circular disc that turns around its centre on a bar called an axle. Wheels carry heavy weights easily. There are giant wheels on big trucks and trains and small wheels on rollerblades.

Axle

▼ Wheels reduce friction, allowing heavy loads to be carried more easily.

▼ Two pulleys together reduce the force needed to lift a heavy girder by one half.

Reversing gears

Sliding rack

Pinion gear

Bevel gears

Slow pinion gear

Screw-shaped worm gear

5 A pulley turns around, like a wheel. It has a groove around its edge for a cable or rope. Lots of pulleys allow us to lift very heavy weights easily. The pulleys on a tower crane can lift huge steel girders to the top of a skyscraper.

▲ Bicycle gears mean you can pedal at the same speed, with the same force, when climbing up a hill or speeding down it.

Pivot

Lever

▲ Gears change the turning direction of a force. They can slow it down or speed it up – and even convert it into a sliding force (rack and pinion).

I DON'T BELIEVE IT!

A ramp is a simple machine called an inclined plane. It is easier to walk up a ramp than to jump straight to the top.

6 Gears are like wheels, with pointed teeth around the edges. They change a fast, weak turning force into a slow, powerful one – or the other way around. On a bicycle, you can pedal up the steepest hill in bottom (lowest) gear, then speed down the other side in top (highest) gear.

When science is hot!

7 Fire! Flames! Burning! Heat! The science of heat is important in all kinds of ways. Not only do we cook with heat, but we also warm our homes and heat water. Burning happens in all kinds of engines in cars, trucks, planes and rockets. It is also used in factory processes, from making steel to shaping plastics.

▲ A firework burns suddenly as an explosive, producing heat, light and sound. The 'bang' is the sound made by the paper wrapper as it is blown apart.

Heat from the drink is conducted up the metal spoon

8 **Heat can move by conduction.** A hot object will pass on, or transfer, some of its heat to a cooler one. Dip a metal spoon in a hot drink and the spoon handle soon warms up. Heat is conducted from the drink, through the metal.

9 **Heat moves by invisible 'heat rays'.** This is called thermal radiation and the rays are infrared waves. Our planet is warmed by the Sun because heat from the Sun radiates through space as infrared waves.

TRUE OR FALSE?

1. Burning happens inside the engine of a plane.
2. A device for measuring temperature is called a calendar.
3. Heat rays are known as infrablue waves.

Answers:
1. True 2. False 3. False

◄ Metal is a good conductor of heat. Put a teaspoon in a hot drink and feel how quickly it heats up.

10 Burning, also called combustion, is a chemical process. Oxygen gas from the air joins to, or combines with, the substance being burned. The chemical change releases lots of heat, and usually light too. If this happens really fast, we call it an explosion.

▲ A burner flame makes glass so hot it becomes soft and bendy, so it can be stretched, shaped and even blown up like a balloon.

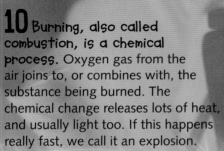

11 Temperature is a measure of how hot or cold something is. It is usually measured in degrees Celsius (°C) or Fahrenheit (°F). Water freezes at 0°C (32°F), and boils at 100°C (212°F). We use thermometers to take our temperatures. Your body temperature is about 37°C (98.6°F).

▶ This thermometer contains alcohol coloured by a red dye. As it warms, the alcohol expands (takes up more space). It moves up the thin tube, showing the temperature on the scale.

12 Heat moves through liquids and gases by convection. Some of the liquid or gas takes in heat, gets lighter, and rises into cooler areas. Then other cooler liquid or gas moves in to do the same and the process repeats. You can see this as 'wavy' hot air rising from a flame.

▶ Hot air shimmering over a candle is a visible sign of the heat being convected away.

Engine power

13 **Imagine having to walk or run everywhere, instead of riding in a car.** Engines are machines that use fuel to do work for us and make life easier. Fuel is a substance that has chemical energy stored inside it. The energy is released as heat by burning or exploding the fuel in the engine.

▼ A jet engine has sets of angled blades, called turbines, that spin on shafts.

Turbines squash incoming air

Jet fuel is sprayed into the air inside the chamber, creating a small explosion

Burning gases spin exhaust turbines

14 **Most cars have petrol engines.** An air and petrol mixture is pushed into a hollow chamber called a cylinder. A spark from a spark plug makes it explode, which pushes a piston down inside the cylinder. This movement is used by gears to turn the wheels. Most cars have four or six cylinders.

15 **A diesel engine doesn't use sparks.** The mixture of air and diesel is squashed in the cylinder, becoming so hot it explodes. Diesel engines are used in machines such as tractors that need lots of power.

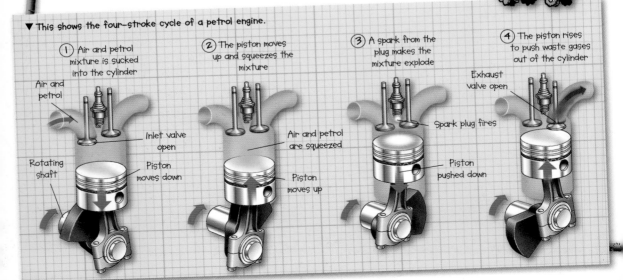

▼ This shows the four-stroke cycle of a petrol engine.

① Air and petrol mixture is sucked into the cylinder

Air and petrol

Inlet valve open

Rotating shaft

Piston moves down

② The piston moves up and squeezes the mixture

Air and petrol are squeezed

Piston moves up

③ A spark from the plug makes the mixture explode

Spark plug fires

Piston pushed down

④ The piston rises to push waste gases out of the cylinder

Exhaust valve open

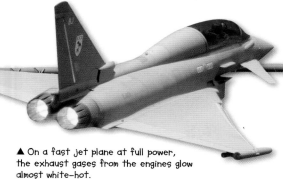

▲ On a fast jet plane at full power, the exhaust gases from the engines glow almost white-hot.

16 A jet engine mixes air and kerosene and sets fire to it in one long, continuous, roaring explosion. Incredibly hot gases blast out of the back of the engine. These push the engine forward – along with the plane.

17 An electric motor passes electricity through coils of wire. This makes the coils magnetic, and they push or pull against magnets around them. The push-pull makes the coils spin on their shaft (axle).

18 Engines that burn fuel give out gases and particles through their exhausts. Some of these gases are harmful to the environment. The less we use engines, the better. Electric motors are quiet, efficient and reliable, but they still need fuel – to make the electricity at the power station.

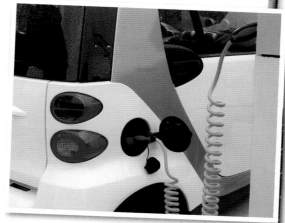

▲ Electric cars have sets of batteries to turn the motor. The batteries are 'filled' with electrical energy by plugging into a recharging point.

▼ Using magnetic forces, an electric motor turns electrical energy into moving or kinetic energy.

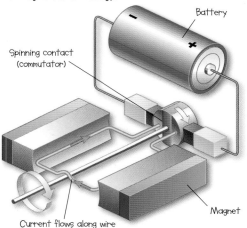

Battery

Spinning contact (commutator)

Magnet

Current flows along wire

QUIZ

1. Are exhaust gases good for the environment?

2. Does a diesel engine use sparks?

3. How many cylinders do most cars have?

4. Do electric cars have batteries?

Answers:
1. No, some of them are harmful
2. No 3. Four or six 4. Yes

21

Science on the move

19 Without science, you would have to walk everywhere, or ride a horse. Luckily, scientists and engineers have developed many methods of transport, most importantly, the car. Lots of people can travel together in a bus, train, plane or ship. These use less energy and resources, and make less pollution than cars.

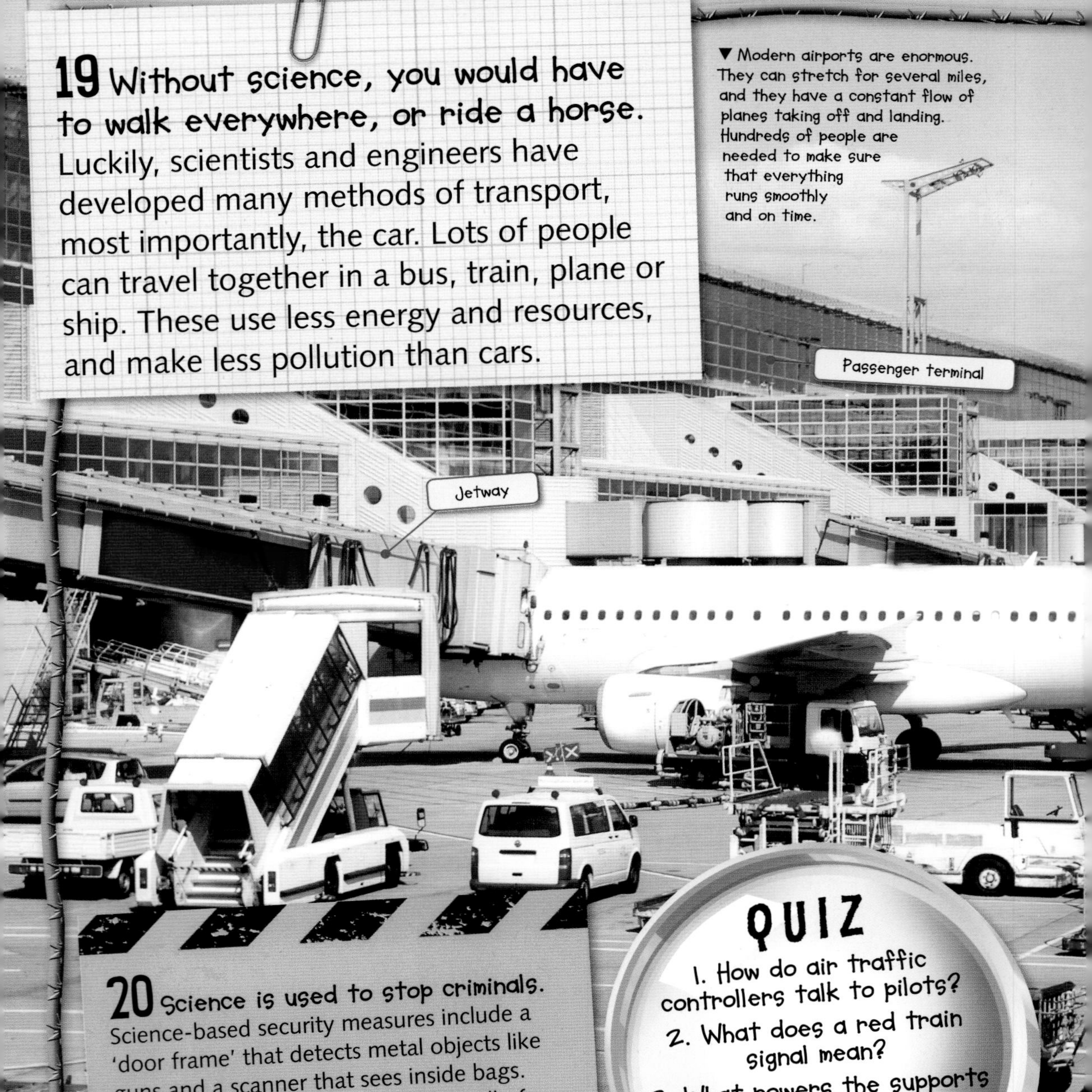

▼ Modern airports are enormous. They can stretch for several miles, and they have a constant flow of planes taking off and landing. Hundreds of people are needed to make sure that everything runs smoothly and on time.

Passenger terminal

Jetway

20 Science is used to stop criminals. Science-based security measures include a 'door frame' that detects metal objects like guns and a scanner that sees inside bags. A sniffer-machine can detect the smell of explosives or illegal drugs.

QUIZ

1. How do air traffic controllers talk to pilots?
2. What does a red train signal mean?
3. What powers the supports that move jetways?

Answers:
1. By radio 2. Stop
3. Electric motors

22

22 Every method of transport needs to be safe and on time. In the airport control tower, air traffic controllers track planes on radar screens. They talk to pilots by radio. Beacons send out radio signals, giving the direction and distance to the airport.

21 Jetways are extending walkways that stretch out from the passenger terminal right to the planes' doors. Their supports move along on wheeled trolleys driven by electric motors.

▶ The radar screen shows each aircraft as a blip, with its flight number or identity code.

23 On the road, drivers obey traffic lights. On a railway network, train drivers obey similar signal lights of different colours, such as red for stop. Sensors by the track record each train passing and send the information by wires or radio to the control room. Each train's position is shown as a flashing light on a wall map.

▼ Train signals show just two colours – red for stop and green for go.

▶ Trackside switches and detectors react to a train going past and automatically change the signals, so that a following train does not get too close.

Noisy science

24 Listening to the radio or television, playing music, shouting at each other — they all depend on the science of sound — acoustics. Sounds are carried by invisible waves in the air. The waves are areas of low pressure, where air particles are stretched farther apart, alternating with areas of high pressure, where they are squashed closer together.

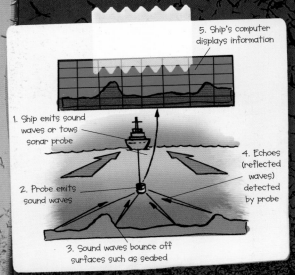

5. Ship's computer displays information

1. Ship emits sound waves or tows sonar probe

2. Probe emits sound waves

3. Sound waves bounce off surfaces such as seabed

4. Echoes (reflected waves) detected by probe

25 Scientists measure the loudness or intensity of sound in decibels, dB. A very quiet sound like a ticking watch is 10 dB. Ordinary speech is 50–60 dB. Loud music is 90 dB. A jet plane taking off is 120 dB. Too much noise damages the ears.

◀ In sonar (echo–sounding), sound waves in the water bounce or reflect off objects, and are detected.

Atomic explosion

26 Whether a sound is high or low is called its pitch, or frequency. It is measured in Hertz, Hz. A singing bird or whining motorcycle has a high pitch. A rumble of thunder or a massive truck has a low pitch. People can hear frequencies from 20 to 20,000 Hz.

Jet plane

Whisper

Express train

▶ The decibel scale measures the intensity, or energy, in sound.

| 0 dB | 40 dB | 80 dB | 120 dB | 180 dB |

27 Sound waves spread out from a vibrating object that is moving rapidly to and fro. Stretch an elastic band between your fingers and twang it. As it vibrates, it makes a sound. When you speak, vocal cords in your neck vibrate. You can feel them through your skin.

28 Sound waves travel about 330 metres every second. This is fast, but it is one million times slower than light waves. Sound waves also bounce off hard, flat surfaces. This is called reflection. The returning waves are heard as an echo.

29 Loudspeakers change electrical signals into sounds. The signals in the wire pass through a wire coil inside the speaker. This turns the coil into a magnet, which pushes and pulls against another magnet. The pushing and pulling make the cone vibrate, which sends sound waves into the air.

◀ The word 'sonic' means making sounds, and the high-pitched noises of bats can be described as 'ultrasonic' – too high for us to hear.

Echoes bouncing back off the moth

Sound waves from the bat

▲ Bats make high-pitched sounds. If the sounds hit an insect they bounce back to the bat's ears. The reflected sound (echo) gives the bat information about the size and location of the insect.

BOX GUITAR

You will need:
shoebox   elastic band
split pins   card

Cut a hole about 10 centimetres across on one side of an empty shoebox. Push split pins through either side of the hole, and stretch an elastic band between them. Pluck the band. Hear how the air and box vibrate. Cover the hole with card. Is the 'guitar' as loud?

Look out — light's about!

30 Almost everything you do depends on light and the science of light, which is called optics. Light is a form of energy that you can see. Light waves are made of electricity and magnetism – and they are tiny. About 2000 of them laid end to end would stretch across this full stop.

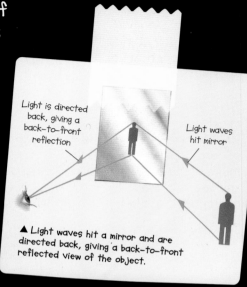

Light is directed back, giving a back-to-front reflection

Light waves hit mirror

▲ Light waves hit a mirror and are directed back, giving a back-to-front reflected view of the object.

▲ A prism of clear glass or clear plastic separates the colours in white light.

32 Like sound, light bounces off surfaces that are very smooth. This is called reflection. A mirror is smooth, hard and flat. When you look at it, you see your reflection.

31 Ordinary light from the Sun or from a light bulb is called white light. But when white light passes through a prism, a triangular block of clear glass, it splits into many colours. These colours are known as the spectrum. Each colour has a different length of wave. A rainbow is made by raindrops, which work like millions of tiny prisms to split up sunlight.

33 Light passes through certain materials, like clear glass and plastic. Materials that let light pass through, to give a clear view, are transparent. Those that do not allow light through, like wood and metal, are opaque.

34 Mirrors and lenses are important parts of many optical (light-using) gadgets. They are found in cameras, binoculars, microscopes, telescopes and lasers. Without them, we would have no close-up photographs of tiny microchips or insects or giant planets – in fact, no photos at all.

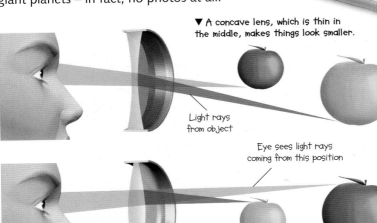

▼ A concave lens, which is thin in the middle, makes things look smaller.

Light rays from object

Eye sees light rays coming from this position

▲ A convex lens, which bulges in the middle, makes things look larger.

35 Light does not usually go straight through glass. It bends slightly where it goes into the glass, then bends back as it comes out. This is called refraction. A lens is a curved piece of glass or plastic that bends light to make things look bigger, smaller or clearer. Spectacle and contact lenses bend light to help people see more clearly.

▲ Glass and water bend, or refract, light waves. This makes a drinking straw look bent where it goes behind the glass and then into the water.

The power of lasers

36 Laser light is a special kind of light. Like ordinary light, it is made of waves, but it has three main differences. Ordinary white light is a mixture of colours, while laser light is one pure colour. Ordinary light waves have peaks (highs) and troughs (lows), which do not line up – laser light waves line up perfectly. Lastly, ordinary light spreads and fades. A laser beam can travel for thousands of kilometres as a strong, straight beam.

◄ The narrow horizontal beam from a laser spirit level can shine all the way across a building site.

▼ Waves of light build up and bounce to and fro inside a laser, then emerge at one end.

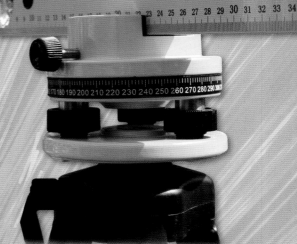

Silver mirror

Part-silver mirror

Particles in ruby crystal

Laser beam emerges

37 To make a laser beam, energy is fed in short bursts into a substance called the active medium. The energy might be electricity, heat or ordinary light. In a red ruby laser, the active medium is a rod of ruby crystal. A strong lamp makes the particles in the crystal vibrate. The energy they give off bounces to and fro inside the crystal. Eventually, the rays vibrate with each other and they are all the same length. The energy becomes so strong that it bursts through a mirror at one end of the crystal.

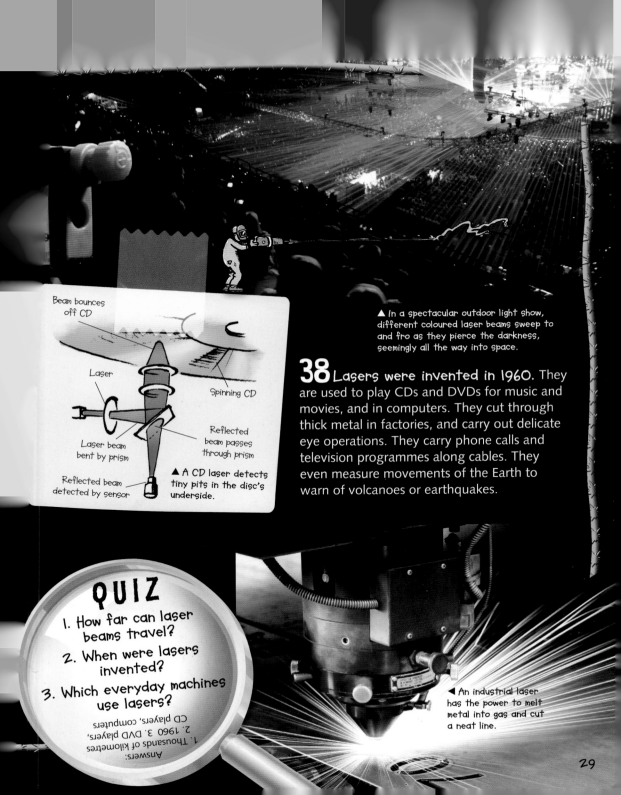

▲ In a spectacular outdoor light show, different coloured laser beams sweep to and fro as they pierce the darkness, seemingly all the way into space.

Beam bounces off CD

Laser

Spinning CD

Laser beam bent by prism

Reflected beam passes through prism

Reflected beam detected by sensor

▲ A CD laser detects tiny pits in the disc's underside.

38 **Lasers were invented in 1960.** They are used to play CDs and DVDs for music and movies, and in computers. They cut through thick metal in factories, and carry out delicate eye operations. They carry phone calls and television programmes along cables. They even measure movements of the Earth to warn of volcanoes or earthquakes.

QUIZ

1. How far can laser beams travel?
2. When were lasers invented?
3. Which everyday machines use lasers?

Answers:
1. Thousands of kilometres 2. 1960 3. DVD players, CD players, computers

◄ An industrial laser has the power to melt metal into gas and cut a neat line.

29

Mysterious magnets

39 Without magnets there would be no electric motors, computers or loudspeakers. Magnetism is an invisible force to do with atoms – tiny particles that make up everything. Atoms are made of even smaller particles, including electrons. Magnetism is linked to the way that these line up and move. Most magnetic substances contain iron. As iron makes up a big part of the metallic substance steel, steel is also magnetic.

▶ For metal recycling, an electromagnet lifts out only iron–containing or ferrous metals, such as steel.

40 A magnet is a lump of iron or steel that has all its electrons and atoms lined up. This means that their magnetic forces all add up. The force surrounds the magnet, in a region called the magnetic field. This is strongest at the two parts of the magnet called the poles.

▲ Maglev (magnetic levitation) trains use pushing or repelling magnetic forces to 'float' above their track.

41 A magnet has two different poles — north and south. A north pole repels (pushes away) the north pole of another magnet. Two south poles also repel each other. But a north pole and a south pole attract (pull together). Both magnetic poles attract any substance containing iron, like a nail or a screw.

42 When electricity flows through a wire, it makes a weak magnetic field around it. If the wire is wrapped into a coil, the magnetism becomes stronger. This is called an electromagnet. Its magnetic force is the same as an ordinary magnet, but when the electricity goes off, the magnetism does too. Some electromagnets are so strong, they can lift whole cars.

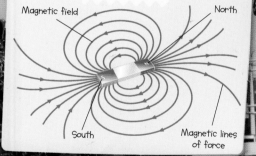

▼ The field around a magnet affects objects that contain iron.

Magnetic field

North

South

Magnetic lines of force

QUIZ

Which of these substances or objects is magnetic?
1. Steel spoon 2. Plastic spoon
3. Pencil 4. Drinks can
5. Food can 6. Screwdriver
7. Cooking foil

Answers:
1. Yes 2. No 3. No 4. No 5. Yes 6. Yes 7. No

Electric sparks!

43 **Flick a switch and things happen.** The television goes off, the computer comes on, lights shine and music plays. Electricity is our favourite form of energy. We send it along wires and plug hundreds of machines into it.

▼ When an electric current flows, the electrons (small blue balls) all move the same way, jumping from one atom to the next. (The red balls are the centres or nuclei of the atoms.)

44 **Electricity depends on electrons.** In certain substances, when electrons are 'pushed', they hop from one atom to the next. When billions do this every second, electricity flows. The 'push' is from a battery or a generator. Electricity only flows in a complete loop or circuit. Break the circuit and the flow stops.

Atom

Electron

▼ Solar panels contain many hundreds of fingernail-sized PV (photovoltaic) cells. These convert light energy ('photo') to electrical energy ('voltaic').

▼ A battery has a chemical paste inside its metal casing.

Positive contact

Negative contact on base

45 **A battery makes electricity from chemicals.** Two different chemicals next to each other, such as an acid and a metal, swap electrons and get the flow going. Electricity's pushing strength is measured in volts. Most batteries are about 1.5, 3, 6 or 9 volts, with 12 volts in cars.

46 **Electricity flows easily through some substances, including water and metals.** These are electrical conductors. Other substances do not allow electricity to flow. They are insulators. Insulators include wood, plastic, glass, card and ceramics. Metal wires and cables have coverings of plastic, to stop the electricity leaking away.

47 Electricity from power stations is carried along cables on high pylons, or buried underground. This is known as the distribution grid. At thousands of volts, this electricity is extremely dangerous. For use in the home, it is changed to 220 volts (in the UK).

▼ Electricity generators are housed in huge casings, some bigger than trucks.

Pylon holds cables off the ground

◄ To check and repair high-voltage cables, the electricity must be turned off well in advance.

MAKE A CIRCUIT

You will need:
lightbulb battery wire
plastic ruler metal spoon dry card

Join a bulb to a battery with pieces of wire, as shown. Electricity flows round the circuit and lights the bulb. Make a gap in the circuit and put various objects into it, to see if they allow electricity to flow again. Try a plastic ruler, a metal spoon and some dry card.

48 Mains electricity is made at a power station. A fuel such as coal or oil is burned to heat water into high-pressure steam. The steam pushes past the blades of a turbine and makes them spin. The turbines turn generators, which have wire coils near powerful magnets, and the spinning motion makes electricity flow in the coils.

Making sounds and pictures

49 The air is full of waves we cannot see or hear, unless we have the right machine. Radio waves are a form of electrical and magnetic energy, just like heat and light waves, microwaves and X-rays. All of these are called electromagnetic waves and they travel at an equal speed – the speed of light.

Satellite

Radio waves

51 Radio waves carry their information by being altered, or modulated, in a certain pattern. The height of a wave is called its amplitude. If this is altered, it is known as AM (amplitude modulation). Look for AM on the radio display.

50 Radio waves are used for both radio and television. They travel vast distances. Long waves curve around the Earth's surface. Short waves bounce between the Earth and the sky.

Aerial

52 The number of waves per second is called the frequency. If this is altered, it is known as FM (frequency modulation). FM radio is clearer than AM, and less affected by weather and thunderstorms.

▼ This range of waves, with different wavelengths, are electrical and magnetic energy. They are called the electromagnetic spectrum.

▲ A radio set picks up radio waves using its aerial or antenna.

Long radio waves

Shorter radio waves (TV)

Microwaves

Infrared waves

Light waves (visible light)

Ultraviolet rays

X-rays

Short X-rays

Gamma rays

53 Radio waves are sent out, or transmitted, from antennae on tall masts or on satellites, to reach a very wide area. A radio receiver converts the pattern of waves to sounds. A television receiver or TV set changes them to pictures and sounds.

I DON'T BELIEVE IT!

You could send and receive radio signals on the Moon, but not in the sea. Radio waves travel easily through space, but only a few metres in water.

▼ A dish-shaped receiver picks up radio waves for TV channels.

54 Digital radio uses incredibly short bursts of radio waves with gaps between them – many thousands each second. Each burst represents the digit (number) 1, and a gap is 0. The order of the 1s and 0s carries information in the form of binary code, as in a computer.

▶ A plasma screen has thousands of tiny boxes, or cells, of three colours – red, green and blue. Electric pulses heat the gas inside for a split second into plasma, which gives out a burst of light. Combinations of these colours gives all the other colours.

▼ Flat-screen TVs can be LCD or plasma. They use less electricity than cathode-ray TVs and produce a better picture.

KEY
① Glowing 'on' cell
② Dark 'off' cell
③ Rear grid of electrical contacts
④ – ⑥ Coloured phosphors inside cells
⑦ Backing plate
⑧ Front grid of electrical contacts
⑨ Transparent front cover

Compu-science

55 **Computers are amazing machines, but they have to be told exactly what to do.** So we put in instructions and information, by various means. These include typing on a keyboard, inserting a disc or memory stick, downloading from the Internet, using a joystick or games controller, or linking up a camera, scanner or another computer.

Flat screen monitor

56 **Most computers are controlled by instructions from a keyboard and a mouse.** The mouse moves a pointer around on the screen and its click buttons select choices from lists called menus.

Silicon 'wafer'

Plastic casing

USB (Universal Serial Bus) sockets

◀ This close up of a slice of silicon 'wafer' shows the tiny parts that receive and send information in a computer.

External monitor (screen) socket

Headphone socket

Wire 'feet' link to other part in the computer

58 **The 'main brain' of a computer is its Central Processing Unit.** It is usually a microchip – millions of electronic parts on a chip of silicon, hardly larger than a fingernail. It receives information and instructions from other microchips, carries out the work, and sends back the results.

57 **Some computers are controlled by talking to them!** They pick up the sounds using a microphone. This is speech recognition technology.

QUIZ

You may have heard of these sets of letters. Do you know what they mean? Their full written-out versions are all here on these two pages.

1. RAM 2. ROM
3. CPU

Answers:
1. Random Access Memory
2. Read Only Memory
3. Central Processing Unit

▲ Launched in 2010, the Apple iPad began a new trend in computerized devices called 'tablets'.

▼ The keys on a keyboard have bendy metal contacts that come together when pressed, allowing electricity to flow.

Top flexible layer

Finger presses down on keypad

Conductive strips (red) not touching – circuit is open (incomplete)

Conductive strips make contact and complete circuit

CD or DVD drive reader

Mouse pad

Keyboard

▲ As well as desktop computers, there are also laptops with a fold-up LCD (liquid crystal display) screen. Touching the mouse pad with a finger controls the cursor or insert point on the screen.

59 Information and instructions are contained in the computer in memory microchips. There are two kinds. Random Access Memory is like a jotting pad. It keeps changing as the computer carries out its tasks. Read Only Memory is like an instruction book. It usually contains the instructions for how the computer starts up and how all the microchips work together.

60 A computer usually displays its progress on a monitor screen. It feeds information to output devices such as printers, loudspeakers and robot arms. Information can be stored on CDs, DVDs, memory sticks (chips), external HDs (hard drive discs), or uploaded to the Internet.

Web around the world

61 The world is at your fingertips — if you are on the Internet. The Internet is one of the most amazing results of science. It is a worldwide network of computers, linked like one huge electrical spider's web.

62 Signals travel between computers in many ways. These include electricity along telephone wires, flashes of laser light along fibre-optic cables or radio waves between tall towers. Information is changed from one form to another in a split second. It can also travel between computers on different sides of the world in less than a second using satellite links.

First 'private' Internet, ARPANET, for the US military

Joint Academic Network (JANET) connects UK universities via their own Internet

Yahoo! Launches as a 'Guide to the World Wide Web' – what we now call a browser or search engine

Animation starts to become common on websites

1969   **1984**   **1994**   **1996**

1961   **1972**   **1989**   **1995**

First ideas for 'packet switching', the basic way the Internet parcels up and sends information in small blocks or packets

First emails, mostly on ARPANET

The birth of the Internet as we know it today, when Tim Berners-Lee and the team at CERN invent the World Wide Web to make information easier to publish and access

eBay and Amazon booksellers begin, and online trade starts to rise

63 The World Wide Web is public information that anyone can find on the Internet, available for everyone to see. However, sometimes you have to pay or join a club to get to certain parts of it. A website is a collection of related information, usually made up of text, videos and pictures. There might be hundreds of web pages within each website. Email is the system for sending private messages from one person to another.

I DON'T BELIEVE IT!

The World Wide Web is the best known and most widely used part of the Internet system. It has billions of pages of information.

▼ Many mobile phones can be used to access the Internet, allowing users to browse web pages, send emails and watch videos.

Facebook has fewer new users signing up — is the slower growth temporary, or the beginning of the end for online social networking?

Half of households in the UK have Internet connections

YouTube is launched, allowing video sharing

The first iPhones bring mobile Internet use for almost anyone

2003 **2005** **2007** **2011**

1998 **2004** **2006** **2010**

Google is launched as a rival to Yahoo!

Facebook is launched, starting the trend for social networking over the Internet

Twitter is launched for posting and sharing text messages, but has a slow start

HD (High Definition) Internet video links become more practical

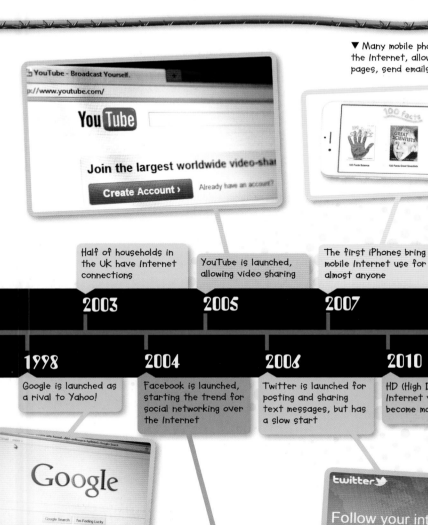

▲ The Web and the Internet interact with other technologies. Twitter is an online public version of text-only messages called 'tweets' developed from mobile phone 'texting' (SMS, Short Message Service).

What's it made of?

64 You wouldn't make a bridge out of straw, or a cup out of bubblewrap! Choosing the right substance for the job is important. All the substances in the world can be divided into several groups. For example, metals such as iron, silver and gold are strong, hard and shiny, and conduct heat and electricity well. They are used to make things that have to be strong and long-lasting.

65 Plastics are made mainly from the substances in petroleum (crude oil). There are so many kinds – some are hard and brittle while others are soft and bendy. They are usually long-lasting, not affected by weather or damp, and they resist heat and electricity.

KEY

① The front wing is a special shape – this produces a force that presses the car down onto the track

② The main body of the car is made from carbon fibre, a light but very strong material

③ The car's axles are made from titanium – a very strong, light metal

④ The engine is made from various alloys, or mixtures of metals, based on aluminium. It produces up to ten times the power of a family car engine

⑤ Each tyre is made of thick, tough rubber to withstand high speeds

⑥ The rear wing is also carbon fibre composite

▼ A racing car has thousands of parts made from hundreds of materials. Each is suited to certain conditions such as stress, temperature and vibrations.

Metal

Fibre

Ceramic

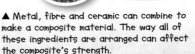

66 Ceramics are materials based on clay or other substances dug from the Earth. They can be shaped and dried, like a clay bowl. Or they can be fired – baked in a hot oven called a kiln. This makes them hard and long-lasting, but brittle and prone to cracks. Ceramics resist heat and electricity very well.

▲ Metal, fibre and ceramic can combine to make a composite material. The way all of these ingredients are arranged can affect the composite's strength.

◄ In 2007, the Interstate 35W bridge collapsed in Minneapolis, USA, killing 13 people. It was due to cracking of small steel connecting plates that were too thin for the weight.

67 Glass is produced from the raw substances limestone and sand. When heated at a high temperature, these substances become a clear, gooey liquid, which sets hard as it cools. Its great advantage is that you can see through it.

68 Composites are mixtures or combinations of different materials. For example, glass strands are coated with plastic to make GRP – glass-reinforced plastic. This composite has the advantages of both materials.

MAKE YOUR OWN COMPOSITE

You will need:
flour   newspaper strips
water   balloon   pin

You can make a composite called pâpier maché from flour, newspaper and water. Tear newspaper into strips. Mix flour and water into a paste. Dip each strip in the paste and place it around a blown-up balloon. Cover the balloon and allow it to dry. Pop the balloon with a pin, and the composite should stay in shape.

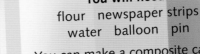

World of chemicals

69 The world is made of chemical substances. Some are completely pure. Others are mixtures of substances – such as petroleum (crude oil). Petroleum provides us with thousands of different chemicals and materials, such as plastics, paints, soaps and fuels. It is one of the most useful, and valuable, substances in the world.

The fumes cool as they rise up the tower, causing them to condense

Fuel gases for burning

Petrol and vehicle fuels

Kerosene and medium fuels (jet fuel)

Heavy oils for lubrication

Furnace

Waxes, tars, bitumens, asphalts

▼ The biggest offshore oil platforms are more than 150 metres tall above the ocean surface. They drill boreholes into the seabed and pump up the crude oil, or petroleum.

Crude oil is super-heated and some parts turn into fumes

▲ The huge tower (fractionating column) of an oil refinery may be 100 metres high.

70 In an oil refinery, crude oil is heated in a huge tower. Some of its different substances turn into fumes and rise up the tower. The fumes condense (turn back into liquids) at different heights inside, due to the different temperatures at each level. Thick, gooey tars, asphalts and bitumens – used to make road surfaces – remain at the bottom.

71 One group of chemicals is called acids. They vary in strength from very weak citric acid, which gives the sharp taste to fruits such as lemons, to extremely strong and dangerous sulphuric acid in a car battery. Powerful acids burn and corrode, or eat away, substances. Some even corrode glass or steel.

72 Another group of chemicals is bases. They vary in strength from weak alkaloids, which give the bitter taste to coffee beans, to strong and dangerous bases in drain cleaners and industrial polishes. Bases feel soapy or slimy and, like acids, they can burn or corrode.

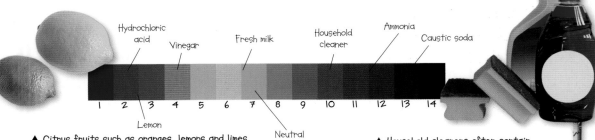

Hydrochloric acid   Vinegar   Fresh milk   Household cleaner   Ammonia   Caustic soda

1 2 3 4 5 6 7 8 9 10 11 12 13 14

Lemon   Neutral

▲ Citrus fruits such as oranges, lemons and limes have a tart taste because they contain a mild acid, called citric acid. It has a pH of 3.

▲ Household cleaners often contain alkalis to help them break down grease and fat. Some cleaners have a pH of 10.

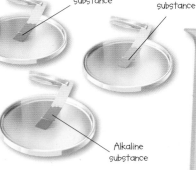

Acidic substance   Neutral substance

▶ Indicator paper changes colour when it touches different substances. Acids turn it red, alkalis make it bluish-purple. The deeper the colour, the stronger the acid or base.

Alkaline substance

FROTHY FUN

You will need:
vinegar   washing soda

Create a chemical reaction by adding a few drops of vinegar to a spoonful of washing soda in a saucer. The vinegar is an acid, the soda is a base. The two react by frothing and giving off bubbles of carbon dioxide gas. What is left is a salt (but not to be eaten).

73 Acids and bases are 'opposite' types of chemicals. When they meet, they undergo changes called a chemical reaction. The result is usually a third type of chemical, called a salt. The common salt we use for cooking is one example. Its chemical name is sodium chloride.

74 The world seems to be made of millions of different substances — such as soil, wood, concrete, plastics and air. These are combinations of simpler substances. If you could take them apart, you would see that they are made of pure substances called elements.

1											
1 H Hydrogen	**2**										
3 Li Lithium	**4** Be Beryllium										
11 Na Sodium	**12** Mg Magnesium	**3**	**4**	**5**	**6**	**7**	**8**	**9**	**10**	**11**	**12**
19 K Potassium	**20** Ca Calcium	**21** Sc Scandium	**22** Ti Titanium	**23** V Vanadium	**24** Cr Chromium	**25** Mn Manganese	**26** Fe Iron	**27** Co Colbalt	**28** Ni Nickel	**29** Cu Copper	**30** Zn Zinc
37 Rb Rubidium	**38** Sr Strontium	**39** Y Yttrium	**40** Zr Zirconium	**41** Nb Niobium	**42** Mo Molybdenum	**43** Tc Technetium	**44** Ru Ruthenium	**45** Rh Rhodium	**46** Pd Palladium	**47** Ag Silver	**48** Cd Cadmium
55 Cs Caesium	**56** Ba Barium	Elements 57–71	**72** Hf Hafnium	**73** Ta Tantalum	**74** W Tungsten	**75** Re Rhenium	**76** Os Osmium	**77** Ir Iridium	**78** Pt Platinum	**79** Au Gold	**80** Hg Mercury
87 Fr Francium	**88** Ra Radium	Elements 89–103	**104** Rf Rutherfordium	**105** Db Dubnium	**106** Sg Seaborgium	**107** Bh Bohrium	**108** HS Hassium	**109** Mt Meitnerium	**110** Ds Darmstadtium	**111** Rg Roentgenium	**112** Uub Ununbium

Atomic number / Chemical symbol

20 Ca Calcium — Name

57 La Lanthanum	**58** Ce Cerium	**59** Pr Praseodymium	**60** Nd Neodymium	**61** Pm Promethium	**62** Sm Samarium	**63** Eu Europium	**64** Gd Gadolinium	**65** Tb Terbium
89 Ac Actinium	**90** Th Thorium	**91** Pa Protactinium	**92** U Uranium	**93** Np Neptunium	**94** Pu Plutonium	**95** Am Americium	**96** Cm Curium	**97** Bk Berkelium

▶ Stars are made mainly of burning hydrogen, which is why they are so hot and bright.

▲ The Periodic Table is a chart of all the elements. In each row the atoms get heavier from left to right. Each column (up–down) contains elements with similar chemical features. Every element has a chemical symbol, name, and atomic number, which is the number of particles called protons in its central part, or nucleus.

75 Hydrogen is the simplest element and it is the first in the Periodic Table. This means it has the smallest atoms. It is a very light gas, which floats upwards in air. Hydrogen was used to fill giant airships. But there was a problem — hydrogen catches fire easily and explodes.

76 About 90 elements are found naturally on and in the Earth. In an element, all of its particles, called atoms, are exactly the same as each other. Just as important, they are all different from the atoms of any other element.

Element types

- ■ Alkali metals
- ■ Alkaline metals
- ■ Transition metals
- ■ Other metals
- ■ Other non-metals
- ■ Halogens
- ■ Inert gases
- ■ Lanthanides
- ■ Actinides
- ■ Trans-actinides

Note: Elements 113–118 are synthetic elements that have only been created briefly, so their properties cannot be known for certain.

					18
					2 **He** Helium
13	14	15	16	17	
5 **B** Boron	6 **C** Carbon	7 **N** Nitrogen	8 **O** Oxygen	9 **F** Fluorine	10 **Ne** Neon
13 **Al** Aluminium	14 **Si** Silicon	15 **P** Phosphorus	16 **S** Sulphur	17 **Cl** Chlorine	18 **Ar** Argon
31 **Ga** Gallium	32 **Ge** Germanium	33 **As** Arsenic	34 **Se** Selenium	35 **Br** Bromine	36 **Kr** Krypton
49 **In** Indium	50 **Sn** Tin	51 **Sb** Antimony	52 **Te** Tellurium	53 **I** Iodine	54 **Xe** Xenon
81 **Ti** Thallium	82 **Pb** Lead	83 **Bi** Bismuth	84 **Po** Polonium	85 **At** Astatine	86 **Rn** Radon
113 **Nh** Nihonium	114 **Fl** Flerovium	115 **Mc** Moscovium	116 **Lv** Livermorium	117 **Ts** Tennessine	118 **Og** Oganesson

66 **Dy** Dysprosium	67 **Ho** Holmium	68 **Er** Erbium	69 **Tm** Thulium	70 **Yb** Ytterbium	71 **Lu** Lutetium
98 **Cf** Californium	99 **Es** Einsteinium	100 **Fm** Fermium	101 **Md** Mendelevium	102 **No** Nobelium	103 **Lr** Lawrencium

78 Uranium is a heavy and dangerous element. It gives off harmful rays and tiny particles. This process is called radioactivity and it can cause sickness, burns and diseases such as cancer. Radioactivity is a form of energy and, under careful control, radioactive elements are used as fuel in nuclear power stations.

▶ Aluminium is a strong but light metal that is ideal for forming the body of vehicles such as planes.

77 Carbon is a very important element in living things — including our own bodies. It joins easily with atoms of other elements to make large groups of atoms called molecules. When it is pure, carbon can be two different forms. These are soft, powdery soot, and hard, glittering diamond. The form depends on how the carbon atoms join to each other.

79 Aluminium is an element that is a metal, and it is one of the most useful in modern life. It is light and strong, it does not rust, and it is resistant to corrosion. Saucepans, drinks cans, cooking foil and jet planes are made mainly of aluminium.

Bond (link)   Atom

◀ Diamond is a form of the element carbon where the atoms are linked, or bonded, in a very strong box–like pattern.

Small science

80 **Many pages in this book mention atoms.** They are the smallest bits of a substance. They are so tiny, even a billion atoms would be too small to see. But scientists have carried out experiments to find out what's inside an atom. The answer is – even smaller bits. These are sub-atomic particles, and there are three main kinds.

81 At the centre of each atom is a blob called the nucleus. It contains two kinds of sub-atomic particles. These are protons and neutrons. Protons are positive, or plus. The neutron is neither positive nor negative. Around the centre of each atom are sub-atomic particles called electrons. They whizz round the nucleus. In the same way that a proton in the nucleus is positive or plus, an electron is negative or minus. The number of protons and electrons is usually the same.

82 Atoms of the various elements have different numbers of protons and neutrons. An atom of hydrogen has just one proton. An atom of helium, the gas put in party balloons to make them float, has two protons and two neutrons. An atom of the heavy metal called lead has 82 protons and 124 neutrons.

I DON'T BELIEVE IT!

One hundred years ago, people thought the electrons were spread out in an atom, like the raisins in a raisin pudding.

▶ The bits inside an atom give each substance its features, from exploding hydrogen to life-giving oxygen.

Hydrogen

Helium

Oxygen

Electron

Proton

Neutron

83 *It is hard to imagine the size of an atom.* A grain of sand, smaller than this o, contains at least 100 billion billion atoms. If you could make the atoms bigger, so that each one becomes as big as a pin head, the grain of sand would be 2 kilometres high!

Electron

Nucleus made from protons and neutrons

Movement of electrons

▲ The protons and neutrons in the nucleus of an atom are held together by a powerful force.

84 *'Nano' means one-billionth (1/1,000,000,000th), and nanotechnology is science at the smallest level – how atoms join to make molecules.* It is fairly new, but it has already produced many useful products, from stronger materials in jet planes and racing cars, to self-cleaning glass and bouncier tennis balls!

◄ This idea for a nano gear-bearing allows the central axle to spin inside the outer collar. It could be used in micromachines.

▼ Buckyballs are ball-shaped structures made of carbon atoms, used in some types of solar panels and medical research.

▶ Like buckyballs, nanotubes are formed mainly of carbon atoms. They can be combined with plastics in hi-tech equipment such as racing bicycles.

Scientists at work

85 **There are thousands of different jobs and careers in science.** Scientists work in laboratories, factories, offices, mines, steelworks, nature parks and almost everywhere else. They find new knowledge and make discoveries using a process called the scientific method.

86 **First comes an idea, called a theory or hypothesis.** This asks or predicts what will happen in a certain situation. Scientists continually come up with new ideas and theories to test. One very simple theory is – if I throw a ball up in the air, will it come back down?

▲ Some scientific work involves handling microbes or dangerous chemicals. This means safety precautions such as wearing gloves and a face mask may be necessary.

▶ In scientific terms, throwing a ball into the air is an experiment. What will be the result?

87 **The scientist carries out an experiment or test, to check what happens.** The experiment is carefully designed and controlled, so that it will reveal useful results. Any changes are carried out one at a time, so that the effect of each change can be studied. The experiment for our simple theory is – throw the ball up in the air.

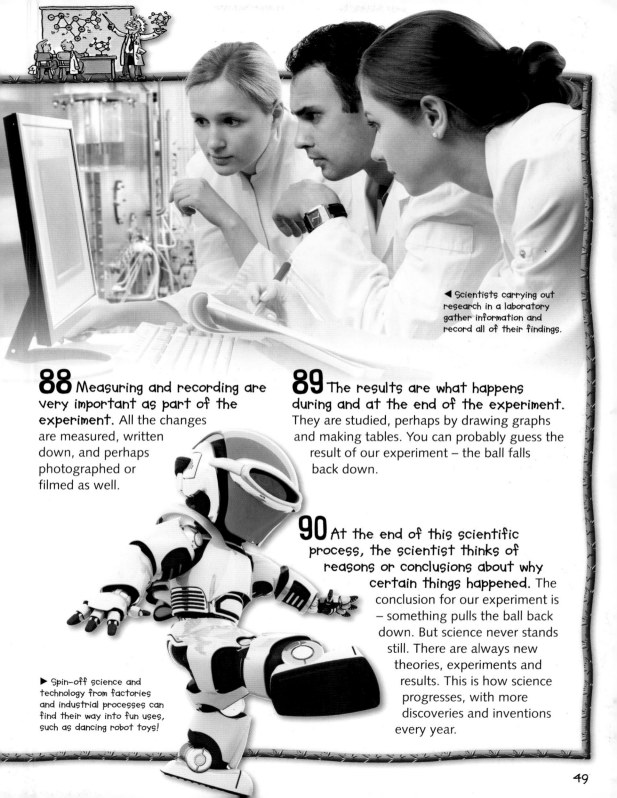

Scientists carrying out research in a laboratory gather information and record all of their findings.

88 Measuring and recording are very important as part of the experiment. All the changes are measured, written down, and perhaps photographed or filmed as well.

89 The results are what happens during and at the end of the experiment. They are studied, perhaps by drawing graphs and making tables. You can probably guess the result of our experiment – the ball falls back down.

90 At the end of this scientific process, the scientist thinks of reasons or conclusions about why certain things happened. The conclusion for our experiment is – something pulls the ball back down. But science never stands still. There are always new theories, experiments and results. This is how science progresses, with more discoveries and inventions every year.

▶ Spin-off science and technology from factories and industrial processes can find their way into fun uses, such as dancing robot toys!

Science in nature

91 Science and its effects are found all over the natural world. Scientists study animals, plants, rocks and soil. They want to understand nature, and find out how science and its technology affect wildlife.

92 One of the most complicated types of science is ecology. Ecologists try to understand how the natural world links together. They study how animals and plants live, what animals eat, and why plants grow better in some soils than others. They count the numbers of animals and plants and may trap animals briefly to study them, or follow the growth of trees in a wood. When the balance of nature is damaged, ecologists can help to find out why.

▼ One of the most important jobs in science is to study damage and pollution in the natural world. Almost everything we do affects wild places and animals and plants. For example, the power station here may make the river water warmer. This could encourage animals and plants accidentally introduced from tropical areas, which change the balance of nature.

▼ The science of ecology involves long periods of studying nature in all kinds of habitats, from rivers to the seabed. For example, observing birds like herons, and fish such as trout, shows which foods they eat. This helps us to understand how changes to the habitat may affect them.

KEY
① Water beetle
② Rainbow trout
③ Water scorpion
④ Banded demoiselle damselfly
⑤ Heron
⑥ Otter
⑦ Warbler
⑧ Power station
⑨ Reedmace

◄ Oil spills and leaks cause vast damage to a region's ecology. Scientists advise on the best ways to clear up the pollution.

93 Ecologists use many forms of high-tech science in their studies. They may fit an animal with a radio-collar so that its movements can be tracked. Special cameras see in the dark and show how night hunters catch their prey. Radar used to detect planes can also follow flocks of birds. The sonar (echo-sounding) equipment of boats can track shoals of fish or whales.

◄ Tracking tigers is vital to know the threats faced by these endangered big cats, and help to save them.

Body science

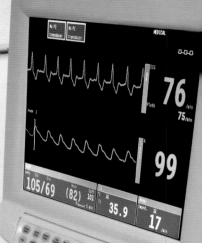

94 **One of the biggest areas of science is medicine.** Medical scientists work to produce better drugs, more spare parts for the body and more machines for use by doctors. They also carry out scientific research to find out how people can stay healthy and prevent disease.

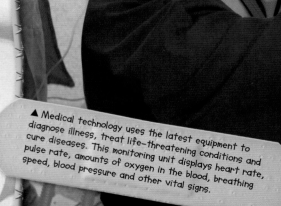

▲ Medical technology uses the latest equipment to diagnose illness, treat life-threatening conditions and cure diseases. This monitoring unit displays heart rate, pulse rate, amounts of oxygen in the blood, breathing speed, blood pressure and other vital signs.

95 As parts of the body work, such as the muscles and nerves, they produce tiny pulses of electricity. Pads on the skin pick up these pulses, which are displayed as a wavy line on a screen or paper strip. The ECG (electro-cardiograph) machine shows the heart beating. The EEG (electro-encephalograph) shows nerve signals flashing around the brain.

Laser beam hits retina inside eye

▶ A laser beam shines safely through the front of the eye to mend inner problems such as a detached retina.

96 Laser beams are ideal for delicate operations, or surgery, on body parts such as the eye. The beam makes very small, precise cuts. It can be shone into the eye and made most focused, or strongest, inside. So it can make a cut deep within the eye, without any harm to the outer parts.

▶ An endoscope is inserted into the body to give a doctor a picture on screen. The treatment can be given immediately.

MAKE A PULSE MACHINE

You will need:
modelling clay   drinking straw

Find your pulse by feeling your wrist, just below the base of your thumb, with a finger of the other hand. Place some modelling clay on this area, and stick a drinking straw into it. Watch the straw twitch with each heartbeat. Now you can see and feel your pulse. Check your pulse rate by counting the number of heartbeats in one minute.

97 The endoscope is like a flexible telescope made of fibre-strands. This is pushed into a body opening such as the mouth, or through a small cut, to see inside. The surgeon looks into the other end of the endoscope, or at a picture on a screen.

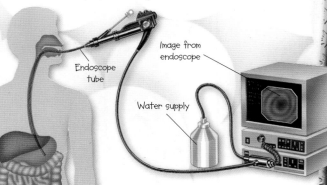

Image from endoscope

Endoscope tube

Water supply

Science in the Future

98 **Many modern machines and processes can cause damage to our environment and our health.** The damage includes acid rain, destruction of the ozone layer and the greenhouse effect, leading to climate change and global warming. Science can help to find solutions. New filters and chemicals called catalysts can reduce dangerous fumes from vehicle exhausts and power stations, and in the chemicals in factory waste pipes.

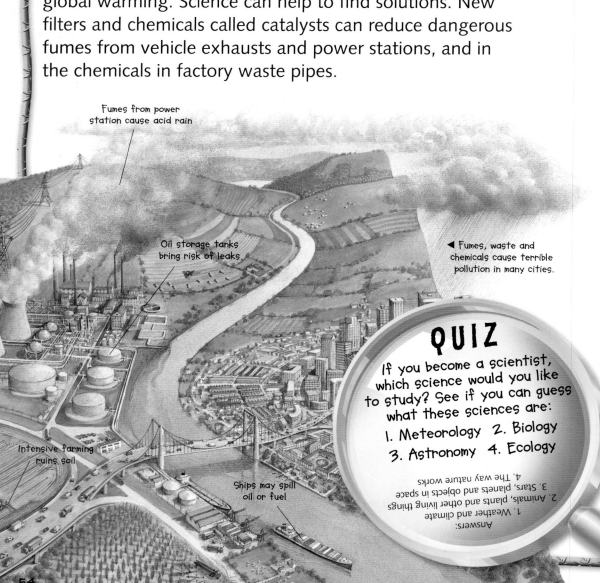

Fumes from power station cause acid rain

Oil storage tanks bring risk of leaks

◀ Fumes, waste and chemicals cause terrible pollution in many cities.

Intensive farming ruins soil

Ships may spill oil or fuel

QUIZ
If you become a scientist, which science would you like to study? See if you can guess what these sciences are:

1. Meteorology 2. Biology
3. Astronomy 4. Ecology

Answers:
1. Weather and climate
2. Animals, plants and other living things
3. Stars, planets and objects in space
4. The way nature works

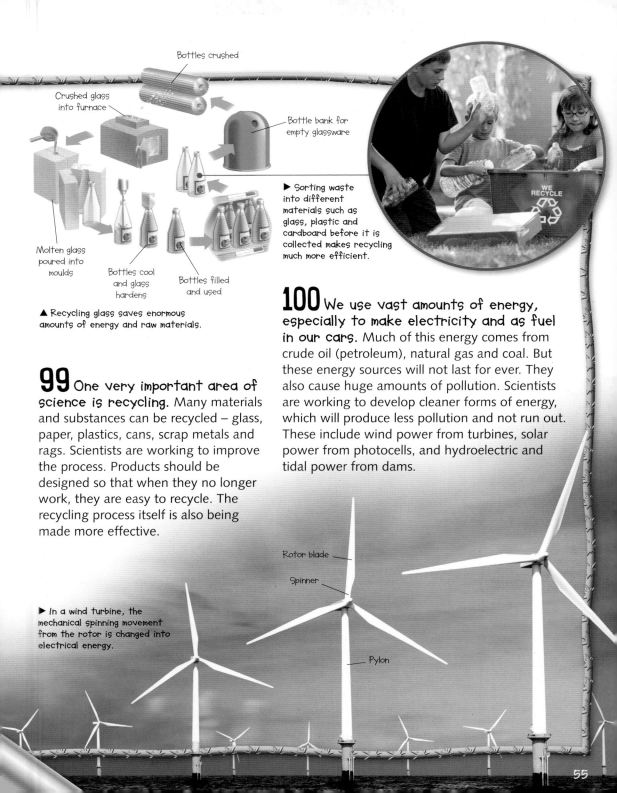

Bottles crushed

Crushed glass into furnace

Bottle bank for empty glassware

Molten glass poured into moulds

Bottles cool and glass hardens

Bottles filled and used

▶ Sorting waste into different materials such as glass, plastic and cardboard before it is collected makes recycling much more efficient.

WE RECYCLE

▲ Recycling glass saves enormous amounts of energy and raw materials.

99 One very important area of science is recycling. Many materials and substances can be recycled – glass, paper, plastics, cans, scrap metals and rags. Scientists are working to improve the process. Products should be designed so that when they no longer work, they are easy to recycle. The recycling process itself is also being made more effective.

100 We use vast amounts of energy, especially to make electricity and as fuel in our cars. Much of this energy comes from crude oil (petroleum), natural gas and coal. But these energy sources will not last for ever. They also cause huge amounts of pollution. Scientists are working to develop cleaner forms of energy, which will produce less pollution and not run out. These include wind power from turbines, solar power from photocells, and hydroelectric and tidal power from dams.

Rotor blade

Spinner

▶ In a wind turbine, the mechanical spinning movement from the rotor is changed into electrical energy.

Pylon

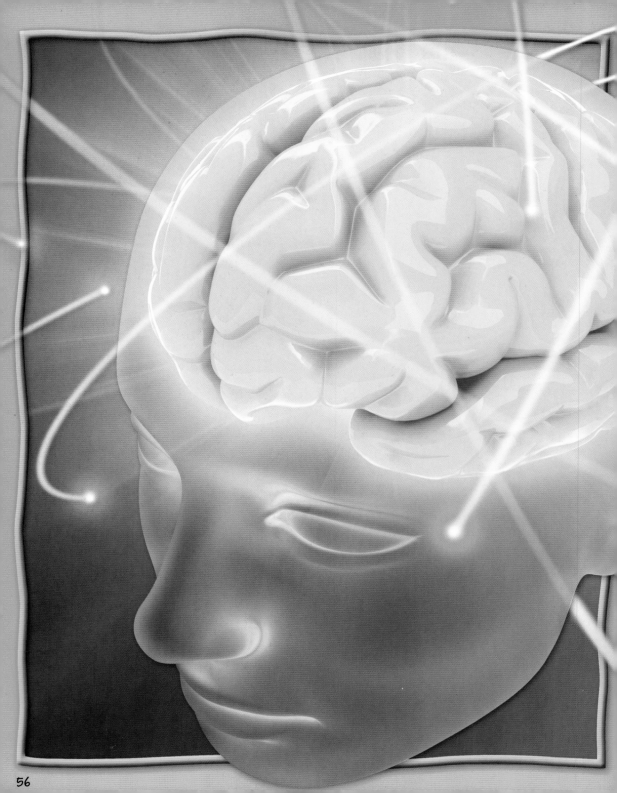

GREAT SCIENTISTS

- Mathematics
- Anatomy
- Microscopic life
- The Laws of Motion
- Natural history
- Chemical elements
- Diseases and cures
- Radiation
- Space and time
- DNA and genetics

Who invented algebra?

What is gravity?

Why do some objects float in water?

Who discovered DNA?

What is at the centre of a black hole?

What is a scientist?

101 **A scientist is someone who studies the world and how it works.** Scientists ask questions then try to answer them with experiments, observations and mathematical reasoning. They also come up with ideas and theories and try to test them in the same way. This is how we find out about the world – from what atoms are to how the Universe works.

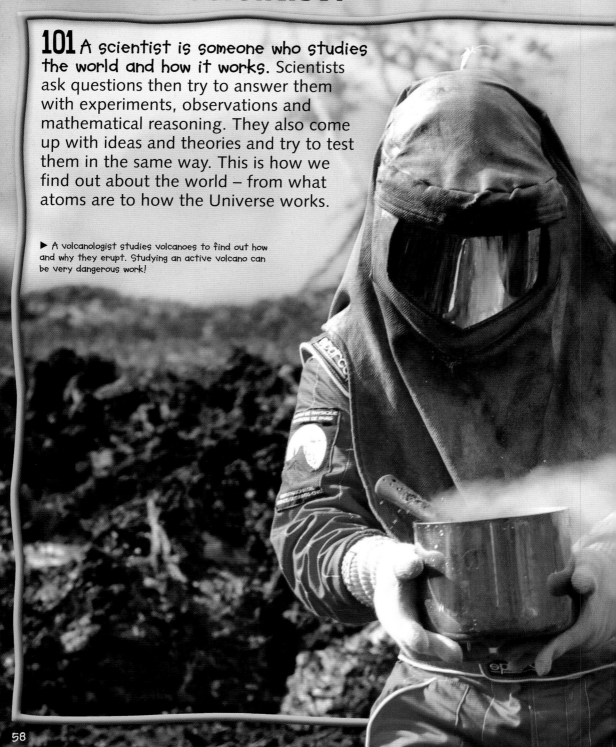

▶ A volcanologist studies volcanoes to find out how and why they erupt. Studying an active volcano can be very dangerous work!

102 Scientific ideas are constantly changing. What scientists think is true in one age may be questioned in the next. Just a century ago, astronomers thought the Universe was no bigger than our Milky Way Galaxy. We now know the Universe is much vaster, with more than 500 billion galaxies.

103 In the past, scientists often studied a wide range of subjects. In fact, the word 'scientist' was not widely used until 1830. Most of the great scientists in this book from before that time were called 'natural philosophers'.

▶ There are many different kinds of scientist. They specialize in different fields, such as particle physicists who study atoms and microbiologists who study microscopic life.

Life Sciences

Botany.............. Botanists study plants in nature and the laboratory

Zoology.............. Zoologists study animals in nature and the laboratory

Genetics............. Genetics is the science of how living things pass on features to offspring

Medicine.............. Medicine is the science of understanding and healing the human body

Physical Sciences

Physics.............. Physicists study matter and forces and how they move through space and time

Chemistry............ Chemists study substances and how they react with each other

Astronomy........... Astronomers study space – from moons and planets to stars and galaxies

Earth Sciences

Geology.............. Geologists study rocks and minerals and how the Earth works

Oceanography........ Oceanographers study the oceans and ocean currents and tides

Palaeontology...... Palaeontologists study prehistoric life and fossils

Meteorology........ Meteorologists study the weather, climate and changes in the atmosphere

Mathematical marvels

104 About 10,000 years ago, people in the Middle East began to farm. They built great civilizations, such as ancient Egypt, and developed numbers, which helped to keep a record of things. They discovered that numbers could be used to work things out, such as fair shares or the area of a field. This is how mathematics began.

▼ The ancient Egyptians built the pyramids with amazing accuracy. They could work out the height of a pyramid just from the length of its shadow.

Euclid
Greek c.300 BC

◀ The Shard in London is a new building, which was completed in 2012. Modern engineers have based their ideas on Euclid's ancient proof.

105 In ancient Greece, mathematicians worked out things such as the areas of triangles. They set out logical proof of their ideas. The greatest mathematician was Euclid, whose book *Elements* still provides basic skills used by engineers and builders today

Archimedes
Greek 287–212 BC

106 Archimedes thought about problems in a scientific way. He came up with theories that could be proved or disproved by experiments and mathematics. Archimedes proved that the power of a lever (a simple machine) to move a load depends on how far from its pivot point (point of rotation) you apply your effort.

107 A story tells how the king of Syracuse suspected impure gold had been used to make his crown. Archimedes was asked to investigate. But how could he tell without melting the crown? He hit on the solution while in his bath, and was so excited he ran naked through the streets shouting, 'Eureka!' (which means, 'I've got it!').

108 Archimedes explained how things float. When an object sinks down in water, the water pushes it back up with a force equal to the weight of water displaced (pushed away). The object has a natural upthrust or 'buoyancy'. He showed that an object sinks until its weight is equal to the weight of water displaced, then it floats.

◀▼ Heavy ships float because they are supported by the weight of water they push out of the way.

The weight of the ship is equal to the water it displaces

When the ships sinks down, the water it displaces thrusts it back up with equal force

109 Archimedes launched a giant ship on his own using levers and pulleys. A pulley turns around like a wheel and has a groove for a cable or rope. Lots of pulleys allow us to lift heavy weights easily.

▼ Archimedes identified three types (classes) of lever, according to where you apply effort in relation to the pivot.

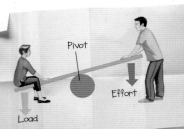

① A class 1 lever has the load and effort on opposite sides of the pivot or fulcrum, like a see-saw

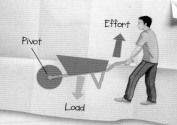

② A class 2 lever has the load and effort on the same side of the pivot, as in a wheelbarrow

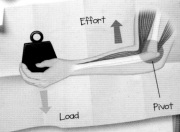

③ A class 3 lever has the effort between the load and the pivot, like a human elbow

Baghdad brilliance

110 When Muhammad began to teach the religion of Islam in the 600s, he charged followers to search for knowledge. Baghdad and other Islamic cities became centres of learning. Ibn Sina studied everything from philosophy to physics. He not only identified the main forms of energy and the idea of force, he wrote a book, *The Canon of Medicine*, which became the doctors' bible for 600 years.

Ibn Sina Avicenna
Persian c.980–1037

Muhammad al-Fazari
Arabic or Persian
Died 796 or 806

QUIZ

1. What did the astrolabe measure?
2. What is distillation used for today?
3. What does algebra use to replace unknown numbers in calculations?

Answers:
1. Angles 2. For refining oil and alcohol 3. Symbols or letters

111 Muslims needed to know the true direction of Muhammad's birthplace. So scientists developed astronomical instruments to map the stars. The astrolabe was invented by astronomer Muhammad al-Fazari. It measured angles by sight, and skilled users could work out directions from the position of stars alone.

▶ Muslim astronomers mapped the stars and their movements very accurately.

112 Jabir ibn Hayyan (Geber) stirred and heated chemicals together in measured quantities to see how they interacted. Jabir also found he could purify liquids by boiling them and collecting the droplets of steam. This is called distillation and is used today for refining oil and alcoholic spirits.

Jabir ibn Hayyan (Geber)
Persian 721–815

▲ As well distillation, Geber discovered acids that were strong enough to dissolve metals.

113 Roman numerals were awkward to use for large numbers. So in the 8th century, after studying Indian Hindu numbers, al-Khwarizmi introduced the Arabic numerals we now use around the world. Roman numerals need seven figures to give a number as small as 38 (XXXVIII). With seven figures, Arabic numerals can give nearly ten million!

al-Khwarizmi
Arabic or Persian
c.780–850

▶ Roman numerals were built up by adding lines. Arabic numerals use symbols for one to 10, which is simpler.

Ancient Roman	Modern Hindu-Arabic
I	1
II	2
III	3
IV	4
V	5
VI	6
VII	7
VIII	8
IX	9
X	10

114 Al-Khwarizmi created the maths known as algebra. Algebra uses symbols or letters to replace unknown numbers in calculations. Mathematicians can work out the unknown numbers by putting the symbols in standard 'recipes' called equations. Algebra is part of nearly all scientific calculations.

115 When al-Khwarizmi's name was written in Latin it was spelt 'Algoritmi'. This name has given us the word 'algorithms'. Algorithms are logical step-by-step mathematical sequences, and it was al-Khwarizmi who first developed the idea. Algorithms are now the basis of all computer programs.

Thinking again

Leonardo da Vinci
Italian 1452–1519

116 In the 1400s, Islamic science reached Europe. The ideas of ancient Greece and Rome were rediscovered, and people like Leonardo da Vinci were excited. They realized that by studying the world, they might learn how it works.

117 You might think helicopters and cars are modern ideas — but Leonardo drew designs for them 500 years ago. His sketches for a hang-glider type flying machine are so detailed that experts recently built one for real — and found that it just about worked.

▼ A scientific genius, Leonardo made brilliant notes and drawings on everything from geology to flying machines.

▼ Leonardo was way ahead of his time, making models to study how rivers flowed.

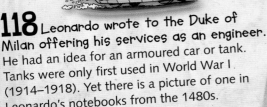

118 Leonardo wrote to the Duke of Milan offering his services as an engineer. He had an idea for an armoured car or tank. Tanks were only first used in World War I (1914–1918). Yet there is a picture of one in Leonardo's notebooks from the 1480s.

119 To draw human figures accurately, artists studied the human body. To show the body's inner layers, Leonardo developed a way of drawing cross-sections and 3D versions of muscles.

▶ Leonardo drew highly accurate diagrams of the human muscular system.

120 Early physicians learned about the body (often wrongly) from ancient books – especially those of Galen (129–199), a Roman doctor. Andreas Vesalius realized the only way to find out was to cut up real corpses (dead bodies). As he did this, he got artist Jan van Calcar to draw what he found. They made the first accurate book of human anatomy (the way the body is put together) in 1543.

▶ As Vesalius carefully cut up bodies, Jan van Calcar made drawings to build up an accurate guide to human anatomy.

Andreas Vesalius
Dutch 1514–1564

121 Many scientists studied in Padua in Italy in the 1500s, including English physician William Harvey. When Harvey returned to England, he studied how blood flowed through the body. He found that it doesn't flow to and fro like tides as Galen said. Instead it is pumped by the heart non-stop around the body through tubes called arteries and veins.

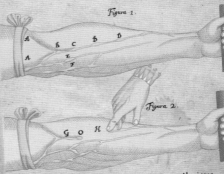

Figura 1.

Figura 2.

▲ Careful experiments showed William Harvey that blood flowed around the body again and again.

William Harvey
English 1578–1657

Microbes and measures

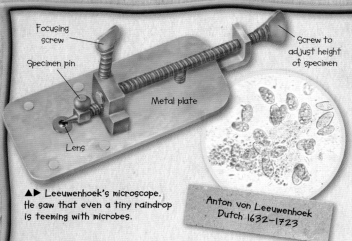

Focusing screw

Screw to adjust height of specimen

Specimen pin

Metal plate

Lens

▲▶ Leeuwenhoek's microscope. He saw that even a tiny raindrop is teeming with microbes.

Anton von Leeuwenhoek
Dutch 1632–1723

123 Robert Hooke was another microscope pioneer and saw that living things are made from tiny 'parcels'. He called them cells, because to him they looked like tiny rows of rooms or cells that monks lived in. Hooke also invented the hearing aid and the anemometer (for measuring wind speed).

▼ Through his microscope, Hooke saw that living things are made up from tiny packages, which he named 'cells'.

122 No one knew there was life too small to see — until Anton von Leeuwenhoek looked through his microscope in the 1670s. Leeuwenhoek made his own microscope, with lenses that could magnify up to 270 times.

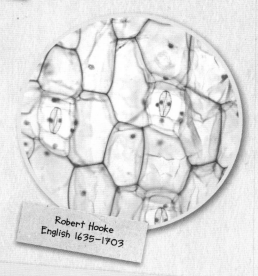

Christiaan Huygens
Dutch 1629–1695

Robert Hooke
English 1635–1703

124 Before the 1600s, people could only tell the time to within ten minutes. But in 1658 Christiaan Huygens perfected a clock that kept time with a swinging weight, or pendulum. It was the world's first accurate clock, so precise it could keep time to within a minute over a week.

◀ Huygens also worked out the maths of pendulums that helps us understand how planets move.

125 Following the pioneering work of Italian astronomer and mathematician Galileo Galilei, Huygens made his own telescope. Through it, he saw that the planet Saturn had a moon, too, later called Titan. He also realized that what had looked to Galileo like ears on Saturn were part of a flat ring running around it.

▼ We now know that Saturn's rings are made up of tiny particles of water, ice and dust.

René Descartes
French 1596–1650

126 French philosopher René Descartes came up with the idea of graphs. Graphs are a way of looking at things that are changing together. When something accelerates, both speed and time change. On a graph, you draw the changes as a simple line called a curve.

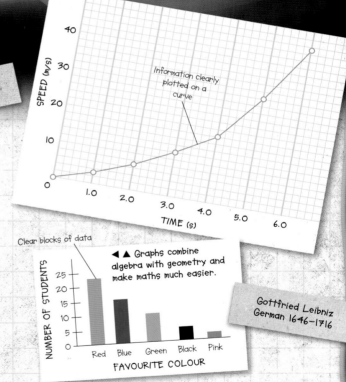

Information clearly plotted on a curve

Clear blocks of data

◄▲ Graphs combine algebra with geometry and make maths much easier.

Gottfried Leibniz
German 1646–1716

I DON'T BELIEVE IT!

There are thought to be millions of types of bacteria, but no one knew they existed until Leeuwenhoek saw them through his microscope.

127 Most things in nature move at varying speeds. To study them, Isaac Newton and Gottfried Leibnitz devised a kind of maths called calculus. Calculus helps you find out how fast something is moving at any one instant – a time so short that it seems to move no distance at all.

Motion man

Sir Isaac Newton
English 1643–1727

128 Isaac Newton discovered that every movement in the Universe obeys three rules, known as the Laws of Motion. They sum up what it takes to get something moving or to stop (1st Law), to make something move faster or slower, or change direction (2nd Law), and how the movement of one thing affects another (3rd Law).

LAW 1: An object won't move unless something forces it to. It will go on moving at the same speed and in the same direction unless forced to change. This is called inertia.

LAW 2: The greater the mass of an object, the more force is needed to make it speed up, slow down or change direction.

▶▲ Scientists can use these laws to work out everything — from the way a diver pushes off from a springboard to the rotation of a galaxy.

129 Newton also discovered gravity — the force of attraction between all matter. He knew that nothing strays from its course without being forced to. So when something starts to fall, it must be forced to. That force is called gravity.

MARBLE MOTION

Demonstrate Newton's Third Law of Motion with marbles or the balls on a pool table. Roll one ball or marble into another — and watch how when they collide, one ball moves one way and the other ball moves the other way.

LAW 3: For every action, there is an equal opposite reaction — in other words, when something pushes off in one direction, the thing it's pushing from is pushed back with equal force in the opposite direction.

130 Sunlight is colourless or white — so where do all the colours come from? Newton realized that sunlight contains all the colours, mixed up. He proved it using a prism, a triangular block of glass.

▼ When sunlight shines through a prism, its rays are bent, each colour to a different degree. When the light emerges from the far side of the prism, it splits into a spectrum — all the colours of the rainbow.

131 Newton was the first modern scientist, but he wrote works of alchemy — a mixture of science, magic and astrology. Alchemists wanted to find the 'philosopher's stone' (a substance that could turn metal to gold) and the 'elixir of life' (a liquid that keeps you young forever). They wrote in code to keep their work secret, so Newton's notebooks are impossible to understand.

Nature's secrets

132 Today, all living things are organized into clear groups — thanks to biologist Carolus Linnaeus. Before this, animals and plants were listed at best alphabetically. Since creatures have different names in different places, this led to chaos.

PARTS OF A FLOWERING PLANT

Anther (male part)

Stigma (female part)

▲ Linnaeus realized that flowering plants can be classified by the shape of their male and female parts.

Carolus Linnaeus
Swedish 1707–1778

▼ A volcanic eruption is a short, sharp force of nature. James Hutton concluded that the landscape is shaped mostly by more gradual forces such as running rivers.

James Hutton
Scottish 1726–1797

HOMEMADE FOSSIL

Make your own fossil by pressing a snail shell or an old bone into tightly compressed fine sand. Take out the shell or bone, then pour runny plaster or wall filler into the mould left behind. Leave the plaster to set, then dig up your fossil!

133 People once thought the Earth was just a few thousand years old and the entire landscape was shaped by a few short, huge disasters. But in his book *Theory of the Earth*, published in 1788, James Hutton showed how the Earth has been shaped gradually over millions of years by milder forces, such as running rivers.

Charles Lyell
English 1797–1875

134 Charles Lyell showed how rocks tell the story of Earth's past. Rock layers form one on top of the other over time and can be read by a geologist like pages in a book. They contain fossils – the remains of once living things turned to stone – showing what creatures were alive when each layer formed.

▲ The first dinosaur fossils were discovered in rock in Lyell's lifetime.

Mary Anning
English 1799–1847

135 Mary Anning hunted for fossils on the shore at Lyme Regis in England, one of the world's richest fossil sites. At the age of 12, she found the skeleton of an ichthyosaur, a dolphin-shaped creature from the time of the dinosaurs – though no one knew about dinosaurs at the time. She went on to find the first fossils of a giant swimming reptile, *Plesiosaurus*, and the first flying reptiles, or pterosaurs.

▲ Mary Anning discovered fossils of a giant swimming reptile, a plesiosaur, which may have looked like this.

William Buckland
English 1784–1856

136 In 1824, William Buckland wrote the first scientific description of a dinosaur fossil, Megalosaurus. This meat-eater was 9 metres long and weighed as much as an elephant. People were astonished such creatures had ever lived, but soon more fossils were found.

▶ Buckland named *Megalosaurus* in 1824. It was not until 1842 that the term 'dinosaur' was first used.

It's chemistry

Robert Boyle
Irish 1627–1691

▲ Boyle's Law shows that the pressure of gases in a diver's suit and body rises as he descends, due to the weight of the water.

Gas molecules

Plunger squeezes gas

Large volume of gas with low pressure

Medium volume of gas with medium pressure

Small volume of gas with high pressure

▲ When a gas is squeezed, the pressure increases in proportion. The more the gas is squeezed, the higher the pressure.

137 **Robert Boyle was the first great chemist of modern times.** With Boyle's Law, he showed that when a gas is compressed its pressure increases at the same rate. He also suggested that everything is made up from basic chemicals or 'elements', which can join together in different ways.

138 People once believed air was not a substance. But Antoine Lavoisier realized substances can exist in three different states – solid, liquid and gas – and if gases are substances, then so is air. He found air is a mix of gases, mostly nitrogen and oxygen.

139 Scientists used to think that everything that burns contained a substance called phlogiston. They thought that as something burned it lost phlogiston. Lavoisier found by careful weighing that tin gains weight when it burns, because it takes in oxygen. So phlogiston couldn't exist. Lavoisier had proved the importance of accurate measurement.

▼ Lavoisier showed that, like solid elements, two gases can join to make a new substance, or compound. Here he is experimenting with hydrogen and oxygen, to produce water.

Antoine Lavoisier
French 1743–1794

Cobalt
Co

Copper
Cu

Molybdenum
Mo

Tungsten
W

Aluminium
Al

140 In 1787, Lavoisier introduced symbols for the different chemical elements. So oxygen is 'O' and hydrogen is 'H'. Lavoisier knew of less than 40 elements. Today, chemists use chemical formulae to identify compounds and the mix of elements of which they are composed. For example, water has the chemical symbol H_2O. This means it has two hydrogen (H) atoms to one oxygen (O).

▲▶ Minerals help to make up rocks. Each of these minerals contains a particular metal. The chemical symbols shown here are for each metal.

Antinomy
Sb

Mercury
Hg

John Dalton
English 1766–1844

141 Chemist John Dalton realized elements are made from solid particles called atoms. Each element is made from atoms of a certain weight. He found hydrogen to be the lightest, so he assigned it an 'atomic weight' of 1. Dalton's atomic theory of the elements is central to chemistry.

142 In 1869, Dmitri Mendeleyev arranged the elements in a table in order of their atomic weight. He placed them from left to right in rows or 'periods' of seven that revealed a pattern. Elements in the same column (from top to bottom) have similar properties. All elements at one end of each row are reactive metals, while those at the other are unreactive gases.

▶ Elements are arranged in rows called periods in the Periodic Table. Mecury is number 80, in row 6.

Atomic number

80

Hg

Symbol for mercury

Mercury
200.59

Atomic weight

Dmitri Mendeleyev
Russian 1834–1907

Sparks of genius

143 In the 1700s, scientists discovered that rubbing things together can give an electrical charge and may create a spark. Benjamin Franklin wondered if lightning was electrical too. He attached a key to a kite, which he flew during a thunderstorm, and got a similar spark from the key.

▼ A spark flew from the key on Franklin's kite, showing that lightning was electrical.

Benjamin Franklin
American 1706–1790

Luigi Galvani
Italian 1737–1798

144 Luigi Galvani made a dead frog's legs twitch with electricity. He believed, incorrectly, that electricity was made by animals' bodies. Alessandro Volta believed this was just a chemical reaction. In 1800, he used the reaction between 'sandwiches' of disks made of the metals copper and zinc in saltwater to create a battery.

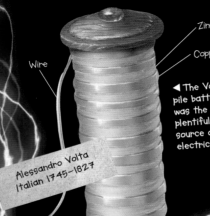

Zinc

Copper

Wire

◀ The Voltaic pile battery was the first plentiful source of electricity.

Alessandro Volta
Italian 1745–1827

Hans Christiaan Øersted
Danish 1777–1851

145 No one realized electricity and magnetism were linked – until physicist Hans Øersted noticed something strange. During a lecture in 1820, he observed that when an electric current was switched on and off, a nearby compass needle swivelled. He went on to confirm with experiments that an electric current creates a magnetic field around it. This effect is known as electromagnetism.

146 Michael Faraday was fascinated by Øersted's discovery. The following year he showed how the interreaction between a magnet and an electrical current can make a wire move. Faraday and others then went on to use this discovery to create the first electric motors.

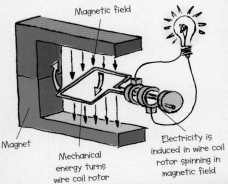

▼ Faraday found that when a wire moves near a magnet, an electric current is generated in it.

Magnetic field

Magnet

Mechanical energy turns wire coil rotor

Electricity is induced in wire coil rotor spinning in magnetic field

147 In 1830, Faraday in London and Joseph Henry in New York found that magnets create electricity. When a magnet is moved near an electric circuit, it creates a surge of electricity. Using this idea, machines could be built to generate lots of electricity.

Joseph Henry
American 1797–1878

148 Faraday's experiments on electricity convinced him that all types of electricity were basically the same. It didn't matter if they were produced naturally in Earth's atmosphere in the form of lightning, artificially by chemical reactions in a battery, or by a rotating copper coil inside a magnetic field.

Faraday showed how a cage of metal wire (known as a Faraday cage) could block electrical discharges and protect a person from lightning.

75

Cured!

Edward Jenner
English 1749–1823

149 People who survived the disease smallpox became immune to a second attack. This meant their bodies could resist the infection. Doctor Edward Jenner injected his gardener's son with cowpox, a milder disease, to see if it gave the same immunity. It did.

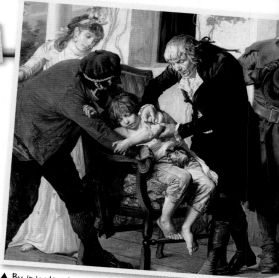

▲ By injecting his gardener's son with cowpox, Edward Jenner had taken the first step towards wiping out the killer disease smallpox.

150 Before 1850, no one knew dirt in hospitals could spread killer germs. Countless patients died of infections. Doctor Ignaz Semmelweiss asked students to wash their hands before dealing with patients. This act of simple hygiene helped reduce the number of deaths.

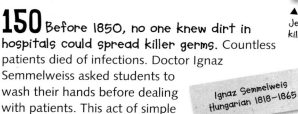

Ignaz Semmelweis
Hungarian 1818–1865

151 Surgeon Joseph Lister introduced soap to his operations to keep things spotlessly clean. Cleanliness cut infections during surgery dramatically, and antiseptic techniques are now a vital part of every operation.

▼ Lister invented a carbolic spray to limit infections during surgery.

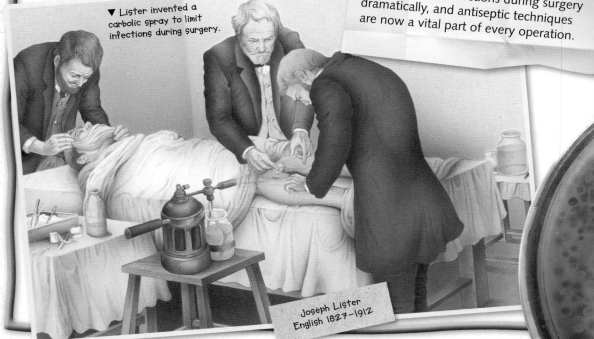

Joseph Lister
English 1827–1912

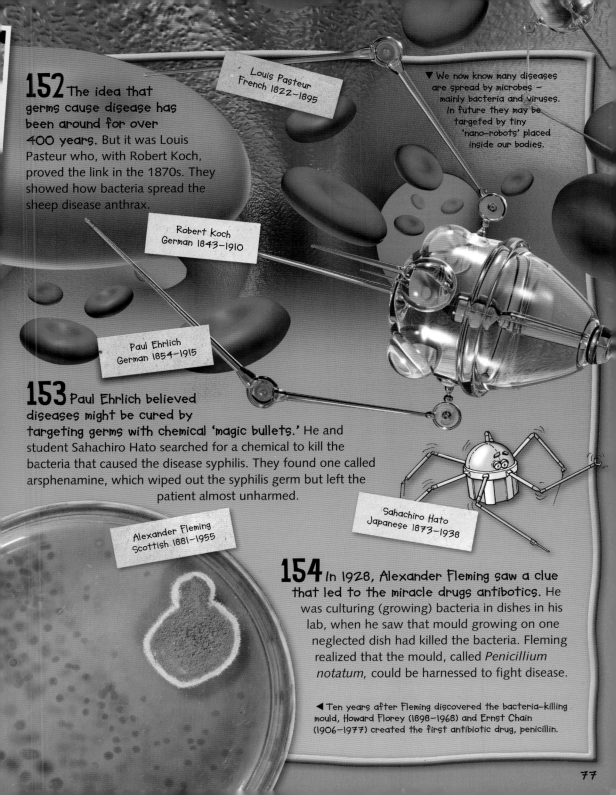

152 The idea that germs cause disease has been around for over 400 years. But it was Louis Pasteur who, with Robert Koch, proved the link in the 1870s. They showed how bacteria spread the sheep disease anthrax.

Louis Pasteur
French 1822–1895

▼ We now know many diseases are spread by microbes — mainly bacteria and viruses. In future they may be targeted by tiny 'nano-robots' placed inside our bodies.

Robert Koch
German 1843–1910

Paul Ehrlich
German 1854–1915

153 Paul Ehrlich believed diseases might be cured by targeting germs with chemical 'magic bullets.' He and student Sahachiro Hato searched for a chemical to kill the bacteria that caused the disease syphilis. They found one called arsphenamine, which wiped out the syphilis germ but left the patient almost unharmed.

Sahachiro Hato
Japanese 1873–1938

Alexander Fleming
Scottish 1881–1955

154 In 1928, Alexander Fleming saw a clue that led to the miracle drugs antibotics. He was culturing (growing) bacteria in dishes in his lab, when he saw that mould growing on one neglected dish had killed the bacteria. Fleming realized that the mould, called *Penicillium notatum*, could be harnessed to fight disease.

◀ Ten years after Fleming discovered the bacteria-killing mould, Howard Florey (1898–1968) and Ernst Chain (1906–1977) created the first antibiotic drug, penicillin.

Dangerous rays

155 In 1886, Heinrich Hertz proved that an electromagnetic current spreads as waves. He made a flickering electric spark jump a gap in an electrical circuit. As the spark flickered, it radiated waves, which set another spark flickering in sync in an aerial receiver. Hertz had discovered radio waves.

Heinrich Hertz
German 1857–1894

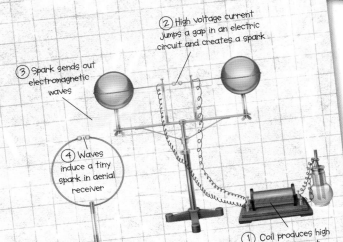

② High voltage current jumps a gap in an electric circuit and creates a spark

③ Spark sends out electromagnetic waves

④ Waves induce a tiny spark in aerial receiver

① Coil produces high voltage current

▲ Hertz's experiments with electricity and electromagnetic waves led to the development of the radio.

I DON'T BELIEVE IT!

Before people realized how dangerous it was, radium was added to products such as toothpaste and hair cream to give them a healthy glow.

▼ We now know that the cathode rays in Crookes' glass tube were actually made up of tiny electrical particles.

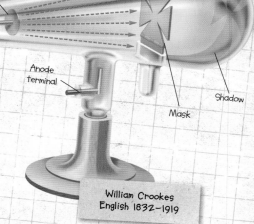

Cathode rays

Cathode terminal

Anode terminal

Mask

Shadow

156 In the 1870s, William Crookes made a glass tube with nearly all the air sucked out of it. When connected to an electric current, the glass tube glowed. This was because electric charge flowed between the terminals, sending out electromagnetic radiation, which Crookes called cathode rays. A metal mask inside the tube cast a shadow, showing that the rays travelled in straight lines.

William Crookes
English 1832–1919

157 In 1895, Wilhelm Röntgen found that even when he covered a Crookes tube, its rays still made a nearby screen glow. Some rays must be shining through the cover. He tried putting other objects in front of the rays (which he called X-rays) and eventually placed his wife's hand. The rays passed through flesh, but were blocked by bone. Röntgen replaced the screen with photo paper and took the first X-ray photo of his wife's hand.

▼ As well as bone, Röntgen discovered that X-rays were blocked by the metal of his wife's jewellery, and a compass!

158 Henri Becquerel found that uranium crystals left on photo paper in a drawer made a photo of themselves. They were releasing or 'radiating' their own energy. He had discovered radioactivity – radiation so energetic it breaks up atoms. This kind of radiation is quite different from electromagnetic radiation and is used to make nuclear bombs.

◄ Marie Curie was the first woman to be awarded a Nobel Prize, in 1903 for physics. She was awarded it again, this time in chemistry, in 1911.

159 Pierre and Marie Curie were fascinated by radioactivity. They discovered two new radioactive elements, radium and polonium. In 1903, they were awarded the Nobel Prize for their work. Marie Curie died from cancer caused by exposure to radioactivity.

Atomic science

160 Scientists once thought atoms were the smallest particles. In 1897, JJ Thomson noticed how magnets bent rays from a cathode ray tube. He realized the rays were streams of particles, much smaller than an atom. Thomson wrongly believed these particles or 'electrons' split off from atoms like currents off a bun.

Sir Ernest Rutherford
New Zealand-born British
1871–1937

161 Ernest Rutherford found that radioactivity is the result of atoms breaking up into different atoms, sending out streams of 'alpha' and 'beta' particles. In 1911, he fired streams of alpha particles at gold foil. Most went straight through, but a few bounced back, pushed by the nuclei inside the gold foil atoms. He realized that atoms aren't solid, but largely empty space with a tiny, dense nucleus (core).

Neils Bohr
Danish 1885–1962

▶ Fortunately, all nuclear explosions since the attack on Japan in 1945 have been tests.

162 In 1912, Niels Bohr suggested that different kinds of atom had a certain number of electrons. He thought they buzzed around an atom's nucleus at varying distances, like planets around the Sun. Atoms give out light and lose energy when electrons fall closer to the nucleus. When atoms absorb light, the electrons jump further out.

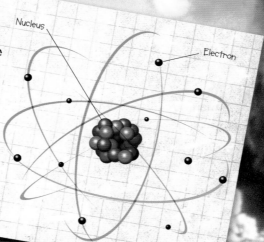

Nucleus

Electron

▶ We now know that electrons are like fuzzy clouds of energy rather than planets.

163 In 1918 Rutherford split atoms for the first time. He fired alpha particles at nitrogen gas and found that hydrogen nuclei chipped off the nitrogen nuclei. He realized that all atomic nuclei are clusters of hydrogen nuclei, which he called protons. Fourteen years later, James Chadwick discovered nuclei also have another kind of particle in the nucleus – the neutron.

James Chadwick
English 1891–1974

164 Enrico Fermi fired neutrons at a uranium atom, to see if they'd stick to form a bigger atom. Instead, the uranium atom split into two smaller atoms and released more neutrons, and heat and light energy. Fermi realized that if these neutrons spun off to split more uranium atoms a 'chain reaction' of splitting could occur.

Enrico Fermi
Italian–American
1901–1954

◀ Enrico Fermi showed how a chain reaction of an atom splitting could begin with the impact of just a single neutron.

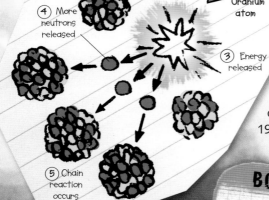

① Neutron fired at nucleus of Uranium atom

② Nucleus splits in two

Uranium atom

④ More neutrons released

③ Energy released

⑤ Chain reaction occurs

165 During World War II (1939–1945) Fermi created a chain reaction of nuclear splitting, or 'fission'. This unleashed energy to create an incredibly powerful bomb. At Los Alamo, New Mexico, Robert Oppenheimer used this idea to make the first nuclear bombs, which were dropped on the Japanese cities of Hiroshima and Nagasaki in August 1945, killing thousands of people outright.

Robert Oppenheimer
American 1904–1967

BOWLING REACTION!

Ask an older relative to take you ten-pin bowling. It's not just fun, it'll show you how a nuclear chain reaction can work, especially if you are lucky enough to strike ten. The ball may only hit one pin directly, but as that pin falls, it can knock down all the rest in turn.

Space and time weirdness

166 In 1900, Max Planck worked out that heat is not radiated in a smooth flow, but in tiny chunks of energy that he called quanta. Albert Einstein realized that all radiation works like this – and that chunks of energy are particles. So a ray of light is streams of particles, not just waves, as everyone thought.

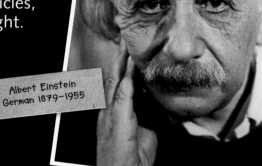

Albert Einstein
German 1879–1955

▲ With his theories of relativity, Einstein overturned our understanding of the nature of time and space.

TRUE OR FALSE?

1. A ray of light is made up of particles.
2. The speed of light can vary.
3. Gravity bends space and time.
4. Paul Dirac's theory was called quantum engines.

Answers:
1. True 2. False, the speed of light is always the same 3. True 4. False, it was called quantum mechanics

167 Speed is always measured compared to something, so the speed of an object varies depending on what you compare it to. In 1887, Einstein showed that light is special – it travels the same speed no matter how you measure it. Speed is the distance something moves through space in a certain time. If light's speed is fixed, Einstein realized that time and space must vary instead. So time and space are not fixed – they are relative and can be distorted. This is Einstein's theory of special relativity.

168 Einstein's theory of special relativity has weird effects for things travelling near the speed of light. For example, time on board a spacecraft travelling near the speed of light would seem to run slower, and the spacecraft would appear to shrink in length and get heavier.

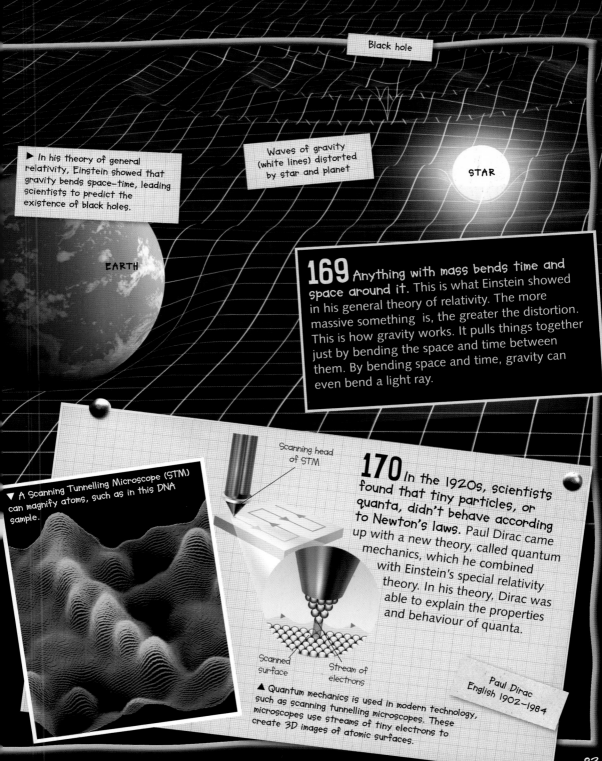

Black hole

▶ In his theory of general relativity, Einstein showed that gravity bends space–time, leading scientists to predict the existence of black holes.

Waves of gravity (white lines) distorted by star and planet

STAR

EARTH

169 Anything with mass bends time and space around it. This is what Einstein showed in his general theory of relativity. The more massive something is, the greater the distortion. This is how gravity works. It pulls things together just by bending the space and time between them. By bending space and time, gravity can even bend a light ray.

Scanning head of STM

▼ A Scanning Tunnelling Microscope (STM) can magnify atoms, such as in this DNA sample.

170 In the 1920s, scientists found that tiny particles, or quanta, didn't behave according to Newton's laws. Paul Dirac came up with a new theory, called quantum mechanics, which he combined with Einstein's special relativity theory. In his theory, Dirac was able to explain the properties and behaviour of quanta.

Scanned surface

Stream of electrons

Paul Dirac
English 1902–1984

▲ Quantum mechanics is used in modern technology, such as scanning tunnelling microscopes. These microscopes use streams of tiny electrons to create 3D images of atomic surfaces.

Star gazers

171 A century ago, astronomers began to wonder if faint clouds in space called nebulae were actually distant galaxies. But were the stars within them really dim or just far away? To find out, astronomers looked for stars of varying brightness called cepheids. Slow varying cepheids are bright, so if they look dim, they must be far away.

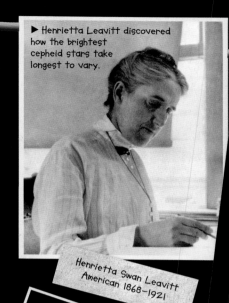

▶ Henrietta Leavitt discovered how the brightest cepheid stars take longest to vary.

Henrietta Swan Leavitt
American 1868–1921

◀ Andromeda was the first galaxy identified using cepheids.

172 In 1923, Edwin Hubble spotted a cepheid in the Andromeda nebula. It took a month to vary in brightness, so by Leavitt's scale it had to be 7000 times brighter than the Sun – and a million trillion kilometres away. So Andromeda must be a separate galaxy. Astronomers know now it is just one of 500 billion or so!

Edwin Hubble
American 1889–1953

▲ Edwin Hubble making observations at the Mount Wilson telescope in California, USA.

173 In 1931, Hubble found that the further away galaxies are, the redder they are. They are redder or 'red-shifted' because light waves are stretched out behind an object that is zooming away from us, just like sound drops in pitch after a car speeds past. So, the further a galaxy is from Earth, the faster it is moving away from us.

Georges Lemaître
Belgian 1894–1966

Arno Penzias
German-American
Born 1933

174 If galaxies are speeding apart now, they must have been closer together in the past. So the Universe is expanding. In the 1920s, Alexander Friedmann and Georges Lemaître suggested that the Universe was once just a tiny point that swelled like a giant explosion. One critic called the idea the Big Bang, and the name stuck.

175 Although the Big Bang theory caught on, there wasn't much proof. Then Arno Penzias and Robert Wilson picked up a faint buzz of radio signals from all over the sky. Astronomers believe that this buzz, called the Cosmic Microwave Background, is the faint afterglow of the Big Bang.

Alexander Friedmann
Russian 1888–1925

Robert Woodrow Wilson
American Born 1936

QUIZ

1. What was the first galaxy to be discovered beyond the Milky Way?
2. What is the theory of the origin of the Universe called?
3. What were pulsars jokingly called?

Answers:
1. The Andromeda Galaxy
2. The Big Bang
3. Little green men

▲ When Burnell first detected the radio pulses from pulsars, the stars were jokingly called 'little green men'.

176 In 1967, Jocelyn Bell Burnell picked up strange radio pulses from certain stars. These pulsing stars, or pulsars, are actually tiny stars spinning at incredible speeds. They were once giant stars that have since collapsed to make a super-dense star just a few kilometres across.

Dame Jocelyn Bell Burnell
Northern Irish Born 1943

Plan for life

177 Gregor Mendel wanted to know why some living things look like their parents and why others look different. In the 1860s, he experimented with pea flowers and their pollen to see which ones gave green peas and which ones gave yellow. Characteristics such as colour, he suggested, are passed to offspring by factors – which we now call genes.

Gregor Mendel
Austrian 1822–1884

▼ Chromosomes are the X-shaped bundles of DNA coiled up in the nucleus of a living cell.

Cell

178 In the 1900s, Thomas Hunt Morgan experimented with fruit flies. He showed that genes are linked to tiny bundles in living cells called chromosomes. By removing materials from a bacterial cell one by one, Oswald Avery later found the one material it needed to pass on characteristics – DNA.

Thomas Hunt Morgan
American 1866–1945

Oswald Avery
Canadian–American
1877–1955

Cell nucleus contains chromosomes

Rosalind Franklin
English 1920–1958

▲ The characteristics in this family group are clear to see, and have been passed on by DNA.

179 Scientists thought DNA's ability to pass on characteristics lay in its shape. Inspired by X-rays taken by Rosalind Franklin, Francis Crick and James Watson worked out in 1953 that the DNA molecule is a double helix (spiral). It's like a twisted rope ladder with two long strands either side linked by thousands of 'rungs'.

James Watson
American Born 1928

Francis Crick
English 1916–2004

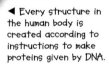
◄ Every structure in the human body is created according to instructions to make proteins given by DNA.

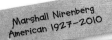
Marshall Nirenberg
American 1927–2010

Har Gobind Khorana
Indian-American
1922–2011

Double spiral
of DNA

Chromosome

A gene is
a section
of DNA

Chemical bases
make up the
rungs of DNA

Arthur Kornberg
American 1918–2007

Werner Arber
Swiss Born 1929

Stanley Cohen
American Born 1922

180 DNA's secret lies in the sequence of four chemical bases that make up its rungs. The sequence creates a code, telling the cell to make different proteins. A gene is just the sequence that gives a particular protein. Marshall Nirenberg, Har Gobind Khorana and Robert Holley went to work to find out which sequence gave which protein. By 1966 they had worked out the entire code.

Robert Holley
American 1922–1993

► By changing its DNA, scientists may be able to 'program' the mosquito that causes malaria to stop breeding.

181 In the 1950s, Arthur Kornberg and Werner Arber found how to chemically copy, cut and paste segments of DNA. Then Stanley Cohen showed how this rewritten DNA could be inserted into bacteria using little DNA snippets called plasmids. In 1972, Cohen inserted plasmids with rewritten toad DNA into bacteria to make the first genetically modified organisms.

182 Most animals have a mix of DNA from both parents, but the DNA of clones is exactly the same. Cloning occurs naturally when bacteria divide. In 1996, Ian Wilmut took DNA from one sheep and placed it in the egg of another to create the first artificially cloned mammal, a sheep named Dolly.

◄ Identical twins are natural clones.

Ian Wilmut
English Born 1944

Frontiers of science

Stephen Hawking
English Born 1942

Tim Berners-Lee
English Born 1955

184 By creating the World Wide Web in 1989, Tim Berners-Lee transformed the way the world communicates. The World Wide Web made the Internet accessible to everyone, anywhere in the world. It worked by turning computer output into web pages that could be read and displayed by any computer.

▲ Hawking suggested that the Big Bang might be a black hole in reverse, expanding from a singularity.

183 Stephen Hawking's work on black holes in space changed our understanding of the Universe. Black holes are places where gravity is so powerful that it draws in even light. At the centre is a minute point called a singularity.

Lene Vestergaard Hau
Danish Born 1959

185 Light is the fastest thing in the Universe. But in 2001 Lene Vestergaard Hau slowed it to a standstill by shining it through sodium atoms in a special cold state called a Bose-Einstein Condensate (BEC). In a BEC, atoms are so inactive there is nothing for particles of light to interact with, forcing them to slow down.

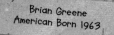

Brian Greene
American Born 1963

Michio Kaku
American Born 1947

Craig Venter
American Born 1946

186 Brian Greene and Michio Kaku are working on a theory that ties together all our ideas about the Universe, matter and energy. They believe everything is made of tiny strings of energy called superstrings. Just as a violin string can make different notes, so a superstring creates particles by vibrating in different ways.

▲ In 2010, Venter created the world's first man-made living cell.

187 Craig Venter was one of many scientists involved in mapping the entire sequence of genes in human DNA. He is also sampling the oceans for micro-organisms to see just how varied DNA is.

▼ Scientists are trying to find the Higgs boson with a massive underground machine at CERN in Switzerland, where they smash atoms together at incredible speeds.

188 Scientists explain how forces such as electromagnetic radiation are transmitted by tiny messenger particles known as bosons. But they don't know why things are heavy and have mass, and why they take force to get going and stop. Peter Higgs suggested it could be down to a mystery particle now called the Higgs boson.

Peter Higgs
English Born 1929

QUIZ

1. What would you find at the centre of a black hole?
2. What's the slowest speed light can travel?
3. Where is CERN?

Answers:
1. A singularity 2. A complete stop 3. Switzerland

INVENTIONS

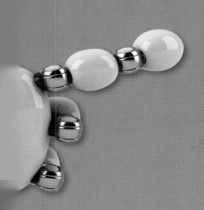

- The first inventions
- Wheels and rails
- Weapons of war
- Exploration by sea
- Renewable energy
- Writing and printing
- Musical instruments
- Communication
- Recording technology
- Inventions at home

When were tools first made?

What is a boneshaker?

Who invented the compass?

What was the first sound ever recorded?

Why were early refrigerators dangerous?

In the beginning

189 **Humans have always been inventors.** More than one million years ago, our ancient relatives made simple stone tools. Around 30,000 years ago our more recent ancestors were much more skilled at tool-making (1) and they had worked out how to sew skins together to make clothes (2). The first musical instruments were made from bone more than 20,000 years ago (3). Early humans lived by hunting animals, and invented bows and arrows to which they added tips of sharp stone. Tools, clothes, weapons, dwellings and other inventions gradually became more complicated and numerous.

▶ Stone Age clothes were made out of animal skins sewn together using a bone needle.

The first inventions

190 **The first inventors lived about 2.5 million years ago.** They were small, human-like creatures who walked upright on two legs. Their first inventions were stone tools. They hammered stones with other stones to shape them. These rough tools have been found in Tanzania in Africa. Scientists call this early relative of ours 'handy man'.

Spear made from wood with tip of sharp flint

191 Stone Age people made really sharp weapons and tools by chipping a stone called flint. They dug pits and tunnels in chalky ground to find the valuable flint lumps. Their digging tools were made from reindeer antlers.

192 Early hunters were able to kill the largest animals. With flint tips on their weapons, they overcame wild oxen and horses and even killed huge, woolly mammoths. They used their sharp flint tools to carve up the bodies. The flint easily sliced through tough animal hides.

▲ Flint tools were shaped to fit comfortably into the hand, with finely chipped cutting edges that could cut through large bones.

▼ Stone Age hunters trapped woolly mammoths in pits and killed them with spears and stones.

Stone

Pit covered with sticks

193 **The axe was a powerful weapon.** A new invention, the axe handle, made it possible to strike very hard blows. Fitted with a sharp stone head, the axe was useful for chopping down trees for firewood and building shelters.

▶ Axe heads were valuable, and were traded with people who had no flint.

MODERN AXE

▶ A modern axe is made of steel but it still has a long, sharp cutting edge and wooden handle.

▶ Saws were made from about 12,000 BC, and had flint 'teeth' held in place by resin.

I DON'T BELIEVE IT!

Some Stone Age hunters used boomerangs! They made them out of mammoth tusks thousands of years before Australian boomerangs, and used them for hunting.

MODERN SAW

▲ Today's steel saws also use many small sharp teeth to slice tough materials.

194 **Saws could cut through the hardest wood.** Flint workers discovered how to make very small flint flakes. They fixed the flakes like teeth in a straight handle of wood or bone. If the teeth broke, they could add new ones. Saws were used to cut through tough bones as well as wood.

Making fire

195 People once used fire created by lightning. The first fire-makers probably lived in East Asia more than 400,000 years ago. As modern humans spread from Africa, over 60,000 years ago, they found that northern winters were very cold, and fire helped them stay warm. They discovered how to twirl a fire stick very fast – by placing the loop of a bowstring around the stick and moving the bow back and forth. After thousands of years, people invented a way to make sparks from steel by hitting it with a flint. Now they could carry their fire-making tinderboxes around with them.

▲ People discovered that very hot flames would harden, or 'fire', pottery in oven-like kilns.

▶ Fire provided early people with warmth, light and heat to cook food. The temperature deep within a cave stays the same whatever the weather outside.

MAKING HEAT

When your hands are cold you rub them together. Do this slowly. They feel the same. Now rub them together really fast. Feel how your hands get warmer. Rubbing things together is called friction. Friction causes heat.

196 Fire makes food taste good. The invention of cooking made food safer, because cooking kills germs. Cooking roots and meat on a fire makes them more tender as well as tastier. Humans are the only animals that cook food.

▲ Some people like cooking outdoors on a fire, as our relatives did over a quarter of a million years ago.

197 Humans invented lamps to light deep, dark caves. The lamps were saucers of clay or stone that burned animal fat, with moss for a wick. Campfire flames kept wild animals away at night. They also cooked food and kept people warm. People could see to make wall paintings in the caves.

New ways of moving

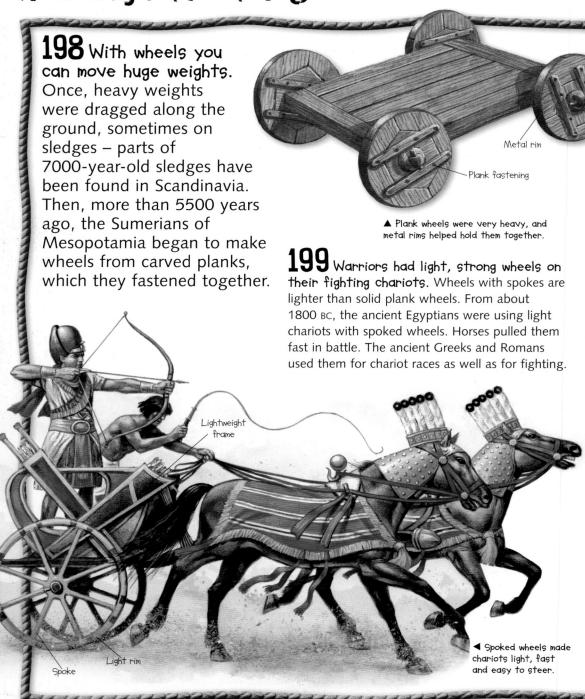

198 With wheels you can move huge weights. Once, heavy weights were dragged along the ground, sometimes on sledges – parts of 7000-year-old sledges have been found in Scandinavia. Then, more than 5500 years ago, the Sumerians of Mesopotamia began to make wheels from carved planks, which they fastened together.

Metal rim

Plank fastening

▲ Plank wheels were very heavy, and metal rims helped hold them together.

199 Warriors had light, strong wheels on their fighting chariots. Wheels with spokes are lighter than solid plank wheels. From about 1800 BC, the ancient Egyptians were using light chariots with spoked wheels. Horses pulled them fast in battle. The ancient Greeks and Romans used them for chariot races as well as for fighting.

Lightweight frame

Spoke

Light rim

◄ Spoked wheels made chariots light, fast and easy to steer.

1818

Hobby

1861

Velocipede (Boneshaker)

Early 1870s

Penny Farthing

1976

Mountain bike

200 Railway lines were once made of wood! Wheels move easily along rails. Horses pulled heavy wagons on these wagonways over 400 years ago. William Jessop invented specially shaped metal wheels to run along metal rails in 1789. Modern trains haul enormous loads at great speed along metal rails.

▲ The first public railway opened in 1825 and was 40 kilometres long. A century later, steam trains like this puffed across whole continents.

▲ Bicycle design has come a long way — early designs were very heavy, and had no pedals or way of steering.

201 In 1861, bikes with solid tyres were called boneshakers! An even earlier version of the bicycle was sometimes called the 'hobby horse'. It had no pedals, so riders had to push their feet against the ground to make it move. The invention of air-filled rubber tyres made cycling more comfortable.

QUIZ

Which came first?
1. (a) the chariot, or (b) the sledge?
2. (a) solid wheels, or (b) spoked wheels?
3. (a) rails, or (b) steam engines?

Answers:
1. b 2. a 3. a

▼ Wheels this size are usually only found on giant dump trucks. These carry heavy loads such as rocks or soil that can be tipped out.

202 Cars with gigantic wheels can drive over other cars! Big wheels give a smooth ride. At some motor shows, trucks with enormous wheels compete to drive over rows of cars. Tractors with huge wheels were invented to drive over very rough ground.

On the farm

203 The first farmers used digging sticks. In the area now called Iraq, about 9000 BC, farmers planted seeds of wheat and barley. They used knives made of flint flakes fixed in a bone or wooden handle to cut the ripe grain stalks. The quern was invented to grind grain into flour between two stones.

▲ Curved knives made of bone or wood were used for harvesting grain.

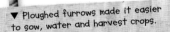

▼ Ploughed furrows made it easier to sow, water and harvest crops.

204 Humans pulled the first ploughs. They were invented in Egypt and surrounding countries as early as 4000 BC. Ploughs broke the ground and turned over the soil faster and better than digging sticks. Later on, oxen and other animals pulled ploughs. The invention of metal ploughs made ploughing much easier.

I DON'T BELIEVE IT!

Some Stone Age people invented the first fridges! They buried spare food in pits dug in ground that was always frozen.

205 For thousands of years, farming hardly changed. Then from about 300 years ago a series of inventions made it much more efficient. One of these was a seed-drill, invented by Englishman Jethro Tull. Pulled by a horse, it sowed seeds at regular spaces in neat rows. It was less wasteful than the old method of throwing grain onto the ground.

Side seed-box

Main seed-box

Coulter bar

▲ Jethro Tull's seed-drill sowed three rows of seed at a time.

206 Modern machines harvest huge fields of wheat and other crops in record time. The combine harvester was invented to cut the crop and separate grain at the same time. Teams of combine harvesters roll across the plains of America, Russia, Australia and many other places, harvesting the wheat. What were once huge areas of land covered with natural grasses now provide grain for bread.

207 Scientists are changing the way plants grow. They have invented ways of creating crop plants with built-in protection from pests and diseases. Other bumper crop plants grow well in places where once they could not grow at all because of the soil or weather.

▼ The latest combine harvesters have air-conditioned, soundproofed cabs and nearly all have sound systems. Some even use satellite navigation (satnav or GPS receivers) to plot their route automatically around fields.

Under attack!

208 Using a spear thrower is like having an arm twice the normal length. They were probably invented over 20,000 years ago. Hunters and warriors used them to hurl spears harder and farther than ever before. People all over the world invented this useful tool, and Australian Aborigines still use it.

▶ One end of the spear thrower is cupped to hold the spear butt.

209 Arrows from a longbow could pass through iron armour. Bows and arrows were invented at least 20,000 years ago. More than 900 years ago, the English longbow was made from a yew branch. Archers used it to fire many arrows a long distance in a short time. By law, all Englishmen had to practise regularly with the longbow. It helped them win many famous battles.

▶ Bowmen often stood behind lines of sharpened stakes that protected them from enemies on horseback.

I DON'T BELIEVE IT!

Longbow archers could aim and fire six arrows per minute. The arrow sometimes went straight through an enemy's armour and out the other side.

210 Crossbows had to be wound up for each shot.
They were invented over 2000 years ago in the Mediterranean
area, and fired a metal bolt or short arrow. They were
powerful and accurate, but much slower than longbows.
Soldiers used them in sieges throughout Europe from about
AD 1000 onwards. But in battles, where speed was important,
crossbows were often beaten by longbows.

▶ Crossbows were the first mechanical
hand weapons, and at one time the
Church tried to ban them.

211 In the Bible, David killed the giant,
Goliath, with a pebble from a sling. The
sling is an ancient weapon probably invented
by shepherds. They used it when guarding their
flocks, and still do in some countries. The
slinger holds the two loose ends, and puts a
pebble in the pouch. Then he whirls it
round his head and lets
go of one end. The
pebble flies out at
the target.

▼ Modern catapults with extra-strong rubber fling
stones 200 metres or more.

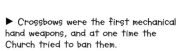

212 Even a small
catapult can do a lot of
damage. The rubber strips are
like bowstrings, which can fire a
pebble from a pouch, like a sling. Some anglers
use a catapult to fire food to attract fish to the
water's surface.

From stone to metal

213 **Sometimes pieces of pure natural gold or copper can be found in the ground.** The first people to work metal lived in the eastern Mediterranean around 8000 BC, and beat these metals with stone tools. They made the first copper weapons and gold ornaments.

► Bronze axe heads were sharper, and less easily damaged, than stone ones.

▲ Gold is quite a soft metal. Early goldsmiths beat it into a variety of shapes and made patterns of hammered indentations on its surface to create beautiful objects.

214 **Blowing air onto flames makes them hotter.** About 8500 years ago people discovered how to melt metals out of the rocks, or ores, containing them. They invented bellows – animal-skin bags, to blow air onto the flames. The hot flames melted the metal out of the ore. We call this 'smelting' the metal.

215 **Bronze weapons stay sharper for longer than copper ones.** About 5500 years ago, metal workers invented bronze by smelting copper ores and tin ores together. They used the bronze to make hard, sharp swords, spearheads and axe heads.

Bellows

Heat source

Molten bronze

Stone mould

◄ Molten bronze was poured into moulds of stone or clay to make tools.

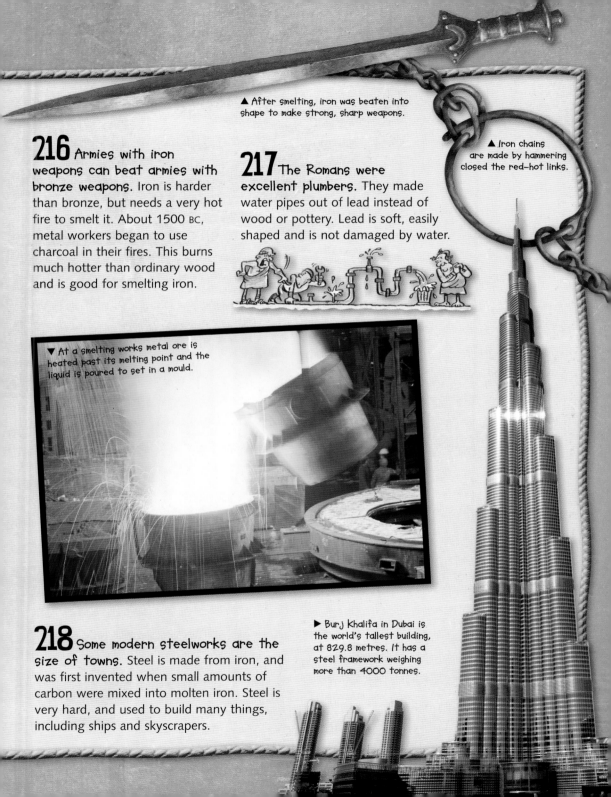

▲ After smelting, iron was beaten into shape to make strong, sharp weapons.

▲ Iron chains are made by hammering closed the red-hot links.

216 Armies with iron weapons can beat armies with bronze weapons. Iron is harder than bronze, but needs a very hot fire to smelt it. About 1500 BC, metal workers began to use charcoal in their fires. This burns much hotter than ordinary wood and is good for smelting iron.

217 The Romans were excellent plumbers. They made water pipes out of lead instead of wood or pottery. Lead is soft, easily shaped and is not damaged by water.

▼ At a smelting works metal ore is heated past its melting point and the liquid is poured to set in a mould.

218 Some modern steelworks are the size of towns. Steel is made from iron, and was first invented when small amounts of carbon were mixed into molten iron. Steel is very hard, and used to build many things, including ships and skyscrapers.

▶ Burj Khalifa in Dubai is the world's tallest building, at 829.8 metres. It has a steel framework weighing more than 4000 tonnes.

Boats and sails

219 Viking explorers reached America 1000 years ago. The world's first boats were log rafts, useful for carrying heavy loads, but very slow. Viking boats were fast, and could travel far across the open sea. Sails were invented at least 5000 years ago, and the Vikings used both sails and oars.

▶ Viking boats were made of long planks fitted onto wooden frames, and steered by means of a long oar fastened near the stern (back of the ship). They could be sailed across deep oceans, or rowed up shallow rivers, and made river journeys from the Baltic as far as the Black Sea.

I DON'T BELIEVE IT!

In 450 BC a merchant called Himilco sailed from North Africa to Britain. He ended up in Cornwall and bought Cornish tin!

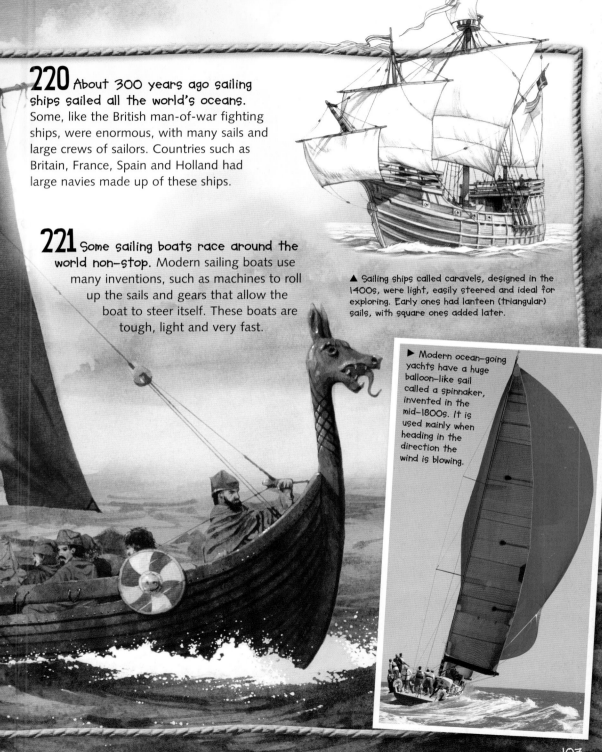

220 About 300 years ago sailing ships sailed all the world's oceans. Some, like the British man-of-war fighting ships, were enormous, with many sails and large crews of sailors. Countries such as Britain, France, Spain and Holland had large navies made up of these ships.

221 Some sailing boats race around the world non–stop. Modern sailing boats use many inventions, such as machines to roll up the sails and gears that allow the boat to steer itself. These boats are tough, light and very fast.

▲ Sailing ships called caravels, designed in the 1400s, were light, easily steered and ideal for exploring. Early ones had lanteen (triangular) sails, with square ones added later.

▶ Modern ocean–going yachts have a huge balloon–like sail called a spinnaker, invented in the mid–1800s. It is used mainly when heading in the direction the wind is blowing.

Wonderful clay

222 Stone Age hunters used baked clay to do magic. At least 30,000 years ago in Central Europe they discovered that some clay went hard in the sun, and even harder in a fire. They made clay figures of animals and humans, and used them in magic spells that they believed helped them catch food. Hardening clay in a fire was the start of the invention of pottery.

◄ By the year AD 500 in South America, Mayan craftsmen were 'firing' elaborate clay sculptures to make them hard and shiny.

▶ Kilns produced much higher temperatures than open fires, and the heat could be controlled.

Clay pot

Heat duct

Fuel

MAKE A COILED POT

Roll modelling clay into a long, 'snake' shape. Coil some of it into a flat circle. Continue to coil, building the coils upward. Try and make a bowl shape, and finally smooth out the ridges.

223 Hard clay bowls changed the way people ate. Early pots were made in China over 15,000 years ago. They were shaped by hand and hardened in fires. They could hold liquid, and were used to boil meat and plants. This made the food tastier and more tender. Around 7000 BC, potters in Southeast Asia used a new invention – a special oven to harden and waterproof clay, called a kiln.

224 Potters' wheels were probably invented before cart wheels. About 3500 BC in Mesopotamia (modern Iraq), potters invented a wheel on which to turn lumps of clay and shape round pots. By spinning the clay, the potter could make smooth, perfectly round shapes quickly.

225 Brick-making was invented in hot countries without many trees. The first brick buildings were built in 9000 BC in Syria and Jordan. House builders made bricks from clay and straw, and dried them in the hot sun. By 3500 BC, bricks hardened in kilns were used in important buildings in Mesopotamia.

▲ As the clay turns around on the disc 'wheel', the potter applies gentle pressure to shape it into a bowl, vase, urn or similar rounded item.

226 Modern factories make thousands of pots at a time. They are 'fired' in huge kilns. Wheels with electric motors are used, though much factory pottery is shaped in moulds. Teams of workers paint patterns.

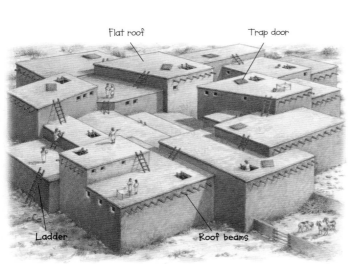

Flat roof

Trap door

Ladder

Roof beams

◀ With the invention of bricks, it was possible to construct large buildings. In 6000 BC, the Turkish town of Çatal Hüyük had houses with rooftop openings connected by ladders instead of doors.

Sailing into the unknown

227 **Early sailors looked at the stars to find their way about.** Around 1000 BC, Phoenician merchants from Syria were able to sail out of sight of land without getting lost. They knew in which direction certain stars lay. The north Pole Star, in the Little Bear constellation (star group), always appears in the north.

▲ Two stars in the Great Bear constellation are called the Pointers. They point to the north Pole Star in the Little Bear constellation.

228 **Magnetic compasses always point north and south.** They allow sailors to navigate (find their way) even when the stars are invisible. The Chinese invented the magnetic compass about 3000 years ago. It was first used in Europe about 1000 years ago.

◄ Compasses have a magnetized needle placed on a pivot so it can turn easily. Beneath this is a card with marked points to show direction.

229 **Early maps showed where sea monsters lived.** The first attempt at a world map was drawn by the Greek Ptolemy in AD 160. Greek maps of around 550 BC showed the known world surrounded by water in which monsters lived. Over 500 years ago, Pacific islanders had maps of sticks and shells, showing islands and currents. The first globe was invented in 1492 by a German, Martin Behaim.

▶ Using stick and shell maps, Pacific islanders successfully crossed thousands of kilometres of ocean.

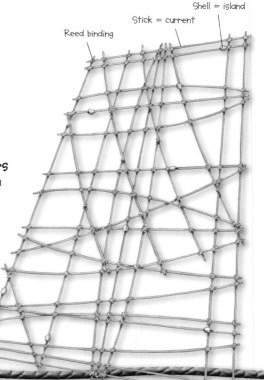

Shell = island
Stick = current
Reed binding

Mirrors

▼ The chronometer was invented by Englishman John Harrison in 1735. It was a reliable timepiece, specially mounted to remove the effect of a ship's motion at sea.

Telescope

Moving arm

▶ The sextant was developed around 1730 and was an important navigation aid until the 1900s.

Scale

230 Eighteenth-century sailors could work out exactly where they were on the oceans. They used an instrument called a sextant, invented around 1730. The sextant measured the height of the Sun from the horizon. The chronometer was an extremely reliable clock that wasn't affected by the motion of the sea.

USING A COMPASS

Take a compass outside and find out which direction is north. Put a cardboard arrow with 'N' on it on the ground pointing in the right direction. Then try to work out the directions of south, west and east.

▼ Modern navigation instruments use signals from several satellites to pinpoint their position.

Antenna (aerial) detects signals from available satellites

Batteries

Receiver compares the available satellite signals and 'locks on' to the three strongest ones

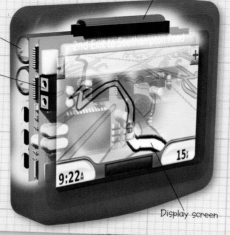

Display screen

231 New direction-finding inventions can tell anyone exactly where they are. A hand-held instrument, called a GPS receiver, receives signals from satellites in space. It shows your position to within a few metres. These receivers can be built into cars, ships, planes – even mobile phones!

Weapons of war

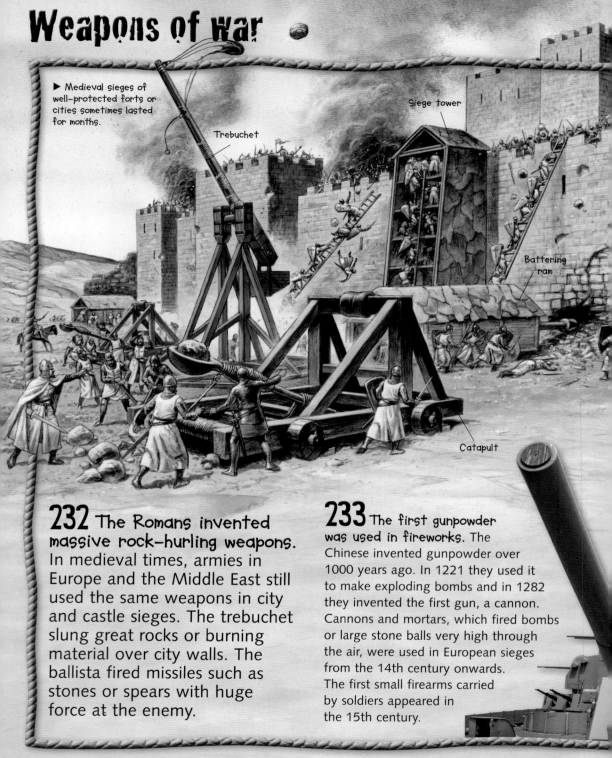

▶ Medieval sieges of well-protected forts or cities sometimes lasted for months.

Trebuchet

Siege tower

Battering ram

Catapult

232 The Romans invented massive rock-hurling weapons. In medieval times, armies in Europe and the Middle East still used the same weapons in city and castle sieges. The trebuchet slung great rocks or burning material over city walls. The ballista fired missiles such as stones or spears with huge force at the enemy.

233 The first gunpowder was used in fireworks. The Chinese invented gunpowder over 1000 years ago. In 1221 they used it to make exploding bombs and in 1282 they invented the first gun, a cannon. Cannons and mortars, which fired bombs or large stone balls very high through the air, were used in European sieges from the 14th century onwards. The first small firearms carried by soldiers appeared in the 15th century.

234 The battering ram could smash through massive city walls and gates. The Egyptians may have invented it in 2000 BC to destroy brick walls. It was a huge tree-trunk, often with an iron head, swung back and forth in a frame. Sometimes it had a roof to protect the soldiers from rocks and arrows from above.

235 Gunpowder was used in tunnels to blow up castle walls. Attackers in a siege dug tunnels under the walls and supported them with wooden props. Then, they blew up or burned away the props so that the walls collapsed.

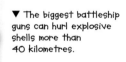

▼ The biggest battleship guns can hurl explosive shells more than 40 kilometres.

236 Greek fire was a secret weapon that burned on water. The Greeks invented it in the 7th century AD to destroy ships attacking Constantinople. A chemical mixture was squirted at enemies through copper pipes. It was still being used many centuries later in medieval sieges, pumped down onto the heads of attackers.

▲ The Gatling gun could fire six bullets a second.

237 Modern machine guns can fire thousands of bullets per minute. Richard Gatling, an American, invented a gun that would later lead to the development of the machine gun in 1862. As in all modern guns, each machine-gun bullet has its own metal case packed with deadly explosives.

Harvesting nature's energy

238 **The first inventions to use wind power were sailing boats.** Invented around 3500 BC by the Egyptians, and also by the Sumerians of Mesopotamia, the first sailing boats had a single square sail. By AD 600, windmills for grinding grain had been invented in Arab countries. Some European windmills, in use from about AD 1100 onwards, could be turned to face the wind.

239 **The first waterwheels invented were flat, not upright.** The ancient Greeks were using upright wheels more than 2100 years ago, and the Romans improved the design with bucket-like containers and gears to slow the turning rate. As well as grinding corn, some were used to drive pumps or saws.

Sail

Direction vane

Main drive

Rotation point

Vertical shaft

Gears

Millstones

Flour chute

▶ Many windmills were made entirely of wood apart from the millstones.

◀ In overshot watermills, the water strikes the top of the millwheel.

The earliest steam engine was totally useless. Around 2000 years ago a Greek engineer invented a steam machine with a spinning metal ball. Unfortunately no one could think of any use for it.

▲ Hydroelectric dams change the energy of moving water into electrical energy.

240 Early steam engines often threatened to explode. Thomas Savery's 1698 steam pump, invented in Devon, England, wasted fuel and was dangerous. Englishman Richard Trevithick developed a steam engine to move on tracks in 1804.

Generator changes the spinning movement from the rotor into electrical energy

The angle of the blades changes according to the speed of the wind

241 Spinning magnets can create an electric current. Michael Faraday and other scientists invented the first magnetic electricity generators (producers) in the 1830s. Today, huge dams use the power of millions of tonnes of flowing water to turn electricity generators, which have spinning electromagnets inside them.

Yaw control pod swings around to keep the rotor blades pointing into the wind

242 The strength of the wind usually increases the higher up you are. Some of the largest wind turbines in use today stand as high as a 50-storey building, with propellers spanning more than the length of a football pitch. They produce enough electricity to power 5000 homes or more.

▶ An increasing number of wind turbines are being built to make electricity.

Rotor blade

Marks on a page

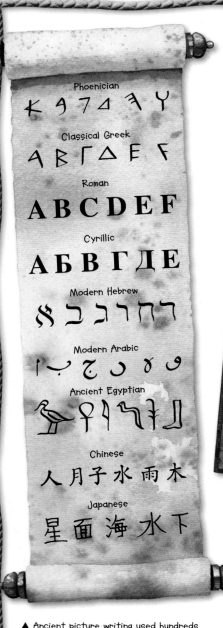

Phoenician

Classical Greek

Roman
ABCDEF

Cyrillic
АБВГДЕ

Modern Hebrew

Modern Arabic

Ancient Egyptian

Chinese
人月子水雨木

Japanese
星面海水下

▲ Ancient picture writing used hundreds of different signs, but most modern alphabets have far fewer letters.

243 **The first writing was made up of pictures.** Writing was invented by the Sumerians 5500 years ago. They scratched their writing onto clay tablets. The most famous word pictures are the 'hieroglyphs' of ancient Egyptians from about 5000 years ago. Cuneiform writing was made up of wedge shapes pressed into clay with a reed. It followed the Sumerian picture writing.

▲ Some of the religious books handwritten by monks were decorated with beautiful illustrations.

244 **The world's earliest books were rolls of paper made from reeds.** The first of this kind was produced in Egypt between 1500 BC and 1350 BC and was called 'The Book of the Dead'. Christian monks used to write their religious books on sheets of parchment made from animal skins.

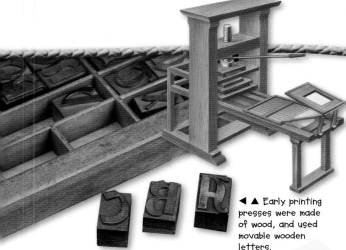

◀ ▲ Early printing presses were made of wood, and used movable wooden letters.

245 Reading suddenly became much more popular after the invention of printing. A German, Johannes Gutenberg, was an early inventor of a printing press with movable letters in the 15th century. By the end of the century there were printing presses all over Europe.

246 Once, people were expert at doing sums on their fingers. The first written numbers were invented about 3100 BC by Middle Eastern traders. Around AD 300, the Chinese invented a counting machine called an abacus. It was a frame with beads strung on wires. Some people still use them.

Container of ink is punched open to release the ink, and pressurized to get the ink into the nozzle area

▼ Modern home printers build up the image as many tiny dots of ink forming a long row or line, and then another line next to it, and so on.

Print head zooms to and fro along a guide rail, squirting out tiny jets of ink

New sheets of paper are fed from the paper tray through a tiny gap by rubber rollers

Printed sheets pile up in the print tray

Power button

▲ Experts can do complicated sums very fast on an abacus.

247 Computers do sums at lightning speed. Early modern computers were invented in the United States and Europe in the 1930s and 1940s. Today, computers are small, cheap and extremely powerful. They can store whole libraries of information. The Internet allows everyone to share information and send messages immediately almost anywhere in the world.

I DON'T BELIEVE IT!

Some early Greek writing was called, 'the way an ox ploughs the ground'. It was written from right to left, then the next line went left to right, and so on, back and forth.

Making things bigger

▲ Spectacles became important as more people began to read books.

248 Small pieces of glass can make everything look bigger. Spectacle-makers in Italy in the 14th century made their own glass lenses to look through. These helped people to read small writing. Scientists later used these lenses to invent microscopes, to see very small things, and telescopes, to see things that are far away.

249 Scientists saw the tiny bacteria that cause illness for the first time with microscopes. The Dutch invented the first microscopes, which had one lens. In the 1590s Zacharias Janssen of Holland invented the first microscope with two lenses, which was much more powerful.

◀ Early microscopes with two or more lenses, like those of English inventor Robert Hooke (1635–1703), were powerful, but the image was unclear.

250 The Dutch tried to keep the first telescope a secret. Hans Lippershey invented it in 1608, but news soon got out. Galileo, an Italian scientist, built one in 1609. He used it to get a close look at the Moon and the planets.

QUIZ

1. Which came first, (a) the telescope, or (b) spectacles?
2. Do you study stars with (a) a microscope, or (b) a telescope?
3. Which are smaller, (a) bacteria, or (b) ants?

Answers:
1.b 2.b 3.a

118

251 Modern microscopes make things look thousands of times bigger. A German, Ernst Ruska, invented the first electron microscope in 1933. It made things look 12,000 times their actual size. The latest microscopes can magnify things millions of times.

◀ An electron microscope shows a tiny parasite in monstrous detail, but this tick is actually less than 15 millimetres long.

252 You cannot look through a radio telescope. An American, Grote Reber, invented the first one and built it in his backyard in 1937. Radio telescopes pick up radio signals from space with a dish-shaped receiver. The signals come from distant stars, and, more recently, from space probes.

▶ Most radio telescope dishes can be moved to face in any direction.

Making music

253 Humans are the only animals that play tunes on musical instruments. Stone Age people made the first percussion instruments, such as rattles, from bones and tusks. Modern versions of these instruments are still used in orchestras today.

▼ The instruments of the modern orchestra are grouped into sections according to type — usually string, woodwind, brass and percussion.

GUIDE TO THE ORCHESTRA

■ **Percussion** instruments, such as drums, produce sound when they are made to vibrate by being hit, rubbed, shaken or scraped.

■ **Brass** instruments, such as horns, are made of curled brass tubes. Sound is produced by blowing into a cup-shaped mouthpiece.

■ **Woodwind** instruments produce sound when a player blows against an edge (as in flutes) or through a wooden reed (as in clarinets).

■ **String** instruments have strings. They produce sound when their strings are plucked or bowed.

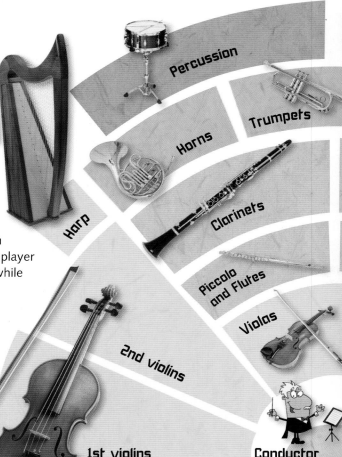

Percussion

Trumpets

Horns

Clarinets

Harp

Piccolo and Flutes

Violas

2nd violins

1st violins

Conductor

254 Over 20,000 years ago Stone Age Europeans invented whistles and flutes. They made them out of bones or antlers. Modern flutes still work in a similar way – the player covers and uncovers holes in a tube while blowing across it.

255 The earliest harps were made from tortoise shells. They were played in Sumeria and Egypt about 5000 years ago. Modern harps, like most ancient harps, have strings of different lengths.

▲ The grand piano's strings are laid out horizontally in a harp-shaped frame.

256 Pianos have padded hammers inside, which strike the strings. The first piano-like instrument was invented in about 1480 and its strings were plucked, not struck, when the keys were pressed. It made a softer sound than a modern piano.

257 The trumpet is among the loudest instruments in the orchestra. A trumpet-like instrument was found in Tutankhamen's tomb in Egypt dating back to 1320 BC. Over 2000 years ago, Celtic warriors in northern Europe blew bronze trumpets shaped like mammoth tusks to frighten their enemies.

Timpani

Trombones

Tubas

Bassoons

Oboes

Double basses

Cellos

◀ The trumpet, played here by award-winning Alison Balsom, has a total tubing length of about 148 centimetres as well as three moveable valves.

258 Bagpipes sound as strange as they look. They were invented in India over 2000 years ago. The Roman army had bagpipe players. In the Middle Ages, European and Middle Eastern herdsmen sometimes played bagpipes while they looked after their animals.

▶ Some modern bagpipes still have a bag of sewn animal skins.

Keeping in touch

259 Some African tribes used to use 'talking drums' to send messages. Native Americans used smoke signals, visible several miles away. Before electrical inventions such as the telephone, sending long-distance messages had to be a simple process.

260 Wooden arms on tall poles across the country sent signals hundreds of miles in 18th-century France. Claude Chappe invented this system, now called semaphore, in 1797. Until recently, navies used semaphore flags to signal from ship to ship. In 1838 American Samuel Morse invented a code of short and long bursts of electric current or light, called dots and dashes. It could send messages along a wire, or could be flashed with a light.

◄ Skilled morse code operators could send 30 words per minute.

▼ Each position of the semaphore signaller's arms forms a different letter. What does this message say?

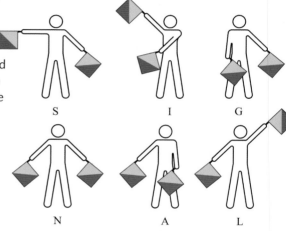

S   I   G

N   A   L

261 The telephone can send your voice around the world. A Scotsman, Alexander Graham Bell, invented it in the 1870s. When you speak, your voice is changed into electric signals that are sent along to a receiver held by the other user. Within 15 years there were 140,000 telephone owners in the United States.

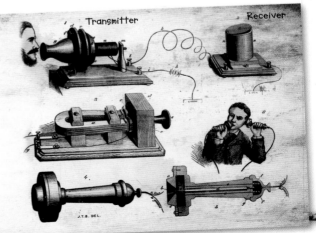

Transmitter   Receiver

► Bell's early telephone (top) in 1876 had one of the first electrical loudspeakers. The modern moving-coil design was invented in 1898 by Oliver Lodge.

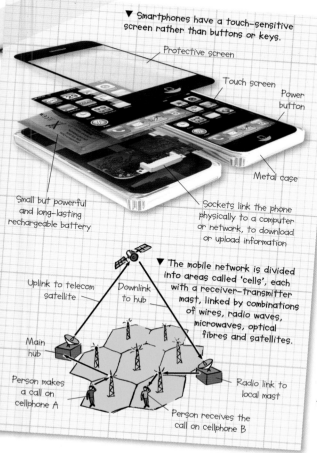

▼ Smartphones have a touch-sensitive screen rather than buttons or keys.

Protective screen

Touch screen

Power button

Metal case

Small but powerful and long-lasting rechargeable battery

Sockets link the phone physically to a computer or network, to download or upload information

▼ The mobile network is divided into areas called 'cells', each with a receiver-transmitter mast, linked by combinations of wires, radio waves, microwaves, optical fibres and satellites.

Uplink to telecom satellite

Downlink to hub

Main hub

Person makes a call on cellphone A

Radio link to local mast

Person receives the call on cellphone B

262 With a mobile or cellphone you can talk to practically anyone wherever you are. Your voice is carried on radio waves or microwaves and passed from antenna to antenna until it reaches the phone you are calling. Some of the antennas are on space satellites.

263 Radio signals fly through the air without wires. An Italian, Guglielmo Marconi, invented the radio or 'wireless' in 1899. Radio stations send signals, carried on invisible radio waves, which are received by an antenna. A Scot, John Logie Baird, invented an early TV system in 1926. TV pictures can travel through the air or along wires.

I DON'T BELIEVE IT!

Early TV performers had to wear thick, clownlike makeup. The pictures were so fuzzy that viewers could not make out their faces otherwise.

▶ Live TV images can be beamed to a satellite in space, then redirected to the other side of the world.

TV camera

Keeping a record

▼ Thomas Edison produced many important inventions, including sound recording, electric light bulbs and an early film-viewing machine.

264 The first sound recording was the nursery rhyme, 'Mary had a little lamb'. In 1877 an American, Thomas Edison, invented a way of recording sounds by using a needle to scratch marks on a cylinder or tube. Moving the needle over the marks again repeated the sounds. Performers spoke or sang into a horn, and the sounds were also played back through it.

265 To play the first disc records, you had to keep turning a handle. Emile Berliner, a German, invented disc recording in 1887. The discs were played with steel needles, and soon wore out. They also broke easily if you dropped them. Long-playing discs appeared in 1948. They had 20 minutes of sound on each side and were made of bendy plastic, which didn't break so easily.

MODERN MUSIC PLAYER

▲ Digital music players can hold over two weeks of sound recording, played through earphones or a dock with speakers.

▼ Early record players had to be wound up between records, and the loudspeaker was a large horn.

QUIZ

1. Were the first recordings on (a) discs, or (b) cylinders?
2. Which came first, (a) movies, or (b) long-playing records?
3. Was the first photograph of (a) flowers, or (b) rooftops?
4. The first movies were viewed through a hole in a box — true or false?

Answers:
1. b 2. a 3. b 4. True

266 It took eight hours to take the world's first photograph in 1826. Frenchman Joseph Nicéphore Niépce was the inventor, and the first photograph was of rooftops. Early cameras were huge, and the photos were on glass plates. In 1881 Peter Houston invented rolls of film, which George Eastman developed for the company Kodak, making photography much easier.

▲ Digital cameras have a display screen that shows the view the lens sees, which is the image that will be stored.

267 Only one person at a time could watch the first movies. The viewer peered through a hole in a box. Thomas Edison's company invented movies in 1888. The invention of a projector in 1895 by the French Lumière brothers allowed a whole audience to watch the film on a screen.

▲ The Lumière brothers, who invented the movie projector, also made films and opened the first public cinema.

► Launched in 2001, the iPod took little more than one year to develop.

268 The forerunner of the MP3 player was the portable laser-based CD player. It was more than ten times bigger and heavier than an iPod. Moving it often made the compact disc (CD) skip.

Round the house

269 **A horse and cart were needed to move the first successful vacuum cleaner around.** An English engineer, Hubert Cecil Booth, invented it in 1902. The first 'Hoover' electric vacuum cleaner was built from a wooden box, an electric fan and an old sack in 1907 in America.

▲ Early vacuum cleaners worked by opening and closing a bellows with a handle.

▼ Refrigerators were once large, noisy and had little food space.

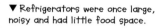

270 **Early refrigerators, invented in the 19th century, killed many people.** They leaked the poisonous gas that was used to cool them. In 1929 the gas was changed to a non-poisonous one called freon. We now know that freon causes damage to the planet's atmosphere, so that has been changed too.

QUIZ

1. Did the first 'Hoover' need (a) a horse, or (b) an electric fan?
2. Were early refrigerators dangerous because (a) they blew up, or (b) they leaked poison gas?
3. The Cretans had china toilets 4000 years ago – true or false?

Answers:
1.b 2.b 3.False

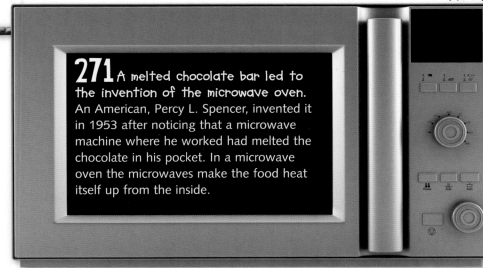

271 A melted chocolate bar led to the invention of the microwave oven. An American, Percy L. Spencer, invented it in 1953 after noticing that a microwave machine where he worked had melted the chocolate in his pocket. In a microwave oven the microwaves make the food heat itself up from the inside.

▲ In a microwave oven the microwaves are deflected by metal vanes down onto the food below.

272 There is no air inside a light bulb. If there was, it would burn out in no time. The first light bulbs failed because air could get in. American Thomas Edison invented an air-tight light bulb in 1879 that could burn for a long time. He opened the first electric light company in 1882.

Vacuum bulb

◀ In a light bulb, electricity causes a wire filament to glow brightly in the airless bulb.

Filament

▲ Energy-saving bulbs make light using fluorescence, where a chemical substance called phosphor lining the tube glows.

273 Four thousand years ago in Crete in Greece the king's palaces had flushing toilets. They used rainwater. In England, toilets that flushed when you pulled a handle were invented in the 18th century. In 1885 Thomas Twyford invented the first all-china flushing toilet.

Screw thread

Power contact

SPACE

- Earth and Moon
- Nearby planets
- Gas giants
- Outer planets
- Space objects
- The life of a star
- Types of galaxy
- The Universe
- Blasting into space
- Astronauts

What is a solar flare?

Why are there craters on the Moon?

Where is the largest volcano in the Solar System?

What is it like on Mercury?

Why does Saturn have rings?

274 Space is all around the Earth, high above the air. Here on the Earth we are surrounded by air. If you go upwards, up a mountain or in an aircraft, the air grows thinner until there is none at all. Space officially begins 100 kilometres up from sea level. It is mostly empty, but there are many exciting things such as planets, stars and galaxies. People who travel in space are called astronauts.

▶ In space, astronauts wear spacesuits to go outside a space station or a spacecraft as it circles the Earth. Much farther away are planets, stars and galaxies.

Our life-giving star

PROMINENCE

PROMINENCE

275 **The Sun is our nearest star.** It does not look like other stars because it is so much closer to us. Most stars are so far away they look like points of light in the sky. The Sun is not solid like the Earth, but is a giant ball of superhot gases, so hot that they glow like the flames of a bonfire.

SOLAR FLARE

◀ The Sun's hot, glowing gas is always on the move, bubbling up to the surface and sinking back down again.

276 **Very little could live on Earth without the Sun.** Deep in its centre the Sun is constantly making energy that keeps its gases hot and glowing. This energy works its way to the surface where it escapes as heat and light. Without it, the Earth would be cold and dark with hardly any life at all.

SUNSPOT

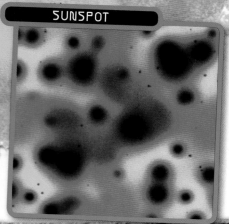

277 **The Sun is often spotty.** Sunspots appear on the surface, some wider than the Earth. They look dark because they are cooler than the rest of the Sun. Solar flares – explosions of energy – suddenly shoot out from the Sun. The Sun also throws huge loops of gas called prominences out into space.

278 When the Moon hides the Sun there is a solar eclipse. Every so often, the Sun, Moon and Earth line up in space so that the Moon comes directly between the Earth and the Sun. This stops the sunlight from reaching a small area on Earth. This area grows dark and cold, as if night has come early.

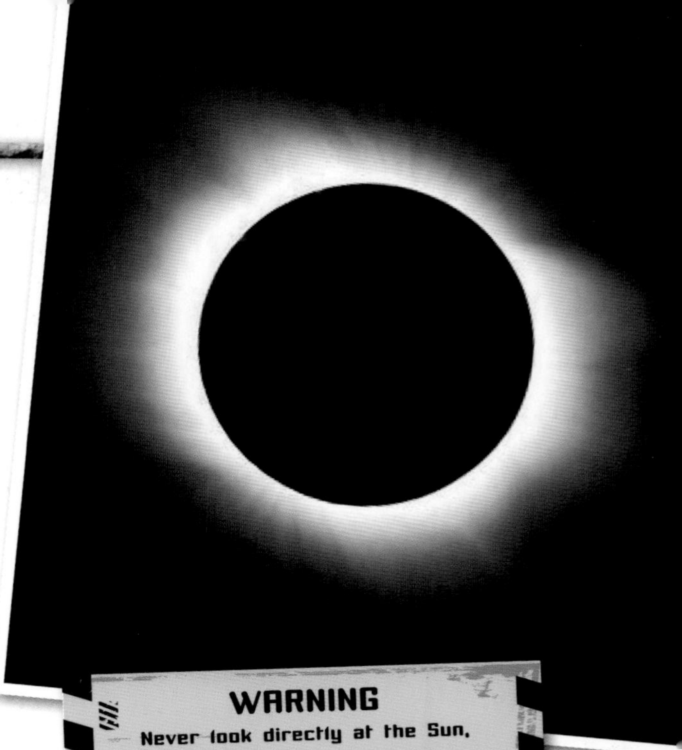

▶ When there is an eclipse, we can see the corona (glowing gas) around the Sun.

Sun

I DON'T BELIEVE IT!
The surface of the Sun is nearly 60 times hotter than boiling water. It is so hot it would melt a spacecraft flying near it.

Moon

Total eclipse

Earth

Shadow of eclipse

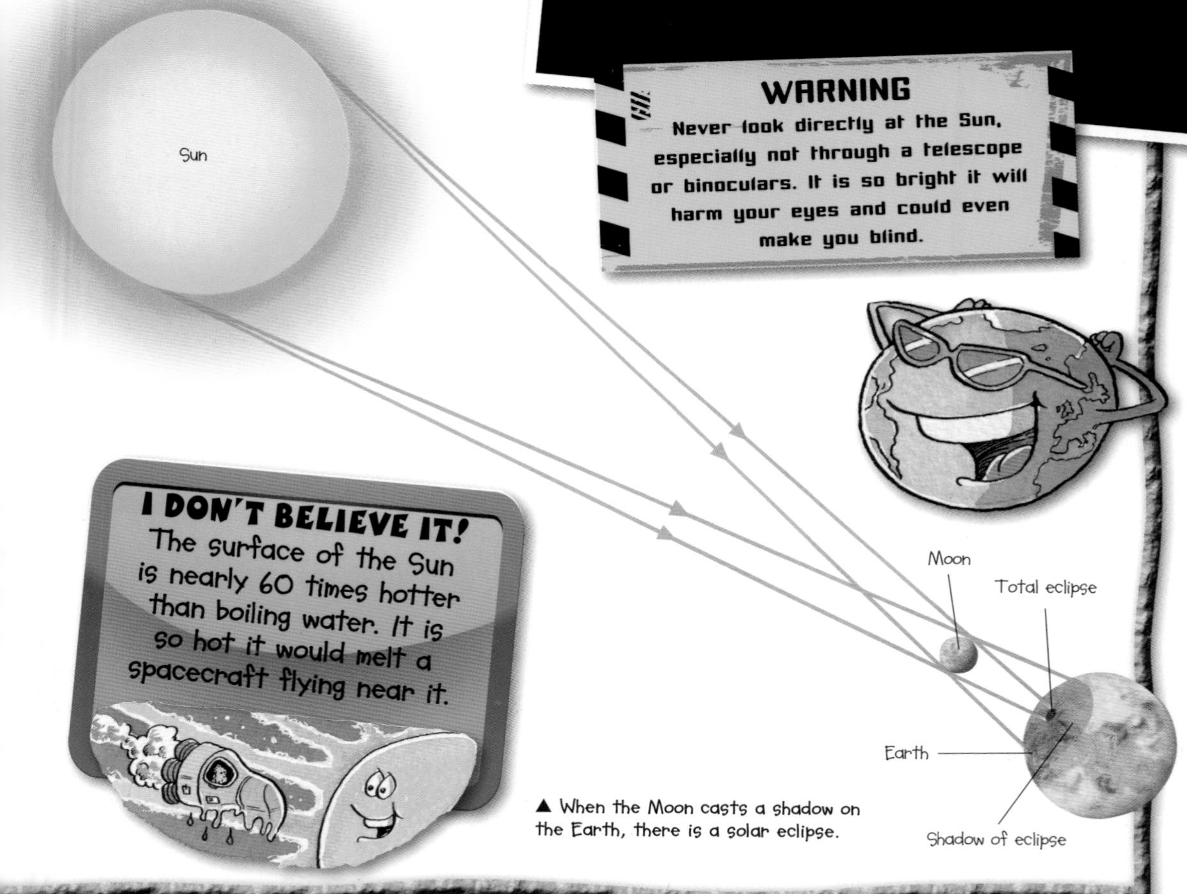

▲ When the Moon casts a shadow on the Earth, there is a solar eclipse.

A family of planets

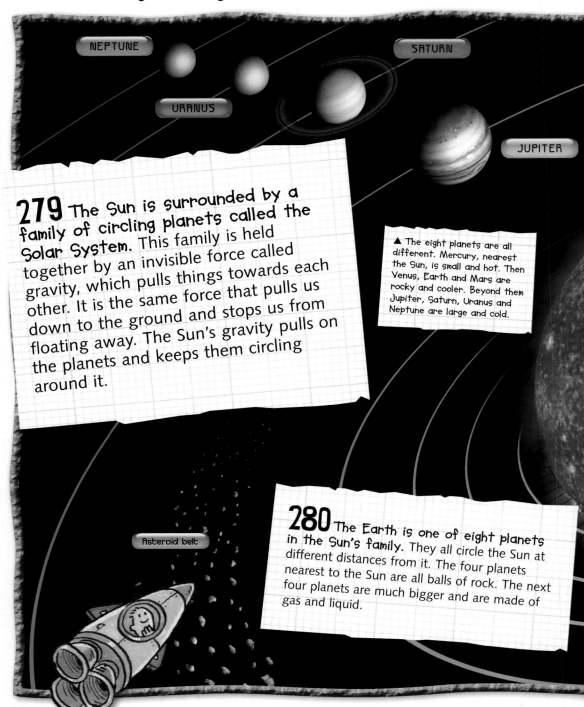

NEPTUNE

URANUS

SATURN

JUPITER

279 The Sun is surrounded by a family of circling planets called the Solar System. This family is held together by an invisible force called gravity, which pulls things towards each other. It is the same force that pulls us down to the ground and stops us from floating away. The Sun's gravity pulls on the planets and keeps them circling around it.

▲ The eight planets are all different. Mercury, nearest the Sun, is small and hot. Then Venus, Earth and Mars are rocky and cooler. Beyond them Jupiter, Saturn, Uranus and Neptune are large and cold.

Asteroid belt

280 The Earth is one of eight planets in the Sun's family. They all circle the Sun at different distances from it. The four planets nearest to the Sun are all balls of rock. The next four planets are much bigger and are made of gas and liquid.

281 Moons circle the planets, travelling with them round the Sun. Earth has one moon. It circles the Earth while the Earth circles round the Sun. Mars has two tiny moons, but Mercury and Venus have none at all. There are large families of moons, like miniature solar systems, around all the large gas planets.

I DON'T BELIEVE IT!
If the Sun was the size of a large beach ball, the Earth would be as small as a pea, and the Moon would look like a pinhead.

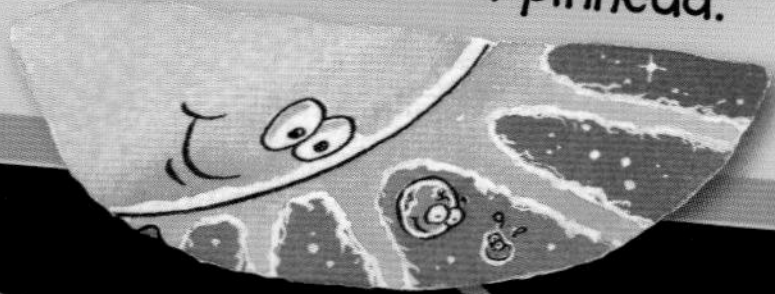

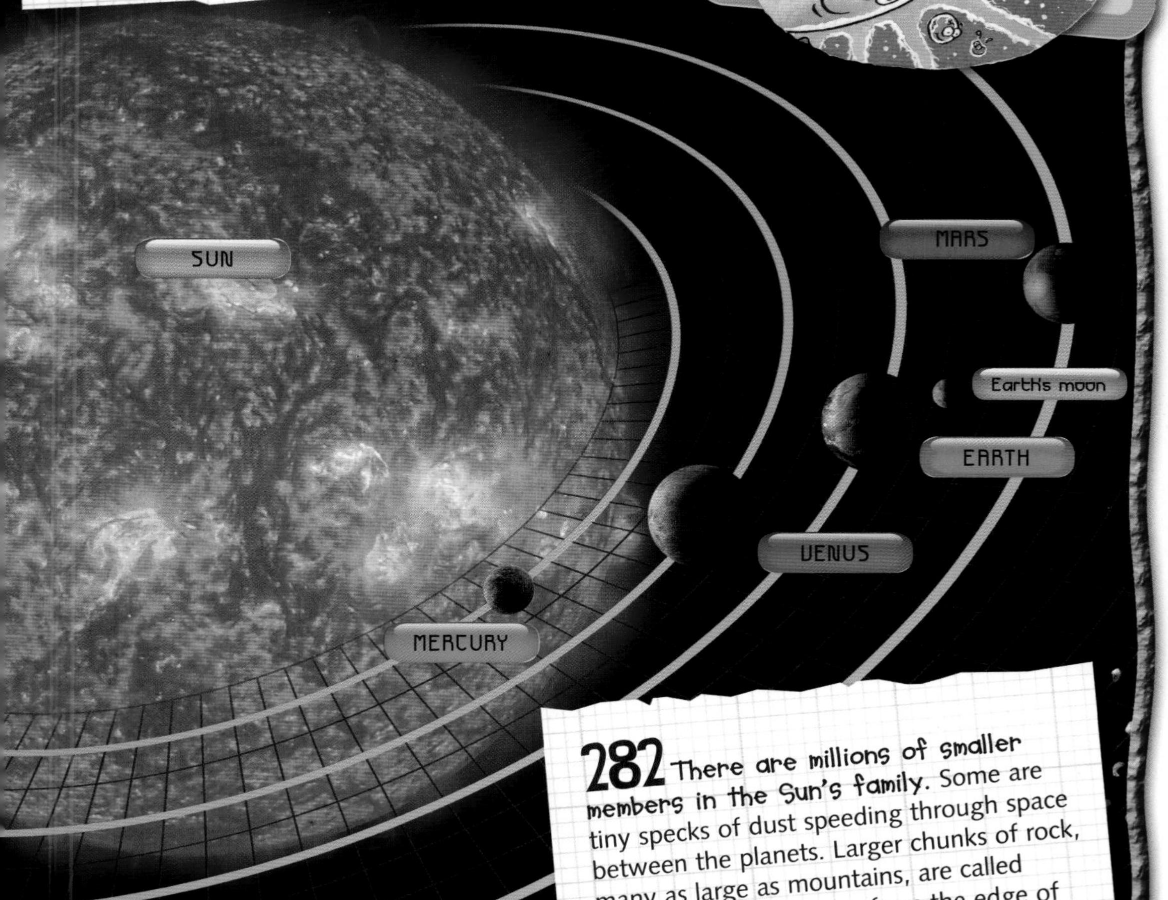

SUN

MARS

Earth's moon

EARTH

VENUS

MERCURY

282 There are millions of smaller members in the Sun's family. Some are tiny specks of dust speeding through space between the planets. Larger chunks of rock, many as large as mountains, are called asteroids. Comets come from the edge of the Solar System, skimming past the Sun before they disappear again.

Planet of life

283 **The planet we live on is the Earth.** It is a round ball of rock. On the outside, where we live, the rock is hard and solid. But deep below our feet, inside the Earth, the rock is hot enough to melt. You can sometimes see this hot rock showering out of an erupting volcano.

284 **The Earth is the only planet with life.** From space the Earth is a blue-and-white planet, with huge oceans and wet masses of cloud. People, animals and plants can live on Earth because of all this water.

285 Sunshine gives us daylight when it is night on the other side of the Earth. When it is daytime, your part of the Earth faces towards the Sun and it is light. At night, your part faces away from the Sun and it is dark. Day follows night because the Earth is always turning.

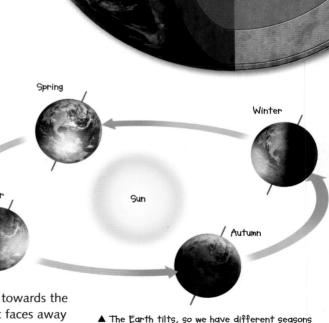

Spring

Winter

Summer

Sun

Autumn

▲ The Earth tilts, so we have different seasons as it moves around the Sun. These are the seasons for the northern half of the Earth.

◄ The inner core at the centre of the Earth is made of iron. It is very hot and keeps the outer core as liquid. Outside this is the mantle, made of thick rock. The thin surface layer that we live on is called the crust.

KEY

1 Inner core
2 Outer core
3 Mantle
4 Crust

286 Craters on the Moon are scars from space rocks crashing into the surface. When a rock smashes into the Moon at high speed, it leaves a saucer-shaped dent, pushing some of the rock outwards into a ring of mountains.

Crater

287 Look for the Moon on clear nights and watch how it seems to change shape. Over a month it changes from a thin crescent to a round shape. This is because sunlight is reflected by the Moon. We see the full Moon when the sunlit side faces the Earth and a thin, crescent shape when most of the sunlit side is facing away from us.

I DON'T BELIEVE IT!
The Moon has no air. When astronauts went to the Moon they had to take air with them in their spacecraft and spacesuits.

The Earth's neighbours

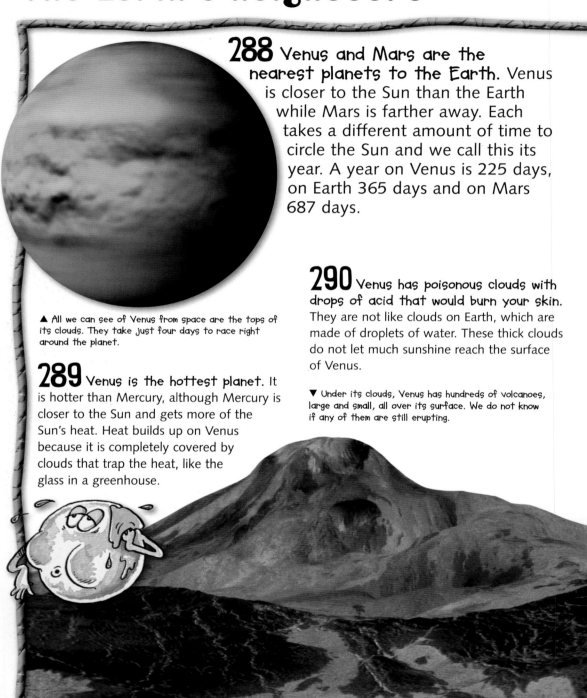

288 Venus and Mars are the nearest planets to the Earth. Venus is closer to the Sun than the Earth while Mars is farther away. Each takes a different amount of time to circle the Sun and we call this its year. A year on Venus is 225 days, on Earth 365 days and on Mars 687 days.

▲ All we can see of Venus from space are the tops of its clouds. They take just four days to race right around the planet.

289 Venus is the hottest planet. It is hotter than Mercury, although Mercury is closer to the Sun and gets more of the Sun's heat. Heat builds up on Venus because it is completely covered by clouds that trap the heat, like the glass in a greenhouse.

290 Venus has poisonous clouds with drops of acid that would burn your skin. They are not like clouds on Earth, which are made of droplets of water. These thick clouds do not let much sunshine reach the surface of Venus.

▼ Under its clouds, Venus has hundreds of volcanoes, large and small, all over its surface. We do not know if any of them are still erupting.

Radio aerial

Solar panel

Camera

▲ *Mariner 9* was the first space probe to circle another planet. Since that time more than 30 other crafts have travelled to Mars and several have soft-landed, including four rovers.

292 Winds on Mars whip up huge dust storms that can cover the whole planet. Mars is very dry, like a desert, and covered in red dust. When a space probe called *Mariner 9* arrived there in 1971, the whole planet was hidden by dust clouds.

291 Mars has the largest volcano in the Solar System. It is called Olympus Mons and is three times as high as Mount Everest, the tallest mountain on Earth. Olympus Mons is an old volcano and it has not erupted for millions of years.

PLANET-SPOTTING
See if you can spot Venus in the night sky. It is often the first bright 'star' to appear in the evening, just above where the Sun has set. Because of this we sometimes call it the 'evening star'.

Olympus Mons

293 There are plans to send astronauts to Mars but the journey would take six months or more. The astronauts would have to take with them everything they need for the journey there and back and for their stay on Mars.

Valles Marineris

◀ An enormous valley seems to cut Mars in half. It is called Valles Marineris. To the left is a row of three huge volcanoes and beyond them you can see the largest volcano, Olympus Mons.

The smallest of all

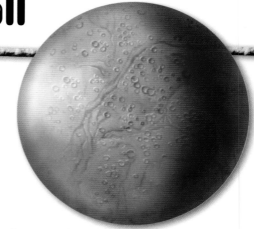

294 Tiny Pluto is so far away, it was not discovered until 1930. In 2006, Pluto was classed as a dwarf planet. It is less than half the width of the smallest planet, Mercury. In fact Pluto is smaller than our Moon.

▲ Pluto is too far away to see any detail on its surface, but it might look like this.

295 Pluto is further from the Sun than the eight main planets. It is so far from the Sun that if you stood on its surface, the Sun would not look much brighter than the other stars. Pluto gets little heat from the Sun and is completely covered with ice.

297 *New Horizons* is the first space probe to visit Pluto. It blasted off in 2006 and reached the dwarf planet in July 2015. It is now travelling to the outer region of the Solar System, called the Kuiper Belt.

296 No one knew Pluto had a moon until 1978. An astronomer noticed what looked like a bulge on the side of the dwarf planet. It turned out to be a moon half the width of Pluto, called Charon. In 2005 two more tiny moons were found, Nix and Hydra.

▼ If you were on Pluto, its moon Charon would look much larger than our Moon does, because Charon is so close to Pluto.

298 Mercury looks like our Moon.
It is a round, cratered ball of rock. Although a little larger than the Moon, like the Moon it has no air.

◄ Mercury's many craters show how often it was hit by space rocks. One was so large that it shattered rocks on the other side of the planet.

▼ The Sun looks huge as it rises on Mercury. A traveller to Mercury would have to keep out of its heat.

299 The sunny side of Mercury is boiling hot but the night side is freezing cold.
Being the nearest planet to the Sun, the sunny side can get twice as hot as an oven. But Mercury spins round slowly so the night side has time to cool down, and there is no air to trap the heat. The night side becomes more than twice as cold as the coldest place on Earth – Antarctica.

The biggest of all

300 Jupiter is the biggest planet, more massive than all the other planets in the Solar System put together. It is 11 times as wide as the Earth although it is still much smaller than the Sun. Saturn, the next largest planet, is more than nine times as wide as the Earth.

301 Jupiter and Saturn are gas giants. They have no solid surface for a spacecraft to land on. All that you can see are the tops of their clouds. Beneath the clouds, the planets are made mostly of gas (like air) and liquid (water is a liquid).

302 The Great Red Spot on Jupiter is a 300-year-old storm. It was first noticed about 300 years ago and is at least twice as wide as the Earth. It rises above the rest of the clouds and swirls around like storm clouds on Earth.

▼ Jupiter's fast winds blow the clouds into coloured bands around the planet.

▼ There are many storms on Jupiter but none as large or long lasting as the Great Red Spot.

▼ Jupiter's Moon Io is always changing because its many volcanoes throw out new material from deep inside it.

JUPITER'S MOON IO

THE GREAT RED SPOT

CLOUDS

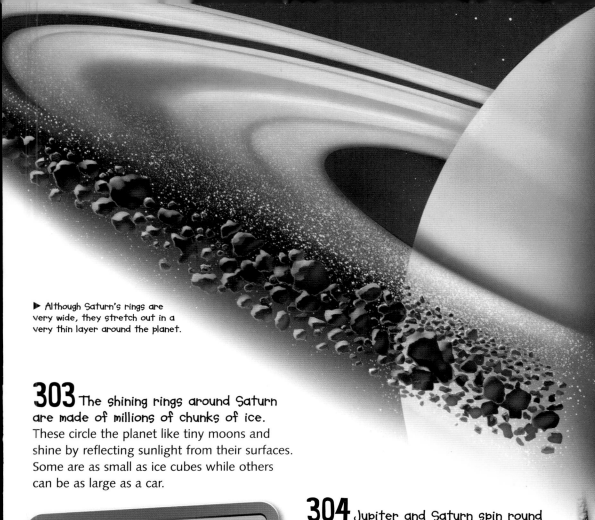

▶ Although Saturn's rings are very wide, they stretch out in a very thin layer around the planet.

303 The shining rings around Saturn are made of millions of chunks of ice. These circle the planet like tiny moons and shine by reflecting sunlight from their surfaces. Some are as small as ice cubes while others can be as large as a car.

I DON'T BELIEVE IT!
For its size, Saturn is lighter than any other planet. If there was a large enough sea, it would float like a cork.

304 Jupiter and Saturn spin round so fast that they bulge out in the middle. This can happen because they are not made of solid rock. As they spin, their clouds are stretched out into light and dark bands around them.

305 Jupiter's moon Io looks a bit like a pizza. It has many active volcanoes that throw out huge plumes of material, making red blotches and dark marks on its orange-yellow surface.

So far away

▼ There is very little to see on Uranus, just a few wisps of cloud above the greenish haze.

306 Uranus and Neptune are gas giants like Jupiter and Saturn. They are the next two planets beyond Saturn but are much smaller, being less than half as wide. They too have no hard surface. Their cloud tops make Uranus and Neptune both look blue. They are very cold, being so far from the Sun.

307 Uranus seems to 'roll' around the Sun. Unlike most of the other planets, which spin upright like tops, Uranus spins on its side. It may have been knocked over when something crashed into it millions of years ago.

308 Uranus has more than 25 moons, and there are probably more to be discovered. Most are very small, but Titania, the largest, is 1575 kilometres across, which makes it the eighth largest moon in the Solar System.

▶ Miranda is one of Uranus' moons. It looks as though it has been split apart and put back together again.

309 **Neptune had a storm that disappeared.** When the *Voyager 2* space probe flew past Neptune in 1989 it spotted a huge storm like a dark version of the Great Red Spot on Jupiter. When the Hubble Space Telescope looked at Neptune in 1994, the storm had gone.

310 **Neptune is sometimes farther from the Sun than Pluto.** Planets and dwarf planets go around the Sun on orbits (paths) that look like circles, but Pluto's path is more squashed. This sometimes brings it closer to the Sun than Neptune.

▼ Several dwarf planets orbit farther away than Neptune and Pluto. Eris is probably 2300 kilometres across, about the same size as Pluto.

311 **Neptune has bright blue clouds that make the whole planet look blue.** Above these clouds are smaller white streaks. These are icy clouds that race around the planet. One of the white clouds seen by the *Voyager 2* space probe was called 'Scooter' because it scooted around the planet so fast.

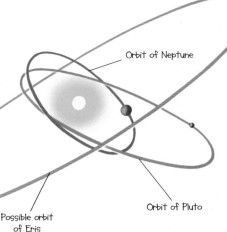

Orbit of Neptune

Orbit of Pluto

Possible orbit of Eris

▲ Like all the gas giant planets, Neptune has rings, although they are much darker and thinner than Saturn's rings.

QUIZ

1. How many moons does Uranus have?
2. Which is the biggest planet in our Solar System?
3. Which planet seems to 'roll' around the Sun?
4. What colour are Neptune's clouds?

Answers:
1. More than 25 2. Jupiter
3. Uranus 4. Blue

Comets, asteroids and meteors

312 There are probably billions of tiny comets at the edge of the Solar System. They circle the Sun far beyond Neptune and even Pluto. Sometimes one is disturbed and moves inwards towards the Sun, looping around it before going back to where it came from. Some comets come back to the Sun regularly, such as Halley's comet, which returns every 76 years.

313 A comet is often called a dirty snowball because it is made of dust and ice mixed together. Heat from the Sun melts some of the ice. This makes dust and gas stream away from the comet, forming a huge tail that glows in the sunlight.

▲ The solid part of a comet is hidden inside a huge, glowing cloud that stretches into a long tail.

314 Comet tails always point away from the Sun. Although it looks bright, a comet's tail is extremely thin so it is blown outwards, away from the Sun. When the comet moves away from the Sun, its tail goes in front of it.

315 Asteroids are chunks of rock that failed to stick together to make a planet. Most of them circle the Sun between Mars and Jupiter where there would be room for another planet. There are millions of asteroids, some the size of a car, and others as big as mountains.

ASTEROIDS

Asteroids travel in a ring around the Sun. This ring is called the asteroid belt and can be found between Mars and Jupiter.

316 Meteors are sometimes called shooting stars. They are not really stars, just streaks of light that flash across the night sky. Meteors are made when pebbles racing through space at high speed hit the top of the air above the Earth. The pebble gets so hot it burns up. We see it as a glowing streak for a few seconds.

▼ At certain times of year there are meteor showers, when you can see more shooting stars than usual.

QUIZ

1. Which way does a comet tail always point?

2. What is another name for a meteor?

3. Where is the asteroid belt?

Answers:
1. Away from the Sun
2. Shooting star
3. Between Mars and Jupiter

A star is born

317 Stars are born in clouds of dust and gas called nebulae. Astronomers can see these clouds as shining patches in the night sky, or dark patches against the distant stars. These clouds shrink as gravity pulls the dust and gas together. At the centre, the gas gets hotter and hotter until a new star is born.

318 Stars begin their lives when they start making energy. When the dust and gas pulls tightly together it gets very hot. Finally it gets so hot in the middle that it can start making energy. The energy makes the star shine, giving out heat and light like the Sun.

KEY

1 Clumps of gas in this nebula start to shrink into the tight round balls that will become stars.

2 The gas spirals round as it is pulled inwards. Any left over gas and dust may form planets around the new star.

3 Deep in its centre, the new star starts making energy, but it is still hidden by the cloud of dust and gas.

4 The dust and gas are blown away and we can see the star shining. Maybe it has a family of planets like the Sun.

STAR CLUSTER

This cluster of young stars, with many stars of different colours and sizes, will gradually drift apart, breaking up the cluster.

319 Young stars often stay together in clusters. When they start to shine they light up the nebula, making it glow with bright colours. Then the starlight blows away the remains of the cloud and we can see a group of new stars, called a star cluster.

QUIZ

1. What is a nebula?
2. How long has the Sun been shining?
3. What colour are large hot stars?
4. What is a group of new young stars called?

Answers:
1. A cloud of dust and gas in space 2. About 4.5 billion years 3. Bluish-white 4. Star cluster

▲ Large white star

▲ Medium-sized star

▲ Small red star

320 Smaller stars live much longer than huge stars. Stars use up their gas to make energy, and the largest stars use up their gas much faster than smaller stars. The Sun is about halfway through its life. It has been shining for about 4.5 billion years and will go on shining for another 4.5 billion years.

BUTTERFLY NEBULA

At the end of its life a red giant star threw out this glowing cloud of gas.

321 Large stars are very hot and white, smaller stars are cooler and redder. A large star can make energy faster and get much hotter than a smaller star. This gives them a very bright, bluish-white colour. Smaller stars are cooler. This makes them look red and shine less brightly. Ordinary in-between stars like our Sun look yellow.

Death of a star

322 **Stars begin to die when they run out of gas to make energy.** The middle of the star begins to shrink but the outer parts expand, making the star much larger.

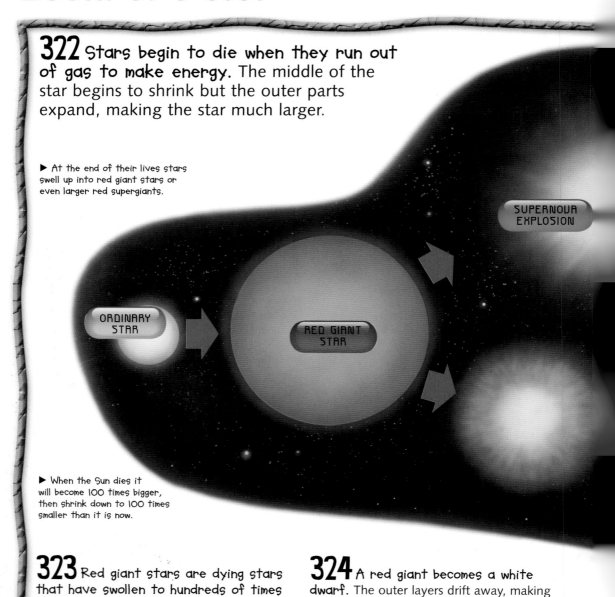

▶ At the end of their lives stars swell up into red giant stars or even larger red supergiants.

SUPERNOVA EXPLOSION

ORDINARY STAR

RED GIANT STAR

▶ When the Sun dies it will become 100 times bigger, then shrink down to 100 times smaller than it is now.

323 Red giant stars are dying stars that have swollen to hundreds of times their normal size. Their expanding outer layers get cooler, making them look red. When the Sun is a red giant it will be large enough to swallow up the nearest planets, Mercury and Venus, and perhaps Earth.

324 A red giant becomes a white dwarf. The outer layers drift away, making a halo of gas around the star. The starlight makes this gas glow and we call it a planetary nebula. All that is left is a small, hot star called a white dwarf, which cannot make energy and gradually cools and dies.

BLACK HOLE

WHITE DWARF STAR

BLACK DWARF STAR

325 Very heavy stars end their lives in a huge explosion called a supernova. This explosion blows away all the outer parts of the star. All that is left is a tiny hot star in the middle of the shell.

◀ After a supernova explosion, a giant star may end up as a very tiny hot star or even a black hole.

I DON'T BELIEVE IT!
One of the main signs of a black hole is flickers of very hot gases near one just before they are sucked in.

SUPERNOVA

326 After a supernova explosion the largest stars may end up as black holes. The remains of the star fall in on itself. As it shrinks, its gravity gets stronger. Eventually the pull of its gravity can get so strong that nothing near it can escape. This is called a black hole.

When a supernova occurs gas rushes outwards in all directions, making a glowing shell.

327 **The Sun is part of a huge family of stars called the Milky Way Galaxy.** There are billions of other stars in our Galaxy, as many as the grains of sand on a beach. We call it the Milky Way because it looks like a very faint band of light in the night sky, as though someone has spilt some milk across space.

▲ This huge spiral galaxy contains billions of stars. Our Milky Way Galaxy would look like this if we could see it from above.

328 **Curling arms give some galaxies their spiral shape.** The Milky Way has arms made of bright stars and glowing clouds of gas that curl round into a spiral shape. Some galaxies, called elliptical galaxies, have a round shape like a squashed ball. Other galaxies have no particular shape.

I DON'T BELIEVE IT!
If you could fit the Milky Way onto these two pages, the Sun would be so tiny, you could not see it.

329 There are billions of galaxies outside the Milky Way. Some are larger than the Milky Way and many are smaller, but they all have more stars than you can count. The galaxies tend to stay together in groups called clusters.

330 There is no bump when galaxies collide. A galaxy is mostly empty space between the stars. But when galaxies get very close they can pull each other out of shape. Sometimes they look as if they have grown a huge tail stretching out into space, or their shape may change into a ring of glowing stars.

A CLUSTER OF GALAXIES

▲ These two galaxies are so close that each has pulled a long tail of bright stars from the other.

Astronomers have nicknamed this interesting cluster of galaxies the 'Bullet Cluster'. It is made up of two colliding groups of galaxies.

▼ From left to right these are spiral, irregular, and elliptical galaxies, and a spiral galaxy with a bar across the middle.

What is the Universe?

331 **The Universe is the name we give to everything we know about.** This means everything on Earth, from tiny bits of dust to the highest mountain, and everything that lives here, including you. It also means everything in space – all the billions of stars in the billions of galaxies.

▼ Astronomers suspect that the universe is primarily made up of dark matter (purple) – a mysterious and unproven substance.

332 **The Universe started with a massive explosion called the Big Bang.** Astronomers think that this happened about 13.7 billion years ago. A huge explosion sent everything racing outwards in all directions. To start with, everything was packed incredibly close together. Over time it has expanded (spread out) into the Universe we can see today, which is mostly empty space.

333 **The Universe's matter includes planets, stars and gas, and its energy includes light and heat.** Scientists suspect that it also contains unknown dark matter and dark energy, which we are unable to detect. These may affect what finally happens to the Universe.

334 The galaxies are still racing away from each other. When astronomers look at distant galaxies they can see that other galaxies are moving away from our galaxy, and the more distant galaxies are moving away faster. In fact all the galaxies are moving apart from each other. We say that the Universe is expanding.

335 We do not know what will happen to the Universe billions of years in the future. It may keep on expanding. If this happens, old stars will gradually die and no new ones will be born. Everywhere will become dark and cold.

DOTTY UNIVERSE

You will need:

balloon   pen

Blow up a balloon a little, holding the neck to stop air escaping. Mark dots on the balloon with a pen, then blow it up some more. Watch how the dots move apart from each other. This is like the galaxies moving apart as the Universe expands.

KEY

1 All the parts that make up the Universe were once packed tightly together. No one knows why the Universe started expanding with a Big Bang.

2 As everything moved apart in all directions, stars and galaxies started to form.

3 Today there are galaxies of different shapes and sizes, all moving apart. One day they may start moving towards each other.

4 The Universe could stop expanding and stay the same, or shrink and end with a Big Crunch.

Three, two, one...Lift off!

336 To blast into space, a rocket has to travel nearly 40 times faster than a jumbo jet. If it goes any slower, gravity pulls it back to Earth. Rockets are powered by burning fuel, which makes hot gases. These gases rush out of the engines, shooting the rocket forwards.

▼ In 2007, the *Dawn* spacecraft started its journey to the asteroid belt tucked inside the nose cone at the top of a *Delta II* rocket.

Satellite goes into space

Third stage

First stage

Second stage

Booster rockets drop away

▲ Each stage fires its engine to make the rocket go faster and faster until it puts the satellite into space.

337 A single rocket is usually not powerful enough to launch a satellite or spacecraft. So most have two or three stages, which are really separate rockets mounted on top of each other, each with its own engines. When the first stage has used up its fuel it drops away, and the second stage starts. Finally the third stage takes over to go into space.

United S

▼ The shuttles were blasted into space by three rocket engines and two huge booster rockets.

338 The space shuttles were re-usable spaceplanes. The first was launched in 1981 and there were over 130 missions before the shuttles were retired in 2011. The shuttle took off straight up like a rocket, carrying a load of up to 24 tonnes. To land it swooped down to glide onto a runway.

▼ The shuttle puts down its wheels and lands on the runway. A parachute and speed brake bring the shuttle to a standstill.

Living in space

339 Space is a dangerous place for astronauts. It can be boiling hot in the sunshine or freezing cold in the Earth's shadow. There is also dangerous radiation from the Sun. Dust, rocks and bits from other rockets race through space at such speed, they could easily make a small hole in a spacecraft, letting the air leak out.

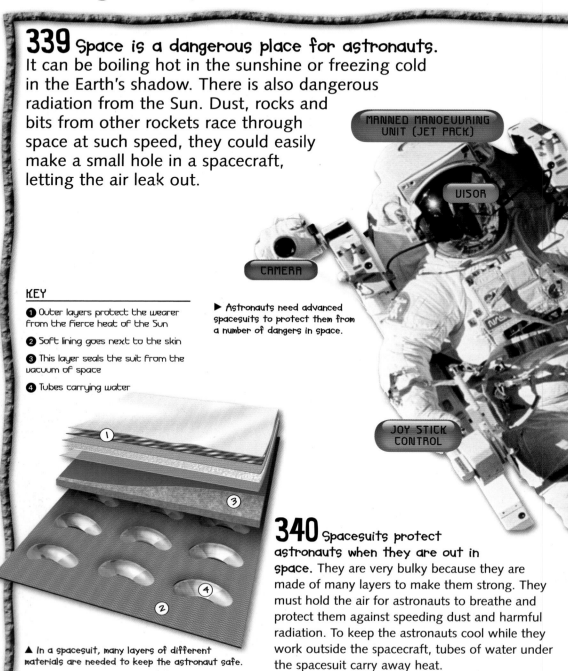

MANNED MANOEUVRING UNIT (JET PACK)

VISOR

CAMERA

JOY STICK CONTROL

► Astronauts need advanced spacesuits to protect them from a number of dangers in space.

KEY

1 Outer layers protect the wearer from the fierce heat of the Sun

2 Soft lining goes next to the skin

3 This layer seals the suit from the vacuum of space

4 Tubes carrying water

▲ In a spacesuit, many layers of different materials are needed to keep the astronaut safe.

340 Spacesuits protect astronauts when they are out in space. They are very bulky because they are made of many layers to make them strong. They must hold the air for astronauts to breathe and protect them against speeding dust and harmful radiation. To keep the astronauts cool while they work outside the spacecraft, tubes of water under the spacesuit carry away heat.

SPACE MEALS

You will need:

dried noodles   boiling water

Buy a dried snack such as noodles, which just needs boiling water added. This is the kind of food astronauts eat. Most of their meals are dried so they are not too heavy to launch into space.

341 Everything floats around in space as if it had no weight. So all objects have to be fixed down or they will float away. Astronauts have footholds to keep them still while they are working. They strap themselves into sleeping bags so they don't bump into things when they are asleep.

GLOVE

342 Astronauts must take everything they need into space with them. Out in space there is no air, water or food so all the things that astronauts need to live must be packed into their spacecraft and taken with them.

▶ Sleeping bags are fixed to walls so sometimes astronauts look as though they are asleep standing up.

SPACESUIT

Home from home

343 A space station is a home in space for astronauts and cosmonauts (Russian astronauts). It has a kitchen for making meals, and cabins with sleeping bags. There are toilets, wash basins and sometimes showers. There are places to work, and controls where astronauts can check that everything is working properly.

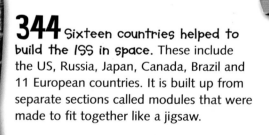

344 Sixteen countries helped to build the ISS in space. These include the US, Russia, Japan, Canada, Brazil and 11 European countries. It is built up from separate sections called modules that were made to fit together like a jigsaw.

I DON'T BELIEVE IT!
The US space station Skylab, launched in 1973, fell back to Earth in 1979. Most of it landed in the ocean but some pieces hit Australia.

KEY
1 Solar panels for power
2 Space shuttle
3 Docking port
4 Control module
5 Living module
6 Soyuz ferry

345 Each part was launched from Earth and added to the ISS in space. They were fitted by astronauts at the ISS using the shuttle's robot arm. Huge panels of solar cells were added. These turn sunlight into electricity to provide a power supply for the space station.

▼ The International Space Station provides astronauts with a home in space.

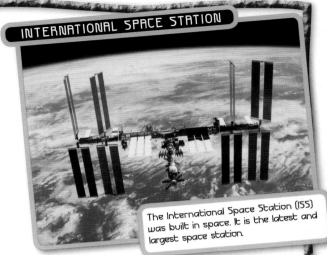

INTERNATIONAL SPACE STATION

The International Space Station (ISS) was built in space. It is the latest and largest space station.

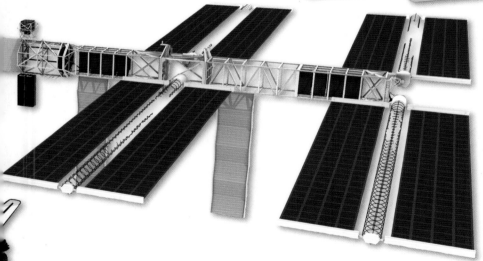

346 The crew live on board the ISS for several months at a time. The first crew of three people arrived at the space station in November 2000 and stayed for over four months. The station now has sleeping quarters for six astronauts, and many modules for living and working.

347 People and supplies can travel to the ISS in Russian Soyuz spacecraft. There are also robot ferries with no crew, including Russian Progress craft and European ATVs (Automated Transfer Vehicles). In 2001, American Dennis Tito became the first space tourist, staying on the ISS for eight days.

348 Hundreds of satellites circle the Earth in space. They are launched into space by rockets and may stay there for ten years or more.

▼ Weather satellites look down at the clouds and give warning when a violent storm is approaching.

349 Communications satellites carry TV programmes and telephone messages around the world. Large aerials on Earth beam radio signals up to a space satellite that then beams them down to another aerial, half way round the world. This lets us talk to people on the other side of the world, and watch events such as the Olympics Games while they are happening in faraway countries.

▼ Communications satellites can beam TV programmes directly to your home through your own aerial dish.

350 Weather satellites help the forecasters tell us what the weather will be like. These satellites can see where the clouds are forming and which way they are going. They watch the winds and rain and measure how hot the air and the ground are.

▶ The different satellites each have their own job to do, looking at the Earth, or the weather, or out into space.

351 Earth-watching satellites look out for pollution. Oil slicks in the sea and dirty air over cities show up clearly in pictures from these satellites. They can help farmers by showing how well crops are growing and by looking for pests and diseases. Spotting forest fires and icebergs that may be a danger to ships is also easier from space.

▶ Satellite telescopes let astronomers look far out into the Universe and discover what is out there.

▼ Pictures of the Earth taken by satellites can help make very accurate maps.

352 Satellite telescopes let astronomers look at exciting things in space. They can see other kinds of radiation, such as X-rays, as well as light. X-ray telescopes can tell astronomers where there may be a black hole.

I DON'T BELIEVE IT!
Spy satellites circling the Earth take pictures of secret sites around the world. They can listen to secret radio messages from military ships or aircraft.

353 The first men landed on the Moon in 1969. They were two astronauts from the US *Apollo 11* mission. Neil Armstrong was the first person to set foot on the Moon. There were five other Apollo missions that landed on the Moon.

354 The giant *Saturn 5* rocket launched the astronauts on their journey to the Moon. It was the largest rocket that had ever been built. Its three huge stages lifted the astronauts into space, and then the third stage gave the spacecraft an extra boost to send it to the Moon.

Command Module

Lunar Module

Legs folded for journey

◄ The distance from the Earth to the Moon is nearly 400,000 kilometres. That is about as far as travelling round the Earth ten times.

355 The Command Module that carried the astronauts to the Moon had no more room than an estate car. The astronauts were squashed inside it for the journey, which took three days to get there and another three to get back. On their return, the Command Module with the astronauts inside, splashed down in the sea.

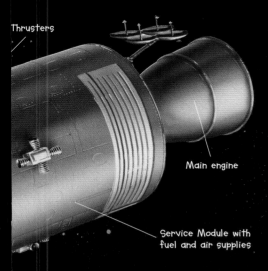

▼ The Lunar and Command Modules travelled to the Moon fixed together, then separated for the Moon landing.

Thrusters

Main engine

Service Module with fuel and air supplies

▲ The longest time that any of the Apollo missions stayed on the Moon was just over three days.

356 No one has been back to the Moon since the last Apollo mission left in 1972. Maybe one day people will return to the Moon and build bases where they can live and work.

357 The Lunar Module took two of the astronauts to the Moon's surface. Once safely landed they put on spacesuits and went outside to collect rocks. Later they took off in the Lunar Module to join the third astronaut who had stayed in the Command Module, circling above the Moon on his own.

358 The Lunar Rover was a moon car for the astronauts to ride on. It looked like a buggy with four wheels and two seats. It could only travel about as fast as you can run. The astronauts drove for up to 20 kilometres at a time, exploring the Moon's hills, valleys, flat plains and cliffs.

I DON'T BELIEVE IT!
On the way to the Moon an explosion damaged the Apollo 13 spacecraft, leaving the astronauts with little heat or light.

Are we alone?

359 The only life we have found so far in the Universe is here on Earth. Everywhere you look on Earth from the frozen Antarctic to the hottest, driest deserts, on land and in the sea, there are living things. Some are huge, such as whales and elephants, and others are much too small to see. But they all need water to live.

▼ On Earth, animals can live in many different habitats, such as in the sea, the air, in deserts and jungles, and icy lands. Try and list as many animals as you can that live in the habitats below.

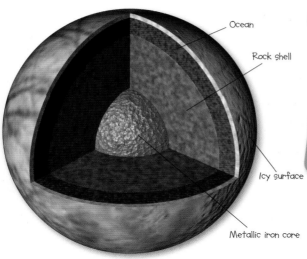

Ocean

Rock shell

Icy surface

Metallic iron core

▲ Deep beneath the cracked, icy surface of Europa, it may be warm enough for the ice to melt into water.

360 There may be an underground ocean on Europa, one of Jupiter's moons. Europa is a little smaller than our Moon and is covered in ice. However, astronomers think that there may be an ocean of water under the ice. If so, there could be strange living creatures swimming around deep underground.

DESERT

SEA

POLAR LANDS

RAINFOREST

362 Astronomers have found planets circling other stars, called exoplanets. Most of them are large, like Jupiter. But perhaps some could be smaller, like Earth. They could have a rocky surface that is not too hot or too cold, and suitable for liquid water – known as 'Goldilocks planets' after the fairytale character who tried the three bears' porridge. These planets could support some kind of life.

▲ No one knows what other exoplanets would be like. They could have strange moons or colourful rings. Anything that lives there might look very strange to us.

361 Mars seems to have had rivers and seas billions of years ago. Astronomers can see dry riverbeds and ridges that look like ocean shores on its surface. This makes them think Mars may have been warm and wet long ago and something may once have lived there. Now it is very cold and dry with no sign of life.

I DON'T BELIEVE IT!
It would take thousands of years to get to the nearest stars with our present spacecraft.

▲ This message could tell people living on distant planets about the Earth, and the people who live here.

363 Scientists have sent a radio message to a distant group of stars. They are hoping that anyone living there will understand the message about life on Earth. However, it will take 25,000 years to get to the stars and another 25,000 years for a reply to come back to Earth!

EXPLORING SPACE

- The first satellites
- Apollo Moon landings
- Planning a mission
- Escape velocity
- Flyby missions
- Engines and fuel
- Orbiters
- Landing on a new world
- Exploring Mars
- Missions to the Sun

Where are spacecraft tested?
What does a spectrometer do?
What has been found on Mars?
Where did Voyager 2 go?
Why are some crafts designed to crash?

To boldly go...

364 **For thousands of years people gazed up at the night sky and wondered what it would be like to explore space.** This became a reality around 50 years ago, and since then humans have been to the Moon, and unmanned spacecraft have visited all of the planets in the Solar System. Spacecraft have also explored other planets' moons, asteroids and glowing comets. These amazing discoveries help us to understand the Universe.

▶ ESA's Integral satellite (launched in 2002) is deployed from a Proton rocket to observe invisible gamma rays in space. Since 1957, humans have sent spacecraft to all eight planets in the Solar System, as well as more than 50 moons, asteroids and comets.

Who explores, and why?

365 Exploring space involves sending craft, robots, equipment and sometimes people to planets, moons, asteroids and comets. Some craft fly near to their targets, while others land. As they explore, they gather information to send back to Earth.

I DON'T BELIEVE IT!
The *Cassini–Huygens* mission to Saturn is the most expensive mission ever. It cost more than $3.3 billion – the price of 12 Airbus A380 super jumbo jets.

Vandenberg Air Force Base and Spaceport, California, USA

NORTH AMERICA

NASA Headquarters, Washington D.C., USA

Kennedy Space, Center, Florida, USA

Alcantara Launch Center, Sao Luis, Brazil

Guiana Space Center, Kourou, French Guiana

SOUTH AMERICA

366 Space exploration is different from other space sciences. For example, astronomy is the study of objects in space including planets, stars and galaxies, as well as the Universe as a whole. Much of this is done using telescopes, rather than travelling out into space.

▼ Astronomers use huge, extremely powerful telescopes to observe outer space from Earth.

▲ Space mission headquarters and launch sites are spread across the world.

367 Space exploration is complicated and expensive. Generally, only large nations, such as the USA, Russia, Japan and Europe, send craft into space. Recently, China and India have also launched exploratory missions.

368 Sending even a small spacecraft into space costs vast amounts of money. The Japanese *Hayabusa* mission to bring back samples of the comet Itokawa began in 2003. It lasted seven years and cost around $170 million. Sending the *Phoenix* lander to Mars in 2008 was even more expensive, at $450 million.

▶ The comet-visiting *Hayabusa* spacecraft blasted off from Uchinoura Space Centre, Japan, in 2003. It returned to Earth in 2010, carrying samples of comet dust.

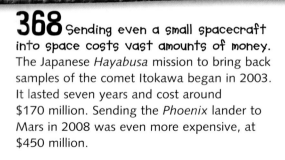

European Space Agency Headquarters, Paris, France

Roscomos Headquarters, Moscow, Russia

EUROPE

ASIA

Uchinoura Space Center, Japan

Xichang Satellite Launch Center, China

Balkonur Cosmodrome (Russian), Kazakhstan

AFRICA

Shar Space Launch Center, Sriharikota Island, India

Tanegashima Space Center, Japan

▼ Recent observations in space suggest faraway stars could have planets forming around them from bits of gas, dust and rock – similiar to our own Solar System.

369 If the costs are so great, why do we explore space? Exploring the unknown has long been a part of human nature. Space exploration provides clues that may help us to understand how the Universe formed. Progress in space technology can also help advances on Earth.

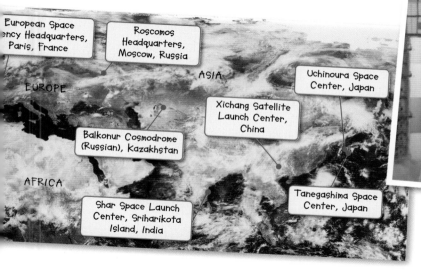

Early explorers

370 The Space Age began in 1957 when Russia launched Sputnik I, the first Earth-orbiting satellite. It was a metal, ball-shaped craft that could measure pressure and temperature, and send radio signals back to Earth.

371 In 1958, the USA launched the satellite Explorer I. As it orbited the Earth it detected two doughnut-shaped belts of high-energy particles, known as the Van Allen Belts. They can damage spacecraft and interfere with radio signals.

◄ The Van Allen belts are made up of particles, trapped by Earth's natural magnetic field.

Inner belt

Outer belt

▼ Tracking Sputnik I's orbit showed how the upper atmosphere of the Earth fades into space.

Heat-resistant outer casing

Inner casing

Batteries

Antennas

Ventilation fan

372 In 1959, Russia's *Luna I* spacecraft was aiming for the Moon, but it missed. Later that year, *Luna 2* crashed into the Moon on purpose, becoming the first craft to reach another world. On its way down the craft measured the Moon's gravity and magnetism.

QUIZ
Early exploration was a 'Space Race' between the USA and the Soviet Union. Which had these 'firsts'?
1. First satellite in space
2. First person in space
3. First craft on the Moon
4. First person on the Moon

Answers:
1, 2, 3 – Russia, 4 – USA

Hatch

Heat shield covering

Long range antenna

◀ Gagarin's *Vostok 1* spacecraft was ten times larger than the Sputnik 1 satellite, and 50 times heavier.

Descent module – only this ball–shaped part came back to Earth

Oxygen and nitrogen gas tanks for fuel and for Gagarin to breathe

Retro–thruster

373 The first person in space was Russian cosmonaut Yuri Gagarin. In 1961 he made one orbit of Earth in the spacecraft *Vostok 1*. The furthest he travelled into space was 327 kilometres. Gagarin's trip made news around the world and showed that humans could survive in space.

374 The US sent seven Surveyor craft to the Moon between 1966 and 1968. Five succeeded in soft-landing (landing without being destroyed) on the surface. This was an important stage in planning the most exciting and ambitious mission of all – sending people to another world.

▶ *Surveyor 3* landed on the Moon in April 1967. It was photographed by the *Apollo 12* astronauts in November 1969.

Man on the Moon!

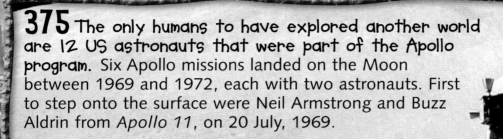

375 The only humans to have explored another world are 12 US astronauts that were part of the Apollo program. Six Apollo missions landed on the Moon between 1969 and 1972, each with two astronauts. First to step onto the surface were Neil Armstrong and Buzz Aldrin from *Apollo 11*, on 20 July, 1969.

376 Each Apollo lunar lander touched down on a different type of terrain. The astronauts stayed on the Moon for three or four days. They explored, carried out experiments and collected samples of Moon dust and rocks to bring back to Earth.

377 The last three Apollo missions took a Lunar Roving Vehicle (LRV), or 'Moon buggy'. The astronauts drove for up to 20 kilometres at a time, exploring the Moon's hills, valleys, flat plains and cliffs.

378 Since the Apollo missions, more than 50 unmanned spacecraft have orbited or landed on the Moon. In 1994, US orbiter *Clementine* took many photographs, gravity readings and detailed maps of the Moon's surface.

◄ *Apollo 15*'s Lunar Module pilot James Irwin salutes the US flag and his Commander David Scott, in 1971. Their Lunar Module lander is behind and the Moon buggy is to the right.

MISSION	DATE	CREW	ACHIEVEMENT
Apollo 11	July 1969	Neil Armstrong (C) Buzz Aldrin (LMP) Michael Collins (CMP)	First humans on another world
Apollo 12	November 1969	Pete Conrad (C) Alan Bean (LMP) Richard Gordon (CMP)	First colour television pictures of the Moon returned to Earth
Apollo 13	April 1970	James Lovell (C) Fred Haise (LMP) Jack Swigert (CMP)	*Apollo 13* turned back after launch because of an explosion. It never reached the Moon, but returned safely to Earth
Apollo 14	January– February 1971	Alan Shepard (C) Edgar Mitchell (LMP) Stuart Roosa (CMP)	Longest Moon walks in much improved spacesuits
Apollo 15	July–August 1971	David Scott (C) James Irwin (LMP) Alfred Worden (CMP)	First use of a Moon buggy allowed astronauts to explore a wider range
Apollo 16	April 1972	John Young (C) Charles Duke (LMP) Thomas Mattingly (CMP)	First and only mission to land in the Moon's highlands
Apollo 17	December 1972	Eugene Cernan (C) Harrison Schmitt (LMP) Ronald Evans (CMP)	Returned a record 49 kilograms of rock and dust samples

379 In 2009, the *Lunar Reconnaissance Orbiter* began mapping the Moon's surface in detail. Its pictures showed parts of the Apollo craft left by the astronauts. In the same year the Indian orbiter *Chandrayaan 1* discovered ice on the Moon.

◄ On each mission, the Commander (C) and the Lunar Module pilot (LMP) landed on the Moon, while the Command Module pilot (CMP) stayed in the orbiting craft.

Plan and prepare

380 **Planning a mission takes many years.** Scientists suggest places to explore, what might be discovered, and the cost. Their government must agree for the mission to go ahead.

▲ In 1961 US space engineer John Houbolt developed the idea of using a three-part spacecraft for the Apollo Moon missions.

381 **There are many types of exploratory missions.** A flyby takes the spacecraft near to its target world, and past. An orbiter circles around the target. A lander mission touches down on the surface. A lander may release a rover, which can travel around on the surface.

▲ For worlds with an atmosphere, parachutes are used to lower a lander gently. This parachute design for a planned mission to Mars is being tested in the world's biggest wind tunnel in California, USA.

382 **The ever-changing positions of Earth and other objects in space mean there is a limited 'launch window' for each mission.** This is when Earth is in the best position for a craft to reach its target in the shortest time. If the launch window is missed, the distances may become too massive.

383 **In space, repairs are difficult or impossible.** Exploring craft must be incredibly reliable, with tested and proven technology. Each piece of equipment needs a back-up, and even if this fails, it should not affect other parts.

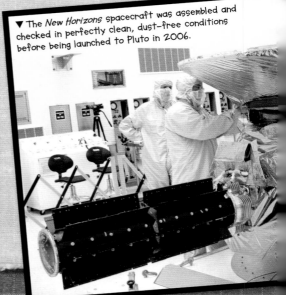

▼ The *New Horizons* spacecraft was assembled and checked in perfectly clean, dust-free conditions before being launched to Pluto in 2006.

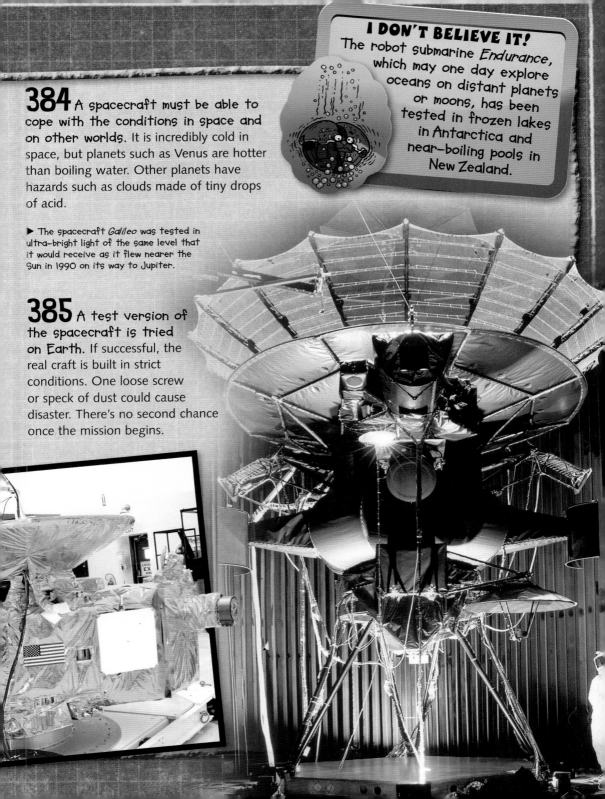

I DON'T BELIEVE IT!
The robot submarine *Endurance*, which may one day explore oceans on distant planets or moons, has been tested in frozen lakes in Antarctica and near-boiling pools in New Zealand.

384 A spacecraft must be able to cope with the conditions in space and on other worlds. It is incredibly cold in space, but planets such as Venus are hotter than boiling water. Other planets have hazards such as clouds made of tiny drops of acid.

▶ The spacecraft *Galileo* was tested in ultra-bright light of the same level that it would receive as it flew nearer the Sun in 1990 on its way to Jupiter.

385 A test version of the spacecraft is tried on Earth. If successful, the real craft is built in strict conditions. One loose screw or speck of dust could cause disaster. There's no second chance once the mission begins.

Blast-off!

386 A spacecraft is blasted into space by its launch vehicle, or rocket. The rocket is the only machine powerful enough to reach 'escape velocity' – the speed needed to break free from the pull of Earth's gravity. The spacecraft is usually folded up in the nose cone of the rocket.

387 Spacecraft and other objects carried by the rocket are called the 'payload'. Most rockets take their payload into orbit around the Earth. The nose cone opens to release the craft stored inside. Parts of it unfold, such as the solar panels that turn sunlight into electricity.

Launch point

Escape velocity

Orbit bound by Earth's gravity

◄ Launch vehicles must quickly reach escape velocity – 11,200 metres per second – to shrug off Earth's gravitational pull.

388 Different sizes of rockets are used for different sizes of spacecraft. One of the heaviest was the *Cassini-Huygens* mission to Saturn. At its launch in 1997, with all its fuel and equipment on board, it weighed 5.6 tonnes – almost as much as a school bus. It needed a huge *Titan IV* rocket launcher to power it into space.

SECOND STAGE (S-II)
The middle section of the launcher had five J-2 rocket engines. It was 25 metres tall, and like the first stage, was 10 metres wide.

FIRST STAGE (S-IC)
The bottom part of *Saturn V* was 42 metres tall. The F-1 rocket engines propelled the entire launch vehicle for the first 60 kilomentres.

J-2 rocket engines

F-1 rocket engines

▲ The biggest launchers were the three-stage *Saturn V* rockets used to launch the Apollo missions. Each stage fell away after using up its fuel.

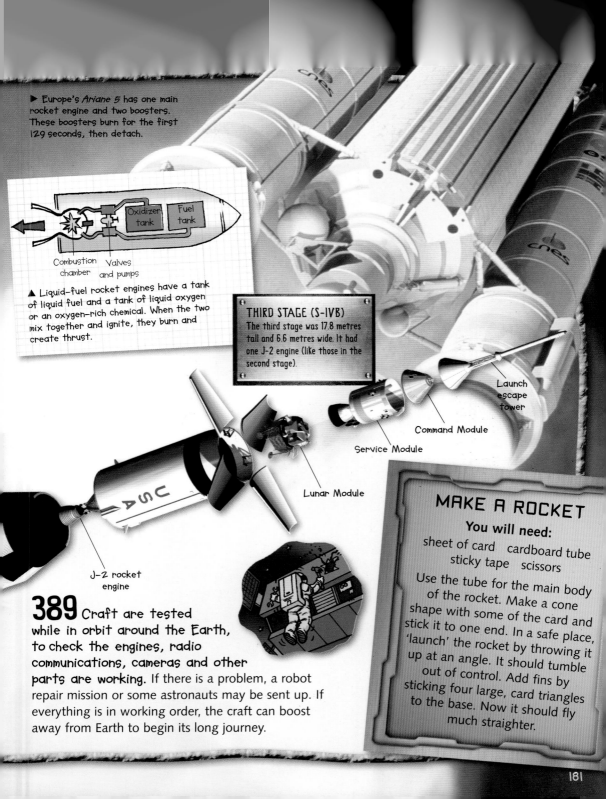

▶ Europe's *Ariane 5* has one main rocket engine and two boosters. These boosters burn for the first 129 seconds, then detach.

Oxidizer tank

Fuel tank

Combustion chamber

Valves and pumps

▲ Liquid-fuel rocket engines have a tank of liquid fuel and a tank of liquid oxygen or an oxygen-rich chemical. When the two mix together and ignite, they burn and create thrust.

THIRD STAGE (S-IVB)
The third stage was 17.8 metres tall and 6.6 metres wide. It had one J-2 engine (like those in the second stage).

Launch escape tower

Command Module

Service Module

Lunar Module

J-2 rocket engine

389 Craft are tested while in orbit around the Earth, to check the engines, radio communications, cameras and other parts are working. If there is a problem, a robot repair mission or some astronauts may be sent up. If everything is in working order, the craft can boost away from Earth to begin its long journey.

MAKE A ROCKET
You will need:
sheet of card   cardboard tube
sticky tape   scissors

Use the tube for the main body of the rocket. Make a cone shape with some of the card and stick it to one end. In a safe place, 'launch' the rocket by throwing it up at an angle. It should tumble out of control. Add fins by sticking four large, card triangles to the base. Now it should fly much straighter.

In deep space

390 Most spacecraft travel for months, even years, to their destinations. The fastest journey to Mars took just over six months, by *Mars Express* in 2003. *Pioneer 10* took 11 years to reach Neptune in 1983.

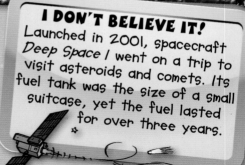

◀ *Mars Express* cruised at a speed of 10,800 kilometres an hour on its way to Mars.

391 Guiding the craft on its course is vital. A tiny error could mean that it misses its distant target by millions of kilometres. Mission controllers on Earth regularly check the craft's position with radio signals using the Deep Space Network (DSN). The DSN is made up of three huge radio dishes located in California, USA, Madrid in Spain, and Canberra, Australia.

▼ This ion thruster is being tested in a vacuum chamber. The blue glow is the beam of charged atoms being thrown out of the engine.

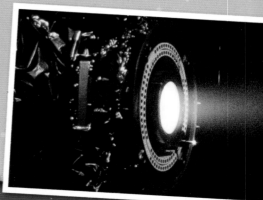

392 Spacecraft only need small engines because there is no air in space to slow them down. Depending on the length of the journey, different kinds of engines and fuels are used. The ion thruster uses magnetism made by electricity. This hurls tiny particles, called ions, backwards, which pushes the craft forwards.

◀ Bowl-shaped antennas (aerials), like *New Horizons'*, exchange radio signals to and from Earth.

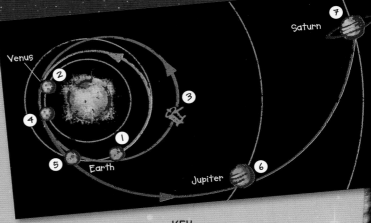

Venus

Saturn

Jupiter

Earth

393 Craft often pass other planets or moons on their journeys. Like Earth, these objects all have a gravitational pull, and this could send a craft off course. However, a planet's gravity may be used to propel the craft in a new direction to save fuel. This is known as a gravity assist flyby or 'slingshot'.

▲ *Cassini–Huygens'* journey to Saturn involved four gravity-assists. The main stages were: launch to first Venus flyby (orange), second Venus flyby (blue), and Earth flyby, past Jupiter to Saturn (purple).

KEY

❶ October 1997 Launch from Earth

❷ April 1998 First Venus flyby

❸ December 1998 Engine fires for 90 minutes to return to Venus

❹ June 1999 Second Venus flyby

❺ August 1999 Earth-Moon flyby

❻ December 2000 Jupiter flyby

❼ July 2004 Arrives in orbit around Saturn

Goldstone, California, USA

◀ ▼ The three Deep Space Network sites are equally spaced around Earth, with 120 degrees between them, making a 360-degree circle.

Madrid, Spain

Canberra, Australia

▶ The Deep Space Network's radio dish at Goldstone near Barstow, California, is 70 metres across.

394 For long periods, much of a craft's equipment shuts down to save electricity. It's like an animal hibernating in winter or a mobile phone on stand-by. When the craft 'hibernates' only a few vital systems stay active, such as navigation.

Ready to explore

395 As the spacecraft approaches its target, its systems power up and it 'comes to life'. Controllers on Earth test the craft's radio communications and other equipment. At such enormous distances, radio signals can take minutes, even hours, to make the journey.

396 Other kinds of camera can 'see' types of waves that are invisible to the human eye. These include infrared or heat rays, ultraviolet rays, radio waves and X-rays. These rays and waves provide information about the target world, such as how hot or cold it is.

▼ *Mars Reconnaissance Orbiter*'s photograph of the 730-metre-wide Victoria Crater was captured by its high-resolution camera and shows amazing detail.

397 Among the most important devices onboard a craft are cameras. Some work like telescopes to take a close-up or magnified view of a small area. Others are wide-angle cameras, which capture a much greater area without magnifying.

The Mars Climate Sounder records the temperature, moisture and dust in the Martian atmosphere

The high-resolution camera captures close-up, detailed photographs of the surface

QUIZ

Spacecraft have many devices, but rarely microphones to detect sound. Why?

A. The chance of meeting aliens who can shout loudly is very small.

B. Sound waves do not travel through the vacuum of space.

C. It's too difficult to change sound waves into radio signals.

Answer:
B

Antenna

398 Magnetometers detect magnetic fields, which exist naturally around some planets, including Earth. Gravitometers measure the target object's pull of gravity. This is especially important in the final stage of the journey – the landing. Some spacecraft also have space dust collectors.

Solar panel

◄ *Mars Reconnaissance Orbiter*, launched in 2005, carries a telescopic camera, wide-angle cameras, sensors for infrared and ultraviolet light and a radar that 'sees' below the surface.

The spectrometer identifies different substances on the surface by measuring how much light is reflected

399 The information from the cameras and sensors is turned into radio signal codes and beamed back to Earth. To send and receive these signals, the craft has one or more dish-shaped antennas. These must be in the correct position to communicate with the dishes located on Earth.

The sub-surface radar can see up to one kilometre below the planet's surface

Flyby, bye-bye

400 On a flyby mission, a spacecraft comes close to its target. It does not go into orbit around it or land – it flies onwards and away into deep space. Some flybys are part of longer missions to even more distant destinations. In these cases the flyby may also involve gravity assist.

LAUNCH
FROM EARTH
20 August, 1977

401 A flyby craft may pass its target several times on a long, lop-sided path, before leaving again. Each pass gives a different view of the target object. The craft's cameras, sensors and other equipment switch on to take pictures and record measurements, then turn off again as it flies away.

JUPITER

Flyby on 9 July, 1979

402 The ultimate flyby craft was *Voyager 2*. It made a 'Grand Tour' of the four outermost planets, which are only suitably aligned every 175 years. *Voyager 2* blasted off in 1977 and flew past Jupiter in 1979, Saturn in 1981, Uranus in 1986 and Neptune in 1989. This craft is still sending back information from a distance twice as far as Pluto is from Earth.

I DON'T BELIEVE IT!
When *Pioneer 11* zoomed to within 43,000 kilometres of Jupiter in 1974, it made the fastest-ever flyby at 50 kilometres per second.

◀ *Voyager 2's* golden disc (like an old vinyl record) is attached to its main body. The disc contains sounds and pictures from Earth for any aliens that may find it.

Flyby on 25 August, 1989

URANUS

▶ *Voyager 2* made the greatest-ever tour of the Solar System. It is still the only spacecraft to fly close to Uranus and Neptune.

Flyby on 24 January, 1986

▼ A heat photograph taken from a distance of 4800 kilometres shows Borelly's tail trailing behind.

SATURN

Flyby on 25 August, 1981

403 In 2001, after visiting the asteroid Braille, *Deep Space 1* flew past Comet Borrelly at 16 kilometres per second! At its closest, the craft was just 2200 kilometres from the comet's solid centre, which is as big as Mount Everest. *Deep Space 1*'s cameras took over 30 pictures before the craft was shut down.

▲ The main body of *Deep Space 1* was about the size of a large double bed.

Into orbit

404 On many exploring missions the craft is designed to go into orbit around its target world. Craft that do this are called orbiters, and they provide a much longer, closer look than a flyby mission.

▶ There are several different types of orbit that craft can make around their targets. Here, they are shown around Earth.

A polar orbit passes over the North and South Poles

An equatorial orbit goes around the middle (Equator)

Most orbits are elliptical, with low and high points

405 One of the most elliptical orbits was made by Mars Global Surveyor. At its closest, it passed Mars at a distance of 171 kilometres, twice in each orbit. The craft's furthest distance away was more than ten times greater.

◀ In 2006, two twin STEREO-craft went into orbit around the Sun. With one in front and one behind Earth, the craft made the first 3D observations of the Sun.

Antenna

ORBITER

You will need:

sock   tennis ball   string (one metre long)

Put the ball in the sock and tie up the top with the string. Go outside. Holding the string half way along its length, whirl the sock above your head so that it 'orbits' you. Gradually lengthen the string – does the 'orbit' take longer?

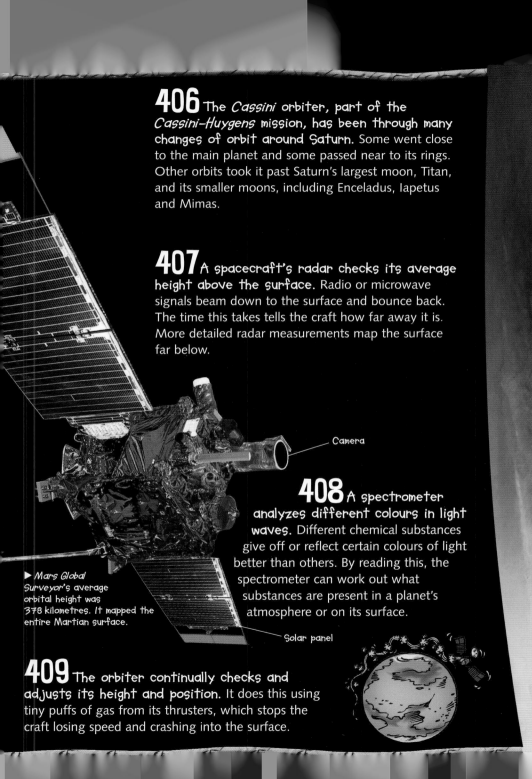

406 The *Cassini* orbiter, part of the *Cassini-Huygens* mission, has been through many changes of orbit around Saturn. Some went close to the main planet and some passed near to its rings. Other orbits took it past Saturn's largest moon, Titan, and its smaller moons, including Enceladus, Iapetus and Mimas.

407 A spacecraft's radar checks its average height above the surface. Radio or microwave signals beam down to the surface and bounce back. The time this takes tells the craft how far away it is. More detailed radar measurements map the surface far below.

Camera

408 A spectrometer analyzes different colours in light waves. Different chemical substances give off or reflect certain colours of light better than others. By reading this, the spectrometer can work out what substances are present in a planet's atmosphere or on its surface.

▶ *Mars Global Surveyor*'s average orbital height was 378 kilometres. It mapped the entire Martian surface.

Solar panel

409 The orbiter continually checks and adjusts its height and position. It does this using tiny puffs of gas from its thrusters, which stops the craft losing speed and crashing into the surface.

Landers and impactors

410 Some missions have landers that touch down onto the surface of their target world. Part of the spacecraft may detach and land while the other part stays in orbit, or the whole spacecraft may land.

① Spacecraft in orbit

② Landing module separates from orbiter

③ First parachute opened, then detached

▶ The later landers of the Russian *Venera* program (1961–1983) used parachutes to slow down in the thick, hot, cloudy atmosphere of Venus.

④ Main parachutes opened at a height of 50 kilometres above the surface

411 The journey down can be hazardous. If the planet has an atmosphere (layer of gas around it) there may be strong winds that could blow the lander off course. If the atmosphere is thick, there may be huge pressure pushing on the craft.

412 If there is an atmosphere, the lander may use parachutes, or inflate its own balloons or air bags, to slow its speed. On the *Cassini-Huygens* mission, the *Huygens* lander used two parachutes as it descended for touchdown on Saturn's moon, Titan.

⑤ Ring-shaped shock absorber filled with compressed gas lessened the impact at touchdown

413 If there is no atmosphere, retro-thrusters are used to slow the craft down. These puff gases in the direction of travel. Most landers have a strong, bouncy casing for protection as they hit the surface, or long, springy legs to reduce the impact.

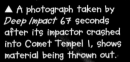

▲ A photograph taken by *Deep Impact* 67 seconds after its impactor crashed into Comet Tempel 1, shows material being thrown out.

414 After touchdown, the lander's solar panels and other parts fold out. Its equipment and systems switch on, and it tests its radio communications with the orbiter and sometimes directly with Earth.

▲ This image shows how *Beagle 2's* solar panels were designed to fold out. However contact with the lander was lost soon after it detached from its orbiter in 2003.

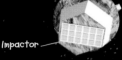

Impactor

415 Some craft are designed to smash into their target, and these are called impactors. The crash is observed by the orbiter and may also be watched by controllers on Earth. The dust, rocks and gases given off by an impact provide valuable information about the target object.

Camera

▶ In 2005, *Deep Impact* released its impactor, watched it strike Comet Tempel 1 and studied the resulting crater.

◀ *Mars Pathfinder* lander being tested on Earth. It used a parachute, retro-thrusters and multi-bubble airbags to land on Mars.

Robotic rovers

416 After touchdown, some landers release small, robotic vehicles called rovers. They have wheels and motors so they can move around on the surface to explore. So far rovers have explored on the Moon and Mars.

Antennas

Laser reflector

Solar panels

▶ In the 1970s, Russia sent two rovers, *Lunokhod 1* and *2*, to the Moon. Each was the size of a large bathtub, weighed almost one tonne and had eight wheels driven by electric motors.

Cameras

Wheels

QUIZ

How were the Mars rovers *Spirit* and *Opportunity* named?

1. Words chosen at random.
2. By a group of space experts.
3. By a 9-year-old girl, who won a competition.

Answer:
3. Siberian-born American schoolgirl Sofi Collis won the 2003 'Name the Rovers' competition

417 Modern rovers are mostly robotic – self-controlled using onboard computers. This is because of the time delay of radio signals. Even when Earth and Mars are at their closest distance to each other, radio signals take over three minutes to travel one way. If a rover was driven by remote control from Earth, it could have fallen off a cliff long before its onboard cameras relayed images of this.

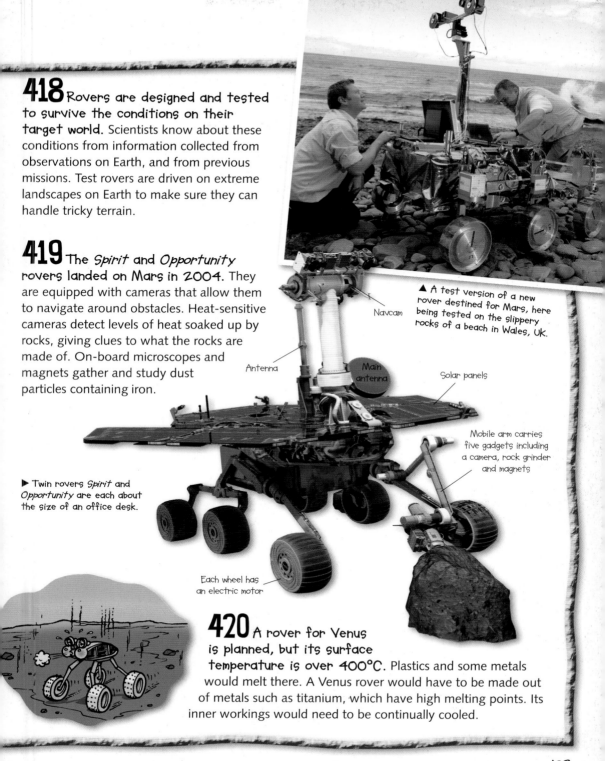

418 Rovers are designed and tested to survive the conditions on their target world. Scientists know about these conditions from information collected from observations on Earth, and from previous missions. Test rovers are driven on extreme landscapes on Earth to make sure they can handle tricky terrain.

419 The *Spirit* and *Opportunity* rovers landed on Mars in 2004. They are equipped with cameras that allow them to navigate around obstacles. Heat-sensitive cameras detect levels of heat soaked up by rocks, giving clues to what the rocks are made of. On-board microscopes and magnets gather and study dust particles containing iron.

▲ A test version of a new rover destined for Mars, here being tested on the slippery rocks of a beach in Wales, UK.

Navcam

Antenna

Main antenna

Solar panels

Mobile arm carries five gadgets including a camera, rock grinder and magnets

▶ Twin rovers *Spirit* and *Opportunity* are each about the size of an office desk.

Each wheel has an electric motor

420 A rover for Venus is planned, but its surface temperature is over 400°C. Plastics and some metals would melt there. A Venus rover would have to be made out of metals such as titanium, which have high melting points. Its inner workings would need to be continually cooled.

Close-up look

▶ In the late 1970s the USA's two *Viking* landers photographed their robotic sampler arms digging into Mars' surface.

Solar panel

421 **Some landers and rovers have robot arms that extend from the main body.** These scoop or drill into the surface to collect samples, which are then tested in the craft's onboard science laboratory. Samples are tested for chemical reactions, such as bubbling or changing colour.

Robotic arm with scoop and camera

Spheres of minerals containing iron, known as 'blueberries'

Circular area ground by tool is 4.5 centimetres across

422 **Most rovers have six wheels.** This design allows them to move quickly around sharp corners, without tipping over. Each wheel has an electric motor, powered by onboard batteries that are charged by the solar panels. If the batteries run down, the rover 'sleeps' until light from the Sun recharges them.

◀ Mars rovers *Spirit* and *Opportunity* are both equipped with a rock-grinding tool. They use it to grind into rocks and gather dust samples.

423 The *Phoenix* Mars lander had several devices on its robotic arm to measure features of Martian soil. It measured how easily it carried (conducted) heat and electricity, and if it contained any liquids. *Phoenix* also had microscopes for an ultra-close view of the surface samples.

I DON'T BELIEVE IT!

One type of rover drill uses heat to melt or burn a hole, which could be useful on icy planets. A thermal rover could even melt its way through ice, perhaps to water beneath, to look for alien life.

Meteorological (weather) station

Gas analyzers

Mini science laboratory

Solar panel

424 Most landers and rovers have mini weather stations. Sensors measure temperatures and pressures through the day and night and record the Sun's brightness. They also take samples of gases if there is an atmosphere, and record weather, such as wind and dust storms.

◀ The *Phoenix* Mars lander of 2008 had a robotic arm, on the left, and a small weather station.

425 The orbiting craft acts as a relay station to receive signals from its lander and send them on to Earth. A lander can in turn be a relay station for a rover. A rover has a small radio set to communicate with the lander and the lander has a slightly larger one to communicate with the orbiter. The orbiter has the biggest radio set to communicate with Earth.

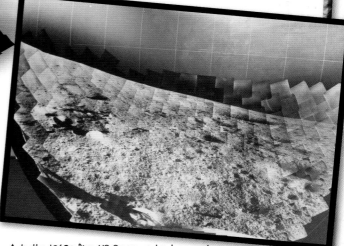

▲ In the 1960s five US Surveyor landers sent back separate close-up photographs of the Moon's surface. These were joined together to make larger scenes.

Exploring Mars

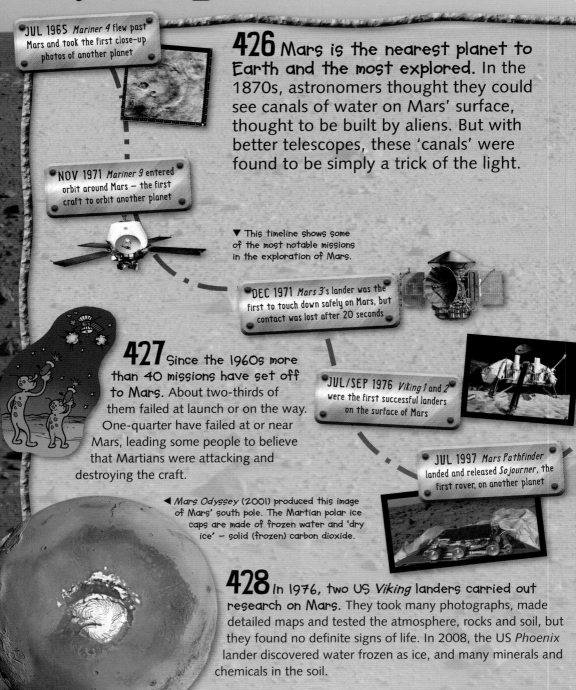

JUL 1965 *Mariner 4* flew past Mars and took the first close-up photos of another planet

426 Mars is the nearest planet to Earth and the most explored. In the 1870s, astronomers thought they could see canals of water on Mars' surface, thought to be built by aliens. But with better telescopes, these 'canals' were found to be simply a trick of the light.

NOV 1971 *Mariner 9* entered orbit around Mars — the first craft to orbit another planet

▼ This timeline shows some of the most notable missions in the exploration of Mars.

DEC 1971 *Mars 3*'s lander was the first to touch down safely on Mars, but contact was lost after 20 seconds

427 Since the 1960s more than 40 missions have set off to Mars. About two-thirds of them failed at launch or on the way. One-quarter have failed at or near Mars, leading some people to believe that Martians were attacking and destroying the craft.

JUL/SEP 1976 *Viking 1 and 2* were the first successful landers on the surface of Mars

JUL 1997 *Mars Pathfinder* landed and released *Sojourner*, the first rover, on another planet

◀ *Mars Odyssey* (2001) produced this image of Mars' south pole. The Martian polar ice caps are made of frozen water and 'dry ice' — solid (frozen) carbon dioxide.

428 In 1976, two US *Viking* landers carried out research on Mars. They took many photographs, made detailed maps and tested the atmosphere, rocks and soil, but they found no definite signs of life. In 2008, the US *Phoenix* lander discovered water frozen as ice, and many minerals and chemicals in the soil.

429 The *Spirit* and *Opportunity* rovers have made an amazing series of explorations and discoveries. They have found evidence that there was once water on Mars, and that it is possibly still there underground. In 2009 *Spirit* got stuck in soft soil but *Opportunity* is still moving, although very slowly.

MAY 2008 *Phoenix* lander touched down. It was the first craft to land in Mars' polar area

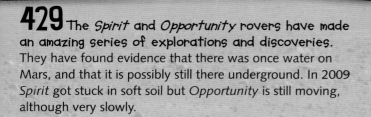

DEC 2003 In orbit, *Mars Express* released its lander, *Beagle 2*, but communications to it were lost

SEP 1997 *Mars Global Surveyor* went into orbit and began detailed, large-scale mapping of the surface

MAR 2006 *Mars Reconnaissance Orbiter* arrived, making a record six working craft in orbit or on the surface of Mars

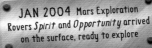

JAN 2004 Mars Exploration Rovers *Spirit* and *Opportunity* arrived on the surface, ready to explore

430 The *Mars Science Laboratory* rover *Curiosity*, which landed in 2012, has a drill, scoop arm and several packages of experiments. It is the biggest-ever rover at almost one tonne in weight. Its aim is to find out if there is, or ever has been, any life on Mars.

◄ *Curiosity* is about the size of a Mini car and has a top speed of 2.5 centimetres per second.

Back on Earth

431 All spacecraft have a mission control centre on Earth. Expert teams monitor a craft's systems, including radio communications, and the data a craft collects from its cameras and instruments.

▲ Mission controllers at NASA's Jet Propulsion Laboratory in California, USA, celebrate as the first images from rover *Opportunity* reach Earth.

432 Missions often run into problems. Controllers must work out how to keep a mission going when faults occur. If power supplies fail, the teams may have to decide to switch off some equipment so that others can continue working.

433 Sample return missions bring items from space back to Earth. In 2004, the *Genesis* craft dropped off its return container. It was supposed to parachute down to Earth's surface, but it crash-landed in Utah, USA. Luckily, some of its samples of solar wind survived for study.

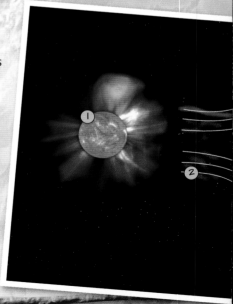

434 Gases, dust, rocks and other items are brought back to Earth to be studied. In the early 1970s the six manned Apollo missions brought a total of 381.7 kilograms of Moon material back to Earth.

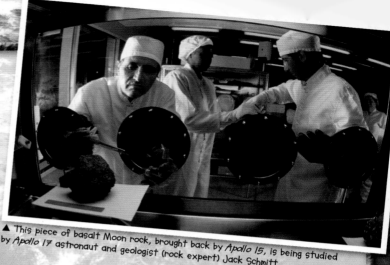

▲ This piece of basalt Moon rock, brought back by *Apollo 15*, is being studied by *Apollo 17* astronaut and geologist (rock expert) Jack Schmitt.

435 Samples returned from space must not be contaminated with material from Earth. Keeping samples clean allows scientists to find out what they contain, and stops any dangerous substances being released on Earth. Spacecraft are ultra-clean at launch to prevent them spreading chemicals or germs from Earth to other worlds.

▼ *Genesis* collected high-energy particles from the Sun's solar wind, which distorts Earth's magnetic field.

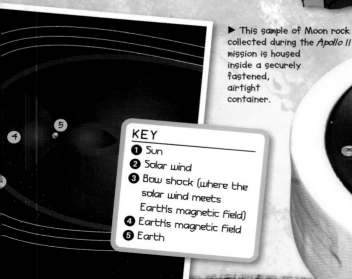

I DON'T BELIEVE IT!

Moon rocks don't look very special, yet over 100 small ones brought back by the Apollo missions have been stolen. More than ten people have been caught trying to sell them.

▶ This sample of Moon rock collected during the *Apollo 11* mission is housed inside a securely fastened, airtight container.

KEY
1. Sun
2. Solar wind
3. Bow shock (where the solar wind meets Earth's magnetic field)
4. Earth's magnetic field
5. Earth

Towards the Sun

◀ This photograph taken by *SOHO* uses a disc with a hole to block out some of the Sun's glare. This reveals vast streaming clouds of superheated matter called plasma.

Corona

Coronal mass ejection (CME) of superheated plasma

1c

HELIOS MISSION

GRENADA

▶ The Helios mission was featured on stamps worldwide.

436 Missions to the Sun encounter enormous heat. In the 1970s the US-German craft *Helios 2* flew to within 44 million kilometres of the Sun. From 1990, the *Ulysses* probe travelled on a huge orbit, passing near the Sun and as far out as Jupiter.

437 In 1995, the *SOHO* spacecraft began studying the Sun from near Earth. Since then, it has found many new comets. In 2015, *Solar Probe Plus* will orbit to within six million kilometres of the Sun, with a shield-like 'sunshade' of heat-resistant, carbon-composite material for protection.

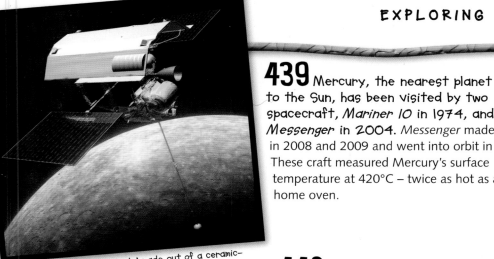

▲ *Messenger* had a 'sunshade' made out of a ceramic–composite material to protect it from the Sun's heat.

439 Mercury, the nearest planet to the Sun, has been visited by two spacecraft, *Mariner 10* in 1974, and *Messenger* in 2004. *Messenger* made flybys in 2008 and 2009 and went into orbit in 2011. These craft measured Mercury's surface temperature at 420°C – twice as hot as a home oven.

440 More than 20 craft have visited Venus, the second planet from the Sun. Its atmosphere of thick clouds, extreme pressures, temperatures over 450°C and acid chemicals, pose huge challenges for exploring craft.

438 Missions to Venus include Russia's Venera series (1961 to 1984), US Mariner probes (1962 to 1973) and *Pioneer Venus* (1978). From 1990 to 1994, *Magellan* used radar to map the surface in amazing detail. In 2006, Europe's *Venus Express* began more mapping. Its instruments also studied Venus' extreme global warming.

◀ Studying Venus' atmosphere may help us understand similar climate processes happening on Earth.

Antenna

Solar panel

Positioning thrusters

Main rocket engine

Gold coating helps to keep out the Sun's heat

▲ *Venus Express* orbits as low as 250 kilometres above the poles of Venus.

I DON'T BELIEVE IT!

The fastest spacecraft, and the fastest man–made object ever, was *Helios 2*. It neared the Sun at 67 kilometres per second!

Asteroids near and far

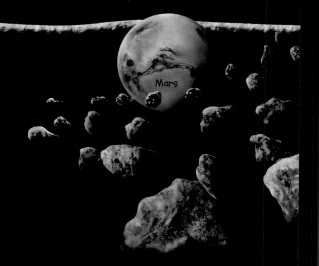

Mars

441 Asteroids orbit the Sun but are far smaller than planets, so even finding them is a challenge. Most large asteroids are in the main asteroid belt between Mars and Jupiter. Much closer to us are near-Earth Asteroids (NEAs), and more than 20 have been explored in detail by flyby craft, orbiters and landers.

Ceres

Vesta

Pallas

Hygiea

442 Orbiting and landing on asteroids is very difficult. Many asteroids are oddly shaped, and they roll and tumble as they move through space. A craft may only discover this as it gets close.

◄ Dwarf planet Ceres and the three largest asteroids in our Solar System, seen against North America for scale. Vesta, the biggest asteroid, is about 530 kilometres across.

443 In 1996, the probe *NEAR–Shoemaker* launched towards NEA Eros. On the way it flew past asteroid Mathilde in the main belt. Then in 2000 it orbited 34-kilometre-long Eros, before landing. The probe discoverd that the asteroid was peanut-shaped, and also gathered information about Eros' rocks, magnetism and movement. In 2008, spacecraft *Rosetta* passed main belt asteroid Steins, and asteroid Lutetia in 2010.

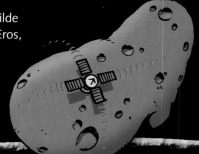

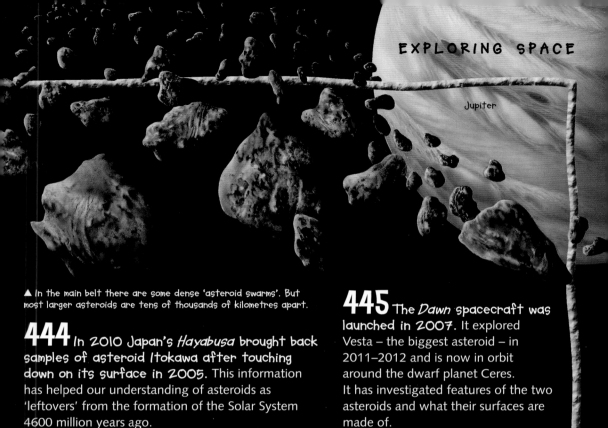

Jupiter

▲ In the main belt there are some dense 'asteroid swarms'. But most larger asteroids are tens of thousands of kilometres apart.

444 In 2010 Japan's *Hayabusa* brought back samples of asteroid *Itokawa* after touching down on its surface in 2005. This information has helped our understanding of asteroids as 'leftovers' from the formation of the Solar System 4600 million years ago.

445 The *Dawn* spacecraft was launched in 2007. It explored Vesta – the biggest asteroid – in 2011–2012 and is now in orbit around the dwarf planet Ceres. It has investigated features of the two asteroids and what their surfaces are made of.

▲ The *Dawn* mission badge shows its two main targets.

▶ *Hayabusa* was designed to gather samples of the asteroid *Itokawa* by firing a metal pellet towards the surface. It could then collect the dust thrown up by the impact.

Comet mysteries

446 Comets travel to and from the edges of the Solar System and beyond as they orbit the Sun. Unlike long-period comets, which may take thousands of years to orbit, short-period comets orbit every 200 years or less and so can be explored.

▶ The Oort cloud surrounds the Solar System and is made up of icy objects. It may be the source of some Sun-orbiting comets.

Sun

Kuiper belt

▶ The Kuiper belt lies beyond Neptune's orbit and is about twice the size of the Solar System. It consists of lots of comet-like objects.

Neptune

447 Like asteroids, comets are difficult to find. Comets warm up and glow only as they near the Sun. Their tails are millions of kilometres long, but consist only of faint gases and dust. The centre, or nucleus, of a comet may give off powerful jets of dust and gases that could blow a craft off course.

▶ A typical comet is mostly dust and ice. It has a glowing area, or coma, around it, and a long tail that points away from the Sun.

Solid rock core

Nucleus is often only a few kilometres across

Jets of gas and dust escape as ice melts

Glowing cloud, or coma, around nucleus is illuminated by sunlight

Dust and ice surrounds core

448 The famous Halley's Comet last appeared in 1986. Several exploring craft, known as the 'Halley Armada', went to visit it. This included Europe's *Giotto* probe, which flew to within 600 kilometres of the comet's nucleus. There were also two Russian-French *Vega* probes, and *Sakigake* and *Suisei* from Japan.

▶ *Stardust* collected comet dust using a very lightweight foam, called aerogel, in a collector shaped like a tennis bat. The collector folded into the craft's bowl–like capsule for return to Earth.

449 In 2008, the *Stardust* probe returned a capsule of dust collected from the comet Wild 2. In 2005, *Deep Impact* visited Comet Tempel 1 and released an impactor to crash into its nucleus and study the dust and gases given off. These craft increase our knowledge of comets as frozen balls of icy chemicals, rock and dust.

DUST COLLECTED FROM COMET WILD 2

Comet dust particles

▲ Under the microscope, a piece of *Stardust's* aerogel (half the size of this 'o') is revealed to have minute dust particles embedded within it.

STARDUST APPROACHING COMET WILD 2

Glowing dust tail illuminated by sunlight

Ion (gas) tail appears bluish

SAMPLE CAPSULE RETURNS TO EARTH

Gas giants

450 The four furthest planets from Earth – Jupiter, Saturn, Uranus and Neptune – are 'gas giants'. These are large planets composed mainly of gases. It takes at least two years to reach Jupiter by the most direct route. But craft usually take longer because they use gravity assist.

▼ *Galileo* orbited Jupiter for more than seven years. It released an atmosphere probe to study the gases that make up almost the whole planet.

451 There have been seven flybys of Jupiter and each one discovered more of the planet's moons. The two US Voyager missions, launched in 1977, discovered that Jupiter has rings like Saturn. US spacecraft *Galileo* arrived in orbit around Jupiter in 1995 and released a probe into the planet's atmosphere.

ON TITAN'S SURFACE

▲ *Huygens'* pictures from the surface of Titan, Saturn's largest moon, show lumps of ice and a haze of deadly methane gas.

452 The ringed planet Saturn had flybys by *Pioneer II* (1979) and *Voyagers 1* and *2* (1980–1981). In 2004 the huge *Cassini-Huygens* craft arrived after a seven-year journey. The orbiter *Cassini* is still taking spectacular photographs of the planet, its rings and its moons.

▼ The *Huygens* lander separated from *Cassini* and headed for Titan. It sent back more than 750 images from the surface.

TITAN

453 The only exploring craft to have visited Uranus and Neptune is *Voyager 2*. During its flyby of Uranus in 1986, *Voyager 2* discovered ten new moons and two new rings. In 1989, the craft passed the outermost planet, Neptune, and discovered six new moons and four new rings.

A heat shield prevented burn–up on entry

Parachutes slowed the lander's descent

Huygens lands on Titan

▼ The four gas giants have many moons – some large, and some very small. This list includes the five largest moons for each (not to scale).

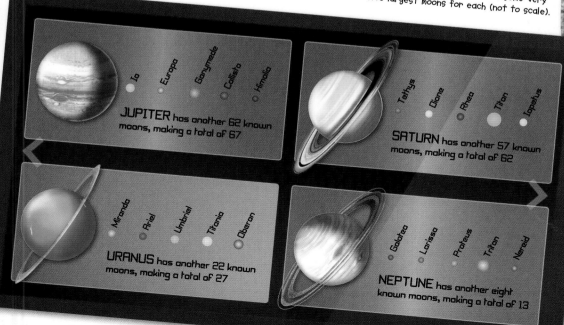

JUPITER has another 62 known moons, making a total of 67
Io · Europa · Ganymede · Callisto · Himalia

SATURN has another 57 known moons, making a total of 62
Tethys · Dione · Rhea · Titan · Iapetus

URANUS has another 22 known moons, making a total of 27
Miranda · Ariel · Umbriel · Titania · Oberon

NEPTUNE has another eight known moons, making a total of 13
Galatea · Larissa · Proteus · Triton · Nereid

Into the future

454 **Sending craft to the edges of the Solar System takes many years.** US spacecraft *New Horizons* set out in 2006 to study the dwarf planet Pluto by performing a flyby. Photos from the craft have revealed Pluto's complex and varied surface, which has bright and dark regions.

455 *New Horizons'* immense nine-year journey was complicated to plan. It included a flyby of tiny asteroid 132534 APL, then a swing around Jupiter for gravity assist and a speed boost. Flybys of Jupiter's moons followed, before the long cruise to tiny Pluto. Without Jupiter's gravity assist, the trip would have taken five years longer.

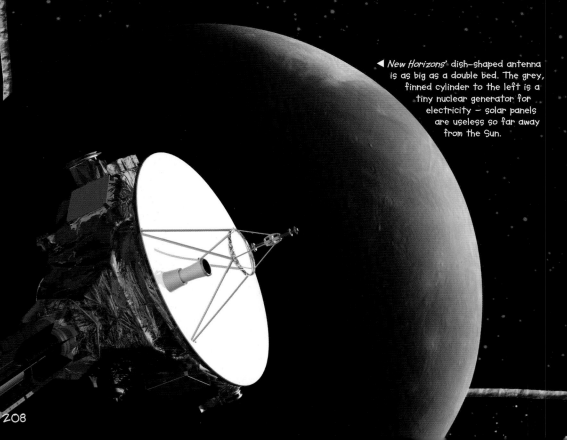

◀ *New Horizons'* dish-shaped antenna is as big as a double bed. The grey, finned cylinder to the left is a tiny nuclear generator for electricity — solar panels are useless so far away from the Sun.

456 Several major explorations are planned for the coming years. The *ExoMars* mission consists of a lander launched in 2016, and a rover, due to launch in 2020. They will look for signs of life on Mars, using a 2-metre-deep drill. The *BepiColombo* mission aims to orbit Mercury and measure the Sun's power.

◄ The *BepiColombo* mission is planned for launch in 2018. The six-year trip will take the craft past the Moon, Earth and Venus before reaching Mercury — the closest planet to the Sun.

Drill

457 What happens to exploring spacecraft? Some are deliberately crashed into other worlds, so that the impact can be observed by other spacecraft or from Earth. Others burn up as they enter the atmosphere of a planet or large moon.

▲ The drill on *ExoMars* rover will pass soil samples to the mini laboratory on board for analysis.

458 Many exploring spacecraft are still travelling in space, and will be for thousands of years. As they run out of power they become silent, either sitting on their target worlds or drifting though empty space – unless they crash into an object.

► The 'Pale Blue Dot' photograph captured in 1990 by *Voyager 1*, was taken from six billion kilometres away. Earth is a tiny speck.

FAR-AWAY EARTH

Earth

459 The most distant craft is *Voyager 1*, launched in 1977. It is now more than 17 billion kilometres from Earth, and is still being tracked.

Space magic and myth

460 Exploring space has long been a favourite subject for story-telling. Even before rockets, there were theories about space travel and aliens. One of the first was *War of the Worlds*, written in 1898 by H G Wells.

▲ H G Wells' original story is brought to life in the 1953 movie *War of the Worlds*, in which martians invade Earth and destroy city after city. Humans can't stop them, but instead, germs eventually wipe out the alien invaders.

◄ The mission statement of *Star Trek*'s starship *Enterprise* was: 'To explore strange new worlds, to seek out new life and new civilizations, to boldly go where no one has gone before.'

461 In the 1950s, as humans began to explore space, tales of sightings of 'flying saucers' and UFOs (Unidentified Flying Objects) soared. Some of these may be explained by secret aircraft or spacecraft being tested by governments. A few people claimed that aliens visited Earth and left signs, such as strange patterns in fields called crop circles.

462 The *Star Wars* (1977 onwards) and *Alien* movies (1979 onwards) are all about adventures in space. This genre grew in popularity at the same time that space exploration was becoming a reality. The *Star Trek* movies (1979 onwards) had several spin-off television series, including *Voyager* and *Deep Space Nine*.

463 In the future, scientists may discover a form of ultra-fast travel involving black holes and wormholes (tunnels through space and time). This could allow humans to travel to distant galaxies to look for other 'Goldilocks' planets similar to Earth. Like the third bowl of porridge in the nursery story, the conditions on a Goldilocks planet are not too hot and not too cold, but 'just right' for life to exist.

QUIZ

1. What was the name of the story written by H G Wells about an alien invasion of Earth?
2. What does UFO stand for?
3. What is a 'Goldilocks' planet?

Answers:
1. *War of the Worlds*
2. Unidentified Flying Object
3. A planet that has the perfect conditions for life to exist – not too hot, not too cold, but 'just right'.

464 Space scientists have suggested new kinds of rockets and thrusters for faster space travel. These could reduce the journey time to the next-nearest star, Proxima Centauri, to about 100 years. But one day we may be beaten to it – aliens from a distant galaxy could be exploring space right now and discover us first!

▼ Virgin Galactic will soon be offering space travel to the general public. A ticket for a flight on *SpaceShipTwo* (below) will cost $200,000!

N339SS

Virgin

211

I-DPCC

PROTEZIONE CIVI

FLIGHT

- Early flying
- The first fighter planes
- Getting airborne
- Engines and propellers
- Controlling a plane
- Passenger planes
- Helicopters
- Balloons and airships
- Supersonic aircraft
- Unusual planes

What was the name of the first jet fighter plane?

Why don't helicopters need runways?

What is an aerofoil?

How many wheels are there on a jumbo jet?

Where is the cockpit?

213

Flying machines

▶ Modern fighter planes such as these Eurofighter Typhoons speed through the skies to attack an enemy.

465 People first tried to fly hundreds of years ago. They made wings from different materials and invented machines to take to the air, but nothing seemed to work. Then it was discovered that a curved wing moving through the air lifted upwards – and the age of flight began. Now huge airliners carry hundreds of passengers halfway around the world, high above the clouds every day – and in the future, passengers may be able to travel into space.

The first flights

466 The first humans to fly went up in a balloon, not a plane. In 1783 in France, the Montgolfier brothers made a large balloon and heated the air inside it by lighting a fire underneath. The balloon rose into the air carrying two passengers who floated over Paris for 25 minutes. They carried a small fire to heat the air and keep the balloon afloat.

▲ In 1783 two volunteers flew to a height of 900 metres in the Montgolfier brothers' balloon.

467 The first planes were gliders with no engines. In the 1890s, a German called Otto Lilienthal experimented with flying by building small gliders that would carry him into the air. He tried using different wing shapes to see which worked best. To become airborne, he launched himself from the top of a hill and glided downwards.

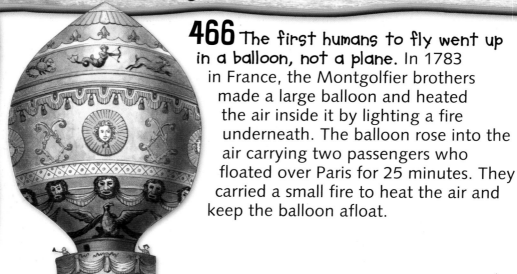

▶ To test his flying machines Otto Lilienthal practised jumping from cliffs, hills and rooftops.

468 The first real plane with an engine flew at a place called Kitty Hawk in the USA in 1903. It was built by Wilbur and Orville Wright and called the *Wright Flyer*. It had two wings, one above the other, and was driven by two propellers behind the wings.

469 The first helicopter looked like a plane with whirling wings. It was built in the 1930s. It had a body like a plane but with no wings. Two rotors were fixed on top, each with blades that whirled round in a circle. They lifted the helicopter straight up so it could hover in the air and move backwards and forwards.

470 The first non-stop flight across the Atlantic from the USA to Europe was in 1919. Two British airmen called John Alcock and Arthur Brown flew a Vickers Vimy, a type of bomber aircraft. The journey took 16.5 hours and they flew through terrible storms. The Vimy had an open cockpit, so gave little protection from the weather.

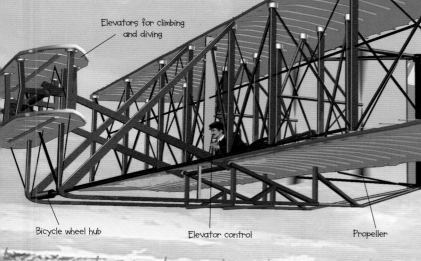

Wing

Elevators for climbing and diving

Bicycle wheel hub

Elevator control

Propeller

Rudder steered right or left

▲ To fly their plane, the Wright brothers had to lie on the lower wing.

Early days of flying

471 **During World War I, planes were used in battle.** Many were biplanes with double wings such as the Sopwith Camel. Fighter planes were built with machine guns to shoot down enemy planes. They could also fire at soldiers on the ground, while larger planes and airships dropped bombs.

▲ A British pilot in his Sopwith Camel watches a burning German plane. The plane got its name from the hump over its guns.

The *Hindenburg*

472 In the 1920s and '30s huge airships carried people between Europe and the USA. These giant oval machines had engines and propellers to push and steer them along. Passengers travelled in cabins below the airship. However the light gas used to lift the airship was often hydrogen, which easily catches fire. In May 1937, the airship *Hindenburg* burst into flames. This put an end to travel by airship.

◀ Thirty-six people died when the *Hindenburg* airship crashed in flames in 1937.

TRUE OR FALSE?

1. A fight between two planes was called a catfight.
2. Jet airliners can fly higher than propeller aircraft.
3. Airships are filled with heavy gas.

Answers:
1. False 2. True 3. False

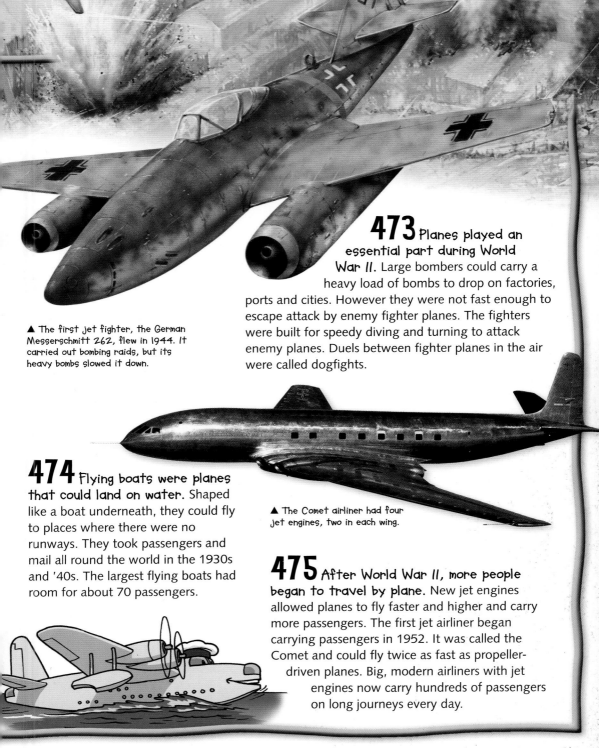

473 Planes played an essential part during World War II. Large bombers could carry a heavy load of bombs to drop on factories, ports and cities. However they were not fast enough to escape attack by enemy fighter planes. The fighters were built for speedy diving and turning to attack enemy planes. Duels between fighter planes in the air were called dogfights.

▲ The first jet fighter, the German Messerschmitt 262, flew in 1944. It carried out bombing raids, but its heavy bombs slowed it down.

474 Flying boats were planes that could land on water. Shaped like a boat underneath, they could fly to places where there were no runways. They took passengers and mail all round the world in the 1930s and '40s. The largest flying boats had room for about 70 passengers.

▲ The Comet airliner had four jet engines, two in each wing.

475 After World War II, more people began to travel by plane. New jet engines allowed planes to fly faster and higher and carry more passengers. The first jet airliner began carrying passengers in 1952. It was called the Comet and could fly twice as fast as propeller-driven planes. Big, modern airliners with jet engines now carry hundreds of passengers on long journeys every day.

Parts of a plane

476 The main body of a plane is usually long and thin, with a pointed nose and smooth shape to cut through the air easily. This is called the fuselage. At the front is the cockpit, or flight deck, where the pilot controls the plane. In a passenger plane, most of the remaining body is taken up by a cabin with seats for passengers. Under the the cabin floor is a hold to store luggage.

▶ An Airbus A380 passenger liner. A typical airliner such as this has a smooth, streamlined body.

Tail

Fuselage

Engine

Cockpit (flight deck)

477 The wings keep the plane up in the air and stick out on either side of the fuselage. They are long and thin with a curved top surface. Engines are usually attached to the wings. Fuel tanks are inside the wings. Along the front and back edges of the wings are moving parts called control surfaces, which can be tilted up or down to steer the plane.

I DON'T BELIEVE IT!
A 747 Jumbo Jet has 18 wheels in total – a set of two wheels under the nose and four sets of four wheels under the body and wings.

220

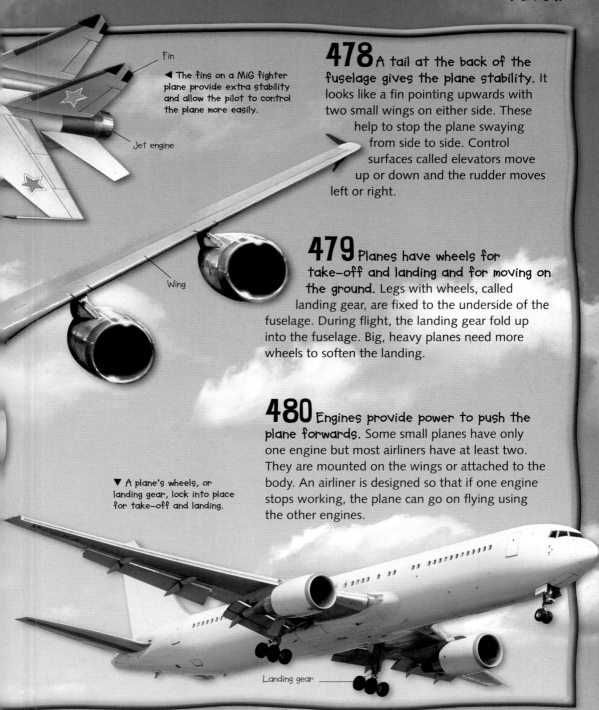

Fin

◀ The fins on a MiG fighter plane provide extra stability and allow the pilot to control the plane more easily.

Jet engine

Wing

478 A tail at the back of the fuselage gives the plane stability. It looks like a fin pointing upwards with two small wings on either side. These help to stop the plane swaying from side to side. Control surfaces called elevators move up or down and the rudder moves left or right.

479 Planes have wheels for take-off and landing and for moving on the ground. Legs with wheels, called landing gear, are fixed to the underside of the fuselage. During flight, the landing gear fold up into the fuselage. Big, heavy planes need more wheels to soften the landing.

480 Engines provide power to push the plane forwards. Some small planes have only one engine but most airliners have at least two. They are mounted on the wings or attached to the body. An airliner is designed so that if one engine stops working, the plane can go on flying using the other engines.

▼ A plane's wheels, or landing gear, lock into place for take-off and landing.

Landing gear

How planes fly

481 **A plane flies by moving through the air.** The engines drive the plane forwards with a force called thrust. However, air pushes in the opposite direction and slows the plane down. This is called drag. Weight is the force that tries to pull the plane down. When moving through the air, the wings give an upward force called lift.

Direction of air flow around wing

▲ As the wing moves forward, air streams under and over it, lifting it up.

482 **Air flowing over the wings gives an upward lift.** The wings are a special shape called an aerofoil. The top curves upwards while the bottom is flatter. As the plane moves forward, air flowing over the top has further to go and is more spread out than the air beneath. The air beneath pushes the wing harder than the air above it, so the wing lifts, taking the plane with it.

A force called lift pulls the plane up

LIFTING FORCE

Wrap a strip of narrow paper around a pencil. Holding one end of the strip, blow hard over the top of it. Watch the free end of the paper lift upwards. This shows how an aircraft wing lifts as it moves through the air, keeping the heavy aircraft in the air. The faster you blow, the higher the paper lifts.

A force called thrust pulls the plane forward

A force called weight pulls the plane down

▲ A flying plane is pushed and pulled by four different forces in four different directions.

▶ Flaps on the wings, called ailerons, direct the air flow up or down.

Aileron

484 As the plane moves forwards it pushes against the air. The air pushes back, which slows the plane down and makes it use more fuel. Aircraft builders try to make the drag as minimal as possible by designing the plane to be smooth and streamlined so it cuts cleanly through the air.

483 The engines give the thrust that drives the plane forwards in the air. As the plane travels faster, the lifting force grows stronger. This force must be equal to the weight of the plane before it can rise into the air and fly. This means that the thrust from the engines must drive the plane quickly to give it enough lift to fly.

485 The weight of a plane is always trying to pull it down. For this reason, planes are built to be as light as possible, using light but strong materials. Even so, a Boeing 747 jumbo jet with all its passengers and luggage can weigh as much as 360 tonnes and still take off.

▼ Jet engines or propellers thrust a plane forwards.

N6436F

A force called drag pulls the plane back

Propeller engine

Jet engine

486 Planes get thrust from jet engines or propellers. Jet engines are more powerful and better for flying high up where the air is thinner. Airliners and fighter planes have jet engines. Propellers are more useful for planes that fly slower and nearer the ground. Most small private planes and some large planes that carry heavy cargo use propeller engines.

Powerful engines

487 **A jet engine thrusts a plane forwards by shooting out a jet of hot gases.** A turbojet engine uses spinning blades called a compressor to suck air into the front of the engine and squeeze it tightly. This air is then mixed with fuel inside the engine, as the fuel requires air to burn. The burning fuel creates hot gases that shoot out of a nozzle at the back of the engine.

BALLOON JET

Blow up a balloon then let it go. Watch the balloon shoot away as the air rushes out. In the same way, a plane shoots forward when gases rush out of its jet engines.

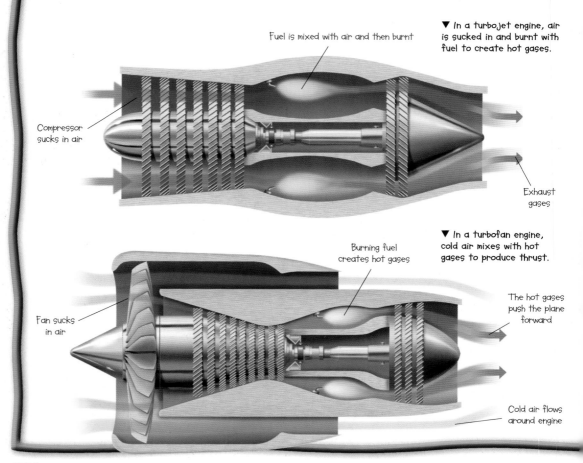

Fuel is mixed with air and then burnt

▼ In a turbojet engine, air is sucked in and burnt with fuel to create hot gases.

Compressor sucks in air

Exhaust gases

▼ In a turbofan engine, cold air mixes with hot gases to produce thrust.

Burning fuel creates hot gases

Fan sucks in air

The hot gases push the plane forward

Cold air flows around engine

488
A turbofan engine is another type of jet engine used by modern airliners. These are less noisy than turbojet engines and cheaper to run. A large fan at the front sucks in air, but not all of it is squeezed and mixed with fuel. Some of the air flows around the outside of the engine and mixes with the hot gases shooting out of the back.

Propeller blade

Hub

▲ When the propellers spin, they pull the plane through the air.

489
Propellers whiz round at high speed, pulling the plane through the air. The propeller has two or more blades sticking out from the centre. Each blade is like a small wing and as it spins, it pushes the air backwards so the plane moves forwards. Small planes have just one propeller at the front, but larger planes may have two or more propellers, each driven by its own engine.

490
Propellers can be driven by two different types of engine. Early planes had engines that worked like the engine in a car. Many small planes still use this type of engine. Turboprop engines are jet engines but the hot gases are used to turn the propeller. This drives the plane instead of a jet of hot gas.

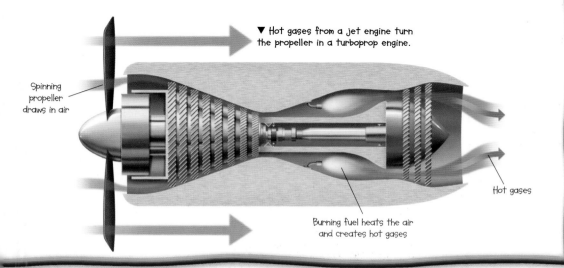

▼ Hot gases from a jet engine turn the propeller in a turboprop engine.

Spinning propeller draws in air

Burning fuel heats the air and creates hot gases

Hot gases

Climbing, diving and turning

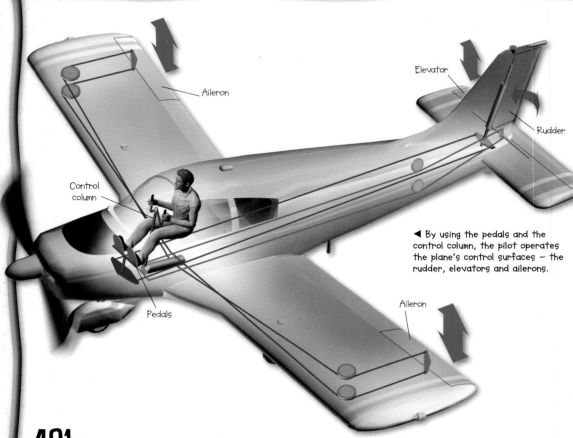

Aileron

Elevator

Rudder

Control column

Pedals

Aileron

◄ By using the pedals and the control column, the pilot operates the plane's control surfaces – the rudder, elevators and ailerons.

491 A pilot controls the plane, making it climb, dive or turn. He uses foot pedals and the control column. These are connected to the control surfaces on the wings and tail, which steer the plane. A plane moves in three directions. 'Yaw' means to turn to the right or left. 'Pitch' tilts the nose up or down and 'roll' is simply to roll from side to side.

492 To make the plane climb higher the pilot pulls the control column towards him. This makes the elevators, the flaps attached to the back of the tail, tilt upwards. The air flowing over the elevators now pushes the tail down and so the nose goes up and the plane climbs up at an angle. To dive, the pilot pushes the control column forward, tilting the elevators down.

493 Moving the control column to the left or right moves flaps called ailerons on the wings. Pushing to the left makes the left aileron go up and the one on the right go down. This lowers the left wing and lifts the right wing so the plane rolls over to the left. Pushing the control column to the right rolls the plane over to the right.

▲ By operating the control surfaces, a pilot is making this small plane turn in the air.

494 The pedals turn the plane to the right or left. These are connected to the rudder on the fin. Pushing the left pedal swings the rudder to the left. This turns the tail to the right and the nose towards the left, so the plane makes a left turn. The right pedal swings the rudder to the right, and the plane makes a right turn.

Roll
Wing tilts up or down

▶ Once in the air, a plane can move in three ways — roll, pitch and yaw.

Pitch
Nose tilts up or down

Yaw
Turns left or right

495 When the plane turns in the air it must roll at the same time. This is called banking and is similar to a bike tilting over when turning a corner. For a right turn, the control column is moved to the right while the right pedal is pushed, turning and rolling the plane to the right at the same time.

Taking off and landing

496 **Planes take off by speeding along a runway.** The pilot sets the engines for maximum power. He travels down the runway until the plane has enough speed for the wings to lift it and fly. Planes usually take off facing into the wind. This gives a faster air flow over the wings and more lift.

▶ After take-off, a plane climbs steeply until it reaches its cruising height.

Wheels for moving on runway

I DON'T BELIEVE IT!

The enormous cargo plane the Antonov AN-225 is so heavy that it needs a run of 3.5 km to get up enough speed to take-off when fully loaded. It has 32 wheels to cushion its landing.

497 **When the plane has enough speed, the pilot pulls the control column back, raising the elevators on the tail.** This lifts the nose and the plane starts to climb into the air. As soon as the plane is climbing steadily the pilot folds the wheels up into the body. This reduces drag and allows the plane to speed up more quickly. It climbs to its cruising height then levels off for the journey. Airliners fly above the clouds where the air is thinner and there is less drag.

◀ This plane has just taken off from an airport close to a holiday resort. Take-off is an impressive sight – but it can be very noisy.

498 Air traffic controllers give the pilot instructions and information so that the plane can take off and land safely. The pilot must always follow the instructions of the air traffic controllers and he cannot land or take-off until he has their permission to do so.

▲ In the control tower, computers show air traffic controllers which planes are ready for take-off and landing.

499 Near the end of the journey, the pilot pushes the control column forward to point the nose down and descend. The pilot lines up the plane along the runway. He slows the engines and lowers the flaps on the wings to help slow the plane. When the wheels touch the ground, the plane may reverse its engines to stop.

500 In fog, when the pilot cannot see very far, planes can land automatically. The plane picks up radio signals from beacons beside the runway. The plane's computers use these signals to line the plane up with the runway and land safely on the runway.

▼ When landing, the wheels under the plane's fuselage touch down on the runway first, followed by the nose wheels.

JORDAN AVIATION

www.jordanaviation.jo

The flight deck

501 **The cockpit is where the pilot sits when he's flying the plane.** In larger planes this is called the flight deck. All around are displays, switches and lights. In front of his seat is the control column and pedals for steering the plane.

◀ A pilot carefully checks the controls on the flight deck of an Airbus A380 before take-off.

502 **The cockpit instruments tell the pilot all he needs to know about the plane.** There are displays showing speed, altitude (height), and whether the plane is climbing, diving or rolling. There is also information about the weather. Warning lights alert the pilot of any problems. Older planes show all this information on dials but many modern planes use computer screens.

503 An automatic pilot can take over from the human pilot and fly the plane. As well as landing a plane automatically, an automatic pilot can fly the plane for much of the journey. The pilot sets the speed, height and direction and a computer controls the plane, making any necessary adjustments to keep it on course.

504 In larger planes, such as passenger airliners and cargo planes, the flight deck has two seats — one for the pilot and the other for the co-pilot. Each seat has its own set of controls with a control column and pedals so the pilot and co-pilot can take over from each other at any time.

505 Fighter planes often have only a single seat for the pilot. Modern fighters usually have a 'glass' cockpit, with the displays on computer screens. Some of these will be 'head-up' displays. This means that the information is shown on a glass screen in front of the pilot's eyes so he doesn't have to look down to see it. He can look out through the screen at the same time to see where he is going. Some head-up displays appear on a special helmet worn by the pilot.

A passenger jet airliner

506 **In a passenger jet airliner, the cabin takes up almost all of the body.** It has seats for the passengers, usually between 200 and 400 altogether. At high altitude, the air outside is too thin for people to breathe. This means that the cabin and cockpit are sealed and filled with air for the passengers and crew to breathe.

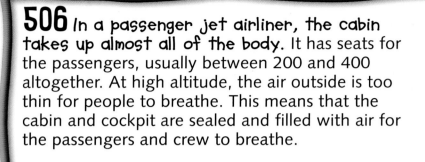

Upper deck and lounge

Windshield

▶ A Boeing 747 jumbo jet has wide wings that provide enormous lift. Its four powerful engines push the plane forward at cruising speeds of 1000 kilometres an hour.

Galley

Porthole

▼ Inside the cabin of a Boeing 747 jumbo jet. There is seating capacity for up to 400 passengers.

Landing gear

507 **Under the floor of the main cabin is the hold, where most of the luggage is stored.** As well as the passengers' baggage, planes often carry cargo in the hold. There is also room inside the cabin for smaller bags. These can go under the seats or in overhead lockers above the seats. Passengers cannot take a lot of very heavy luggage because the plane cannot fly if it is too heavy.

Oxygen cylinders

508 **In the cabin there are small kitchens called galleys.** Here the cabin staff store food and drink for the journey. Meals are prepared beforehand and delivered to the airport ready to serve. At mealtimes the cabin staff serve food from a trolley.

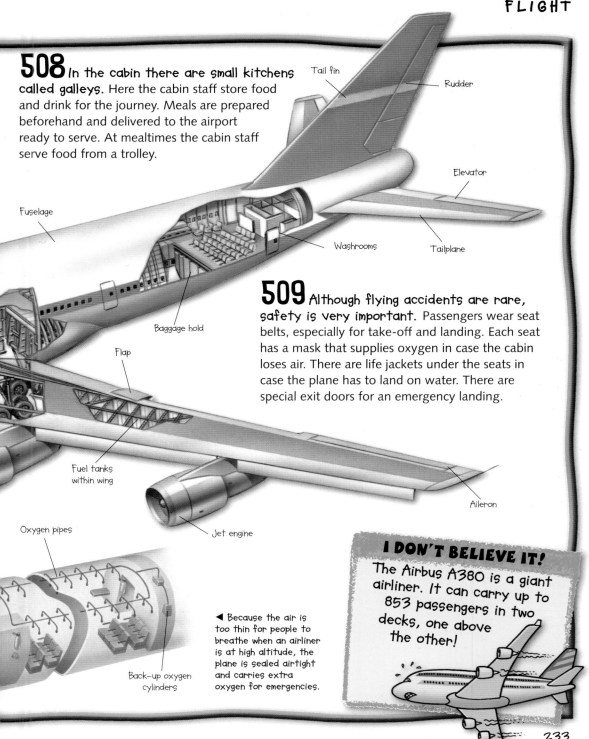

Tail fin

Rudder

Elevator

Fuselage

Washrooms

Tailplane

Baggage hold

Flap

509 **Although flying accidents are rare, safety is very important.** Passengers wear seat belts, especially for take-off and landing. Each seat has a mask that supplies oxygen in case the cabin loses air. There are life jackets under the seats in case the plane has to land on water. There are special exit doors for an emergency landing.

Fuel tanks within wing

Aileron

Oxygen pipes

Jet engine

◀ Because the air is too thin for people to breathe when an airliner is at high altitude, the plane is sealed airtight and carries extra oxygen for emergencies.

Back-up oxygen cylinders

I DON'T BELIEVE IT!

The Airbus A380 is a giant airliner. It can carry up to 853 passengers in two decks, one above the other!

At the airport

510 The most obvious parts of an airport are the terminals and the runways. Most big airports have at least two runways over 3 kilometres long. These allow the largest jets to take off and land. Lights and markings along the runway show the pilot where to touch down.

511 Passengers arrive at the terminal building for their flights. Tickets and passports are checked and luggage is left with the airline staff. Then passengers and their hand luggage are checked by security officers for dangerous objects such as knives. The luggage is also checked. People wait to board their plane in the departure lounge.

Passenger boarding bridge

▶ Airports can be huge and stretch for several miles. They have a constant flow of planes that are taking off and landing.

512 The area around the terminal where the planes park is called the **apron**. In large airports, the passengers walk through a closed bridge directly onto the plane. When everyone is on board and settled in their seats, the doors close and the bridge pulls away. Then the plane moves slowly towards the runway along paths called taxiways. Sometimes a truck called a tug may tow a plane into position on the runway.

513 The control tower ensures planes move safely around the airport. Air traffic controllers keep track of all planes, both on the ground and when they take off and land. Their job is to make sure the planes are far enough apart to avoid accidents. The controller and pilots talk to each other by radio. The pilots wait for the controllers to give permission to take off or land.

Terminal building

I DON'T BELIEVE IT!

About 68 million passengers travel through London's Heathrow airport every year — that's over 180,000 every day. On average, planes take off and land at Heathrow at a rate of one every minute.

514 Between flights, engineers check that everything is working correctly. The plane is cleaned and loaded with fresh food and drink. Luggage is taken out of the hold and the luggage for the next flight is loaded. Tankers refill the onboard tanks with fuel. The planes are given more thorough checks to ensure they are safe to fly.

Helicopters

Forward tilt

Backward tilt

Sideways tilt

Move up

Move down

Rotor hub

Rotor blade

Jet engine

▲ Because they can move in any direction, helicopters are extremely useful. The pilot tilts the blades to change direction.

515 **A helicopter has whirling rotors to lift it into the air.** The rotors have blades that are shaped like long, narrow wings. The engine spins the blades. This lifts the helicopter in the same way as the wings on a plane. A tail rotor stops the helicopter spinning in the opposite direction to the main rotor.

516 Helicopters can move in any direction — up, down, right, left, forwards or backwards. This is done by changing the tilt of the rotor blades. To go forwards, the blades twist as they turn to give more lift at the back. This tilts the tail up and the helicopter moves forwards. It can also spin on the spot using the tail rotor. All this movement makes helicopters very difficult to fly.

517 Helicopters do not need a runway and can land anywhere as long as there is enough room. This makes them very useful, especially for rescuing people from the sea or mountains as they can hover in one place. While hovering, injured or stranded people can be lifted into the helicopter then carried to safety.

▲ A helicopter can hover in one place to enable emergency workers to be lowered to accident scenes to help sick or injured people.

Tail rotor

518 Some helicopters have double rotors to lift heavy loads. The Chinook helicopter has one rotor at the front and one at the back. One is slightly above the other and they turn in opposite directions. These helicopters can carry up to 55 soldiers or heavy military equipment slung underneath the helicopter.

Tailplane and fin

▲ The Black Hawk military helicopter is used to carry troops and supplies during times of combat.

▼ Two large rotors give the Chinook helicopter extra lifting power to carry more people.

MAKE A WHIRLING ROTOR

Take a piece of paper 20 cm by 6 cm and fold it in half. Unfold it then cut from one short edge to the fold to make two strips. Fold these in opposite directions and put a paper clip on the other end. Watch it whirl like a helicopter rotor when you drop it.

237

Lighter than air

519 Balloons and airships can fly because they are lighter than air. They are filled with a very light gas that tries to rise above the heavier air around it. If there is enough gas, it can lift the weight of the balloon or airship so that it floats up into the air.

▶ Hot air balloons are flown for fun and are spectacular to watch. There are competitions held around the world where balloonists can compete in races.

▲ The gas from a burner heats up the air inside a balloon, making the balloon float upwards.

LOOK FOR RISING HOT AIR

Watch the smoke from a BBQ or a bonfire. It always drifts upwards. This is because the hot coal heats the air, which rises up above the surrounding colder air. The tiny smoke particles let us see the air rising.

520 The air inside a hot air balloon is heated to make it lighter than the cool air around it. Burners under the balloon heat the air inside, which spreads out and becomes lighter than the air outside. When the burners are turned on, the balloon rises. With the burners off, the balloon gradually falls as the air inside it cools. To fall more quickly, the pilot opens a vent (hole) and lets out some of the hot air. A balloon can't be steered, it goes where the wind blows it.

◄ The first balloon to fly non-stop around the world was Breitling Orbiter 3.

522 Weather balloons use a light gas called helium to go much higher than hot air balloons. They measure temperatures and winds high above the clouds and send the information back by radio. Helium balloons have also broken records. In 1999 Bertrand Piccard and Brian Jones were the first people to fly a balloon around the world without stopping. It took them nearly 20 days in the Breitling Orbiter 3.

521 Airships are also filled with light gas, but unlike balloons they have engines to steer them. Modern airships use helium gas, which does not burn. The engines and propellers drive the airship and steer it with the help of rudders. There is a cabin for the pilot and passengers called a gondola. Airships are often seen hovering above events such as the Olympic Games, carrying TV cameras to give a view from the air.

► This airship has been fitted with radar and tied to a ship. It will be used to spot icebergs beneath the water, and warn passing ships to steer clear of them.

CANMAR TEAL

Taking off vertically

▼ The American V-22 Osprey takes off like a helicopter, using its two rotors.

524 The V-22 Osprey is a plane with two large propellers at the ends of its wings. These lift the Osprey straight up into the air just like helicopter rotor blades. Then the engines swivel round at the ends of the wings so the propellers are tilted upright. The Osprey then flies like a normal plane. The propellers can also be tilted to allow the V-22 Osprey to hover like a helicopter.

523 Vertical take-off planes do not need a long runway — they take off upwards. There are two main types — planes that use propellers called tilt-rotor planes and those that have jet engines and are often called jump jets. These aircraft are mostly used as military planes. They can land on ships at sea and carry troops and equipment to army bases without a runway.

▶ A spinning fan inside the F-35B acts like a helicopter rotor.

◀ Harrier jump jets operate mainly from aircraft carriers at sea.

525 The new F-35B plane uses a spinning fan and the blast from its jet engines to take off. It needs a short runway. It starts by moving forwards then directs the jet from its engine downwards. With the help of a large fan in the middle of the plane, it lifts up off the runway. Then the plane swivels backwards and flies at supersonic speed. The fan also lets the plane hover in the air and land straight downwards.

526 The Harrier jump jet uses its jet engines to take off upwards. The jet of gas from the engines is directed downwards, pushing the plane up into the air. For normal flight the jets of gas are directed backwards and it flies like any other jet plane. Like the Osprey it can hover in the air and land without a runway. A British plane, the Harrier was first introduced in 1969.

I DON'T BELIEVE IT!

In 1954 a strange experimental object took off vertically. It was nicknamed the Flying Bedstead because that is exactly what it looked like — a metal frame with four legs and two engines. It could take off upwards, hover and move backwards and forwards.

Planes for war

527 In war, planes are used to attack the enemy, drop bombs and carry troops and equipment. Modern military planes often act as both fighter and bomber. They fly fast enough to attack and escape from danger while carrying bombs and missiles. Large bombers can usually fly longer distances than fighter planes.

▲ After dropping its bombs a fighter plane speeds away. Fighters are usually small and agile.

528 Military planes have different weapons depending on the mission. They carry rockets, missiles and bombs as well as guns. Many missiles and bombs can find their own way to the target. Missiles have a rocket engine to home in on the target. 'Smart' bombs have no engine. Instead they glide down using fins to steer onto the target. Pilots can fire their weapons at more than one target at the same time.

▼ A fighter plane (far right) flies next to a bigger tanker plane (below) for refuelling.

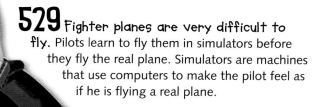

529 Fighter planes are very difficult to fly. Pilots learn to fly them in simulators before they fly the real plane. Simulators are machines that use computers to make the pilot feel as if he is flying a real plane.

◄ Specialized helmets allow fighter pilots to communicate with other pilots and air controllers. The helmet also supplies the pilot with air to breathe.

530 The armed forces use huge cargo planes to carry troops and heavy equipment. They deliver tanks and all the other supplies and equipment needed by an army wherever it is fighting. Cargo planes need a runway to land on, so helicopters take over from planes to carry men and equipment around the battlefield.

▲ *Global Hawk* spy plane is a robot that operates without a pilot.

531 Planes can spy on the enemy. From the air, spy planes use cameras and spying equipment to give a picture of what is happening on the ground and where enemy planes are. A control centre on the plane keeps its own forces informed and tells them what and where to attack. Spy planes also fly over the ocean to spot submarines and warn naval ships.

532 Many military planes can refuel while flying. They often have to fly long distances and there may not be anywhere they can land to refuel. Large tanker planes carrying fuel fly alongside. A pipe links the two planes and delivers fuel from the tanker. This allows the fighter or bomber to fly much further.

I DON'T BELIEVE IT!

Most military planes have ejection seats so the pilot can escape if the aircraft is hit. The whole seat with the pilot sitting in it is catapulted out of the cockpit. A rocket shoots it upwards, then a parachute opens to lower it gently to the ground.

Working planes

533 Transport planes carry cargo around the world. Inside there are no seats, just a huge area to be filled with containers of goods. A Boeing 747 jumbo jet can hold as much as five large trucks. It is loaded through hatches on the side.

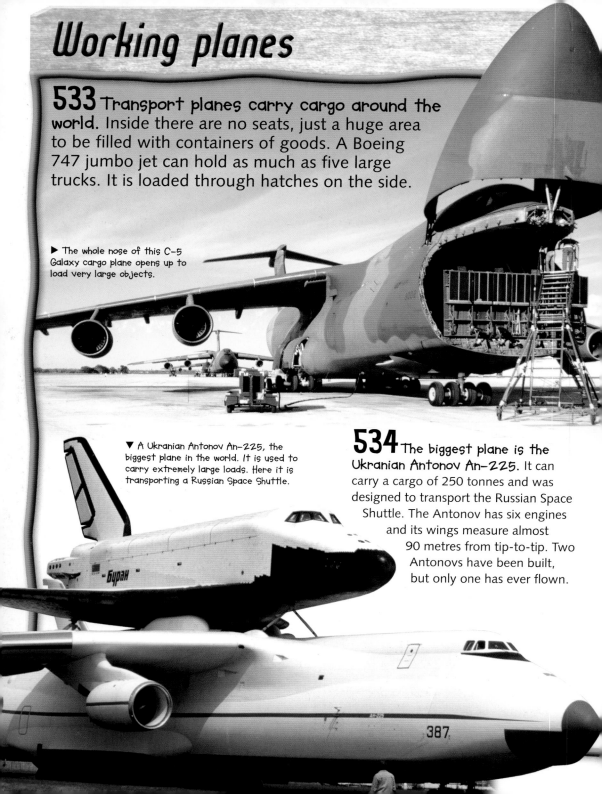

▶ The whole nose of this C-5 Galaxy cargo plane opens up to load very large objects.

▼ A Ukranian Antonov An-225, the biggest plane in the world. It is used to carry extremely large loads. Here it is transporting a Russian Space Shuttle.

534 The biggest plane is the Ukranian Antonov An-225. It can carry a cargo of 250 tonnes and was designed to transport the Russian Space Shuttle. The Antonov has six engines and its wings measure almost 90 metres from tip-to-tip. Two Antonovs have been built, but only one has ever flown.

▶ A firefighting plane dumps its load of red fire retardant in an attempt to put out a forest fire. This is a special substance that will stop the fire spreading.

537 Photographs taken from a flying plane give a good view of the ground. These photos can help people to draw maps. They also help historians by finding forgotten villages and roads. Slight bumps left by the burial of old ruins show up more clearly from the air than from the ground.

535 Planes and helicopters can help put out forest fires by dropping water on the fire. Special water-bombing planes fly very low over the sea or a lake and scoop up water. They then fly over the fire and drop the water. Helicopters carry a large bucket underneath and use this to scoop up and drop the water.

536 Helicopters and small planes can act as ambulances. If a person is badly injured in a road accident, an air ambulance helicopter may be called. The patient is put on a stretcher and whisked away to hospital in the helicopter. In Australia, doctors use small planes to visit remote farms and villages – it would take too long by car.

538 The police use helicopters to watch the traffic and chase criminals. Police in a helicopter can spot an escaping criminal and guide the police on the ground to help catch him, particularly in a car chase. The helicopters also fly over busy roads, reporting back on accidents and traffic jams.

Planes for fun

539 **Some people fly planes just for fun or sport.** They use small planes or gliders that take off from small airfields. They do not need a long concrete runway – a strip of mown grass is often good enough. Most small planes can only carry a few passengers and some only have a seat for the pilot.

▶ The UK Air Force Red Arrows aerobatic team has been giving displays since 1965.

▲ Gliders are made from light materials. They can stay in the air for hours if conditions are right.

540 **The smallest kind of plane is called a microlight.** This plane is very light, with just a wing, a propeller engine and one or two seats in an open cockpit. Some look like very small planes but others look more like large kites, with wings that fold up. A pilot has to pass a test to fly a microlight just like they would for any other sort of plane.

541 **Gliders are planes with no engines.** The shape of a glider is long and thin to slice through the air, with long wings for lift. To become airborne, they are towed along the ground until they are moving fast enough to take off. Some are towed into the air by a plane, which takes off pulling the glider behind it. In the air, the plane drops the tow rope and the glider flies on its own gradually dropping to the ground.

▶ A small propeller behind the pilot drives this microlight.

542 Paragliders and hang gliders do not have engines, and the pilots take off from the top of a hill or cliff. A hang glider is like a large kite with a person hanging below, strapped into a harness. A paraglider is more like a parachute, with a canopy that holds air to make a wing shape. Pilots take off by running into the wind, and gradually glide down to the ground.

543 Gliders use rising currents of air to fly higher. They fly near hills where the wind flows up and over the hill. It lifts the glider up higher so it can stay in the air longer. Gliders also ride on currents of warm air called thermals. These form when air is heated by the warm ground and rises like the hot air in a balloon.

544 Flying a small plane in complicated loops, rolls and turns is called aerobatics. Pilots often perform aerobatics for competitions. Groups of planes flying in formation with coloured smoke streaming out behind them put on spectacular displays at air shows. The pilots need lots of practice and skill to do this safely. Helicopters can also perform aerobatic displays.

MAKE A GLIDER

Fold a piece of A4 paper in half lengthwise then open it out flat. Fold the top corners down to the centre, making an arrow shape. Then fold the two sides in again. Fold the paper back along the original centre fold. Hold the glider's nose with the wings open flat. Throw it to see how far it flies. Try again with a paper clip on the nose.

Planes at sea

545 Military aircraft go to sea on board huge ships called aircraft carriers. These can take planes as close as possible to war zones. The planes use the aircraft carrier like an airport, taking off for a mission then returning to land and refuel. Many planes can fold their wings up when not flying so that more can fit onboard.

546 Vertical take-off planes can operate from smaller aircraft carriers. They do not need a runway, just enough space on the deck to take off and land again. These smaller carriers often have a ramp at the end of the deck for planes that need a short runway to help them take off.

547 The top deck of an aircraft carrier is the flight deck where the planes take off and land. It is like a runway but not as long, so a catapult shoots the planes forward, giving them extra speed to fly from the deck. After landing, the plane is brought to a standstill by a wire hooked across the deck. Below the flight deck is a hangar deck where planes are stored. They go up and down between the decks in a huge lift.

▼ Planes park on the flight deck of an aircraft carrier between flights.

◀ A seaplane floats on the water ready for take-off. These small planes are sometimes used by coast guards in rescue operations.

549 Seaplanes can land on water. These small planes have floats instead of wheels. The floats rest on the surface so the plane is out of the water. Seaplanes can only land and take off if the water is calm. They are sometimes used for flying between islands, or in remote areas where there are lakes to land on but few runways.

548 Helicopters are also used on ships. They only need a small platform called a helipad for taking off and landing. They cannot travel as far or as fast as a plane, but they can ferry people and equipment and act as look outs. Oil rigs out at sea often depend on helicopters to bring new crews and supplies from the mainland.

▶ Helipads provide a landing place at sea.

Flying faster than sound

550 **Supersonic planes fly faster than sound.** Sound travels extremely fast – when you clap your hands the sound moves out in all directions and people hear it almost immediately. Supersonic planes travel faster than this. When a plane starts to travel faster than sound, we say it is breaking the sound barrier.

▶ An American F-16 Fighting Falcon can fly twice as fast as sound.

551 Many military fighter planes are built to fly faster than sound. Their engines often have afterburners for more power and speed. These burn extra fuel in the stream of hot gas coming out of the engine. This gives a plane more power for take-off, or for a short burst of extra speed, and allows it to fly for longer at supersonic speeds.

Sound waves spread outwards as the plane moves

Sound waves become squashed as the plane increases speed

As the plane flies through the sound barrier, a sonic boom is heard

▲ As a plane moves faster, sound waves squash together, eventually creating a sonic boom.

552 When a plane flies at supersonic speed, people on the ground hear a sonic boom. This happens because as it flies, the plane squashes the air in front of it into waves. When the plane reaches the speed of sound, the waves join up, making one shock wave. The shock wave spreads out behind the plane like the wave behind a boat and makes a sound like thunder.

Swept-back wings give a streamlined shape

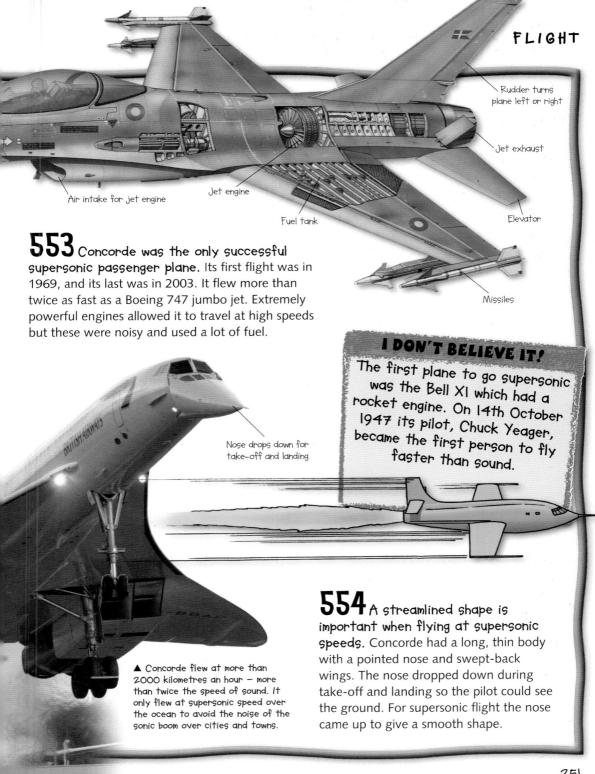

Rudder turns
plane left or right

Jet exhaust

Air intake for jet engine

Jet engine

Fuel tank

Elevator

Missiles

553 Concorde was the only successful
supersonic passenger plane. Its first flight was in
1969, and its last was in 2003. It flew more than
twice as fast as a Boeing 747 jumbo jet. Extremely
powerful engines allowed it to travel at high speeds
but these were noisy and used a lot of fuel.

I DON'T BELIEVE IT!
The first plane to go supersonic
was the Bell XI which had a
rocket engine. On 14th October
1947 its pilot, Chuck Yeager,
became the first person to fly
faster than sound.

Nose drops down for
take-off and landing

▲ Concorde flew at more than
2000 kilometres an hour — more
than twice the speed of sound. It
only flew at supersonic speed over
the ocean to avoid the noise of the
sonic boom over cities and towns.

554 A streamlined shape is
important when flying at supersonic
speeds. Concorde had a long, thin body
with a pointed nose and swept-back
wings. The nose dropped down during
take-off and landing so the pilot could see
the ground. For supersonic flight the nose
came up to give a smooth shape.

Flying in space

555 **Powerful rockets can fly into space.** There is no air in space, so wings are of no use. Rockets are pushed upwards by their powerful engines. Also, without air there is no drag to slow the rocket. Once started by a boost from its motor, the rocket keeps going, only needing extra boosts to change direction or speed.

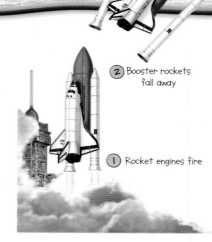

② Booster rockets fall away

① Rocket engines fire

▲ The Shuttle's rocket engines and boosters gave it enough speed to reach space.

◀ The *Ariane 5* rocket launches satellites into space. A new rocket is built for each launch.

Liquid oxygen tank

Liquid hydrogen tank

556 **Rocket engines are similar to jet engines.** Inside the engine the fuel burns, making hot gases rush out through a nozzle at the back, and the rocket shoots forwards. However a rocket carries its own oxygen gas to burn the fuel. A jet engine uses oxygen from the air. This means a jet engine only works in air, but a rocket engine works in air and space.

▲ The solid fuel in the Shuttle's booster rockets burned very rapidly for maximum thrust.

③ Fuel tank separates

557 The Space Shuttle took off as a rocket. It had three rocket engines, but it also used two huge booster rockets. These only fired for two minutes before dropping back to Earth. The engines used fuel from a separate tank that also fell away when the Shuttle reached space. The booster rockets landed in the sea and were used again, but the tank burned up as it dropped into the atmosphere.

④ Return to Earth

⑤ Touch down

558 The Shuttle landed on a runway like a huge glider. When the Shuttle returned to Earth it did not use its rocket engines. It swooped gently downwards and used its wings and tail to slow and guide it towards its long runway. It touched down much faster than an airliner and used a parachute to help it slow down and stop.

Exhaust nozzle

▶ *Orion* does not need wings like the Shuttle because it will not land on a runway.

Solid fuel booster

559 A new spacecraft called *Orion* will replace the Shuttle. It will be launched by a rocket called *Ares*, which is similar to the Shuttle's boosters. Four to six astronauts will travel in the cone-shaped capsule. They will be able to go to the International Space Station, or the Moon – or even the planet Mars. When they return to Earth they will float down using parachutes and land in the sea.

Strange planes

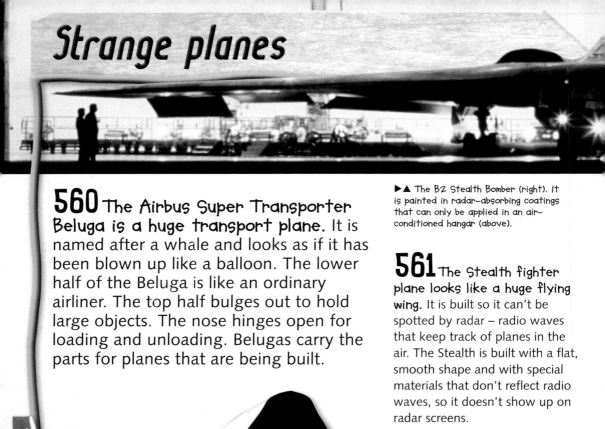

560 The Airbus Super Transporter Beluga is a huge transport plane. It is named after a whale and looks as if it has been blown up like a balloon. The lower half of the Beluga is like an ordinary airliner. The top half bulges out to hold large objects. The nose hinges open for loading and unloading. Belugas carry the parts for planes that are being built.

▶▲ The B2 Stealth Bomber (right). It is painted in radar-absorbing coatings that can only be applied in an air-conditioned hangar (above).

561 The Stealth fighter plane looks like a huge flying wing. It is built so it can't be spotted by radar – radio waves that keep track of planes in the air. The Stealth is built with a flat, smooth shape and with special materials that don't reflect radio waves, so it doesn't show up on radar screens.

◀ Bulky cargo is lifted into a Beluga transport plane. Its oddly shaped nose makes it look like a beluga whale.

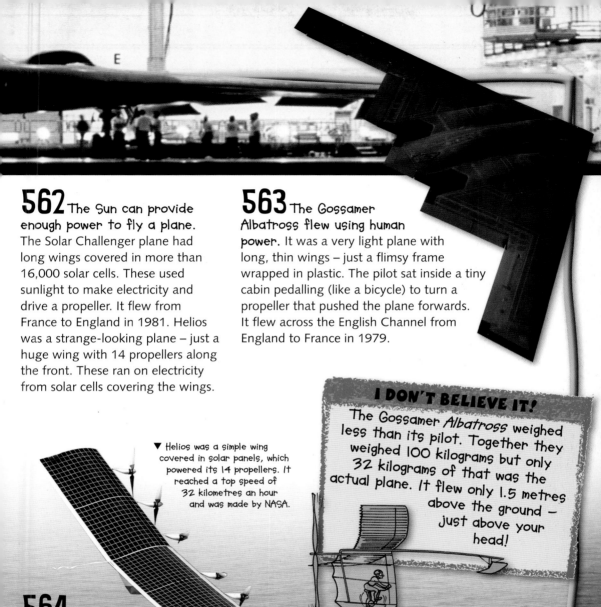

562 The Sun can provide enough power to fly a plane. The Solar Challenger plane had long wings covered in more than 16,000 solar cells. These used sunlight to make electricity and drive a propeller. It flew from France to England in 1981. Helios was a strange-looking plane – just a huge wing with 14 propellers along the front. These ran on electricity from solar cells covering the wings.

563 The Gossamer Albatross flew using human power. It was a very light plane with long, thin wings – just a flimsy frame wrapped in plastic. The pilot sat inside a tiny cabin pedalling (like a bicycle) to turn a propeller that pushed the plane forwards. It flew across the English Channel from England to France in 1979.

▼ Helios was a simple wing covered in solar panels, which powered its 14 propellers. It reached a top speed of 32 kilometres an hour and was made by NASA.

I DON'T BELIEVE IT!
The Gossamer Albatross weighed less than its pilot. Together they weighed 100 kilograms but only 32 kilograms of that was the actual plane. It flew only 1.5 metres above the ground – just above your head!

564 Predator is a robot spy plane. It is the same size as a small plane but with no cabin or pilot. It flies by remote control like a model plane. Cameras show its controllers a view of the enemy. It can also carry missiles to attack enemy targets.

SPEED

- Measuring speed
- Velocity
- Energy
- Speedy animals
- Racing
- Streamlined design
- The land speed record
- Speed machines
- Acceleration and deceleration
- Light speed

Why do racing bikes slow down when cornering?

What is the fastest reptile?

How fast do galaxies move?

What is velocity?

Who holds the world water speed record?

How fast?

565 Speed is how far (the distance) something goes in a certain time. If a jet plane travels 3000 kilometres in three hours, its speed is 1000 kilometres per hour. We describe speed as distance covered – such as metres or kilometres – in one unit or 'piece' of time, such as one minute, one hour or one year.

566 We describe something as 'high speed' if it is very fast, but what we think of as high speed has changed over time. In 1972 the fastest sailing craft was *Crossbow*, a catamaran (yacht with two hulls), at 48.6 kilometres per hour. Just 30 years later the record was 103 kilometres per hour, due to the invention of kitesurfing, in which the sailor rides a modified surfboard while holding on to a special kind of kite.

567 Whether something is 'speedy' or fast depends on what, where and when. Cars on a motorway travel at 110 kilometres per hour. A garden snail crawls along at 18 centimetres per minute. The snail is 10,000 times slower than the car – but speedy compared to other kinds of snails.

▶ Some machines are not only built for speed, they are named after it. Speedboats such as these Vee-Class powerboats go faster than 160 kilometres per hour, their super-streamlined hulls slicing across the wave tops.

P2-9

SCREAM MACHINE

Panasonic SEA TOW MOREHEAD CITY, NC

REN Marine
ountain.com

Panasonic 76

LUCAS OIL PRODUCTS INC.

7

7

259

Units for speed

568 Speed is the distance covered in a set time. A racing car might have a speed of 160 kilometres per hour for one lap of its course, but it might go at 300 kilometres per hour on straights and 50 kilometres per hour around bends. The 160 kilometres per hour is the average speed – total distance divided by total time.

$$SPEED = \frac{DISTANCE}{TIME}$$

569 The knot is used to measure how fast something goes on water. Its name comes from the fact that ships used to measure their speed by letting a rope out into the water. The rope had knots at regular intervals and a float at one end. The more knots that passed over the ship's side in 30 seconds, the faster the speed. One knot is equal to 1.83 kilometres per hour.

Knots
▶ Sailing speeds are still often measured in knots – as are wind speeds.

570 Throughout history, people have measured distance, time and speed in lots of different ways. Long ago, the time for a journey by sailing ship was measured to the nearest day, or even the nearest week! Today, modern jet planes mean the journeys are measured in kilometres per hour.

Miles per hour (mph)
▶ The speed indicator dial on fast cars may go up to 200 miles per hour.

Metres per minute
▶ For a snail or a slug, one metre is a very long distance.

571 Even today there are many different ways to describe speed around the world. In most of Europe, road speed is measured in kilometres per hour (km/h). In the UK and USA it is measured in miles per hour (mph).

Metres per second

▲ Comets travel through space at more than 66,600 metres per second, but seen from Earth, they appear to be hardly moving.

Kilometres per hour (km/h)

▶ Most passenger jet planes have a cruising speed of around 900–950 kilometres per hour.

572 To describe and imagine very fast or slow speeds, we have to change the measuring units we use. A rocket must reach more than 40,300 kilometres per hour to blast away from Earth into space. This is known as escape velocity. It may be easier to imagine as 11.2 kilometres per second, or even 11,200 metres per second.

573 Special units can help us when comparing speeds. A cheetah is much faster than a cockroach, but this is mainly because it is much bigger. However, if we compare each animal's speed to its size, things are rather different. A cockroach covers 50 of its own body lengths per second, but the cheetah covers just 12 of its own body lengths per second.

It's all relative

574 **All speeds are relative.** This is because nothing in the Universe is completely still. Even someone measuring speed is moving! So you can only measure something's speed 'relative' to something else – that is, by how fast it goes past.

575 A single object has many different speeds. A train goes at 100 kilometres per hour relative to its tracks and stations. For a person in a car travelling alongside the track at 60 kilometres per hour, the train's speed is 40 kilometres per hour. For a passenger on a train travelling towards the first train at 100 kilometres per hour, the combined speed is 200 kilometres per hour.

① To a person standing still at a station, the passing train's speed would be 100 kilometres per hour.

② For a driver in a car travelling alongside the train, its relative speed is 40 kilometres per hour.

③ For passengers in an oncoming second train, the combined speed is 200 kilometres per hour.

576 Usually we measure speed as the distance travelled here on Earth, along the surface or through the air – but this is also relative. The Earth's surface is moving as the planet spins once each day. If you could stay put in space, high above the Earth, someone standing still at the Equator (an imaginary line drawn around the mid-point of the Earth) would be moving at 462 metres each second.

▼ ② The Equator is the fastest-moving place on Earth, being the widest part, in the middle of the direction of spin.

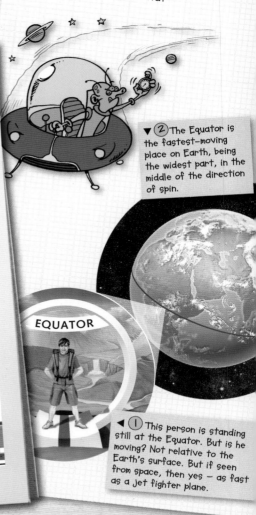

EQUATOR

◄ ① This person is standing still at the Equator. But is he moving? Not relative to the Earth's surface. But if seen from space, then yes – as fast as a jet fighter plane.

577 As well as constantly spinning, the Earth travels on its yearly orbit around the Sun. This makes working out speed even more complicated, since Earth's average orbital speed is about 30 kilometres each second.

▼ ③ Like the other planets, Earth zooms at huge speed around the Sun.

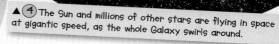

▲ ④ The Sun and millions of other stars are flying in space at gigantic speed, as the whole Galaxy swirls around.

578 Added to this is the speed of the whole Solar System (the Sun and all its planets). It is whirling around the centre of our massive group of stars, the Milky Way Galaxy. This speed is even faster – about 250 kilometres each second.

579 Even if you went into deepest space, there is still nowhere that you can stand to measure 'true' speed. All the galaxies are flying away from each other, some at more than 300 kilometres per second. The whole Universe is moving faster and getting bigger.

Measuring speed

580 Long ago, there were no standard ways of measuring speed because there was no accurate way to measure time. People used devices such as sand clocks (in which sand poured through a small hole) to measure time, and methods such as counting their own steps to measure distance. The only way of comparing the speed of two or more things, such as horses, was a head-to-head race.

▼ The Olympics showcase the world's fastest humans in direct competition. Here Vomma Iso-Hollo wins 1932's 3000 metres steeplechase.

581 Gradually, measuring devices became more accurate. The first stopwatch was developed in the 1850s, and by the 1910s it was accurate to 1/100th of one second. During the 1970s, digital stopwatches increased this to 1/1000th of one second.

582 To measure distance, people once used lengths of wood. This gave rise to units of length such as the pole or rod, equivalent to 5.03 metres. Tape measures arrived in the 1700s, and by 1970 laser beams could measure distances more accurately.

▼ Stopwatches used clockwork springs and measured to 1/100th of one second. Electronic timing devices use vibrating crystals to measure to 1/1000th of one second.

▲ A race result may be so close the human eye cannot see who has won. A photo finish uses a sequence of pictures, 1000 or more each second, to pick out the winner, as in this 100 metres sprint.

583 For distance and speed over long distances, such as across seas, people relied on maps and charts. They measured the distance on the map and multiplied it by the scale of the map. But this was not very accurate – a very thin line on the map could be hundreds of metres wide in the real world.

584 From the 1990s the 'satnav' system GPS (which stands for Global Positioning System) meant speed over long distances could be measured much more precisely. GPS satellite clocks are accurate to 14 billionths of one second, and the best GPS receivers can pinpoint position to within 25 centimetres.

Each satellite transmits its identity and position

Some satellites are farther away, so signals arrive at the GPS unit at different times

GPS unit in vehicle is 'tuned in' to the signals from the satellites

▲ A 'satnav' receiver compares the times taken for signals to arrive from at least three GPS satellites.

585 Some sports have special ways to measure speed. The Hawk-Eye system uses several video cameras to record a ball's path from different angles. A computer compares the pictures and calculates the ball's speed and direction. A fast cricket bowl is 160 kilometres per hour, and a tennis serve can be 250 kilometres per hour – 70 metres in one second!

▼ In tennis, the Hawk-Eye tracking system shows the ball's speed, position and direction, and also if it landed on, in or outside the line.

OFFICIAL
REVIEW

What is velocity?

586 Speed is distance covered with time – but it has no direction. To describe speed in a certain direction, we use the term 'velocity'. A swan might have a speed of 60 kilometres an hour when it migrates to its breeding area, but its velocity is 60 kilometres per hour due north.

587 Measuring velocity means measuring time and distance (as for speed), and also position. For long distances this can be done using GPS or 'satnav' equipment. In smaller areas it can be done with a map, perhaps using local landmarks, or with short-range radio signals such as radio beacons used by aircraft.

◀ This grey reef shark's radio tracker gives its position at different times, showing its overall velocity on longer journeys between reefs, and how, for example, ocean currents affect its movements.

588 Velocity gives much more information than speed. It shows changes in speed, direction and location, and how fast and how often they happen. This helps aircraft pilots to work out the fuel needed to climb to cruising height, go around storms, and circle or 'stack' waiting to land.

▶ As the plane passes through each criss-cross radio 'grid', the pilots work out its velocity to land safely.

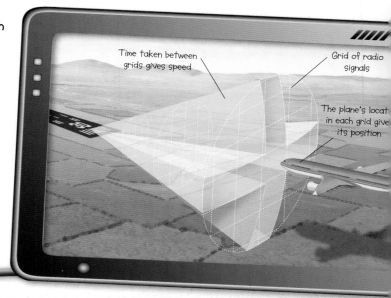

Time taken between grids gives speed

Grid of radio signals

The plane's locat in each grid give its position

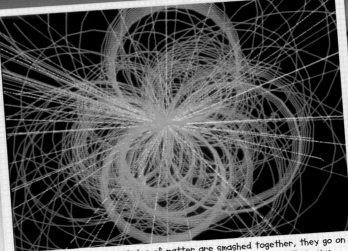

▲ When the smallest particles of matter are smashed together, they go on amazingly complicated curved pathways or tracks. These show their size, speed and structure.

589 On the huge scale of space travel, knowing about speed and direction, and so velocity, is vital. As a space probe sets off for a distant planet it must aim exactly in the right direction. Otherwise, after a journey of perhaps 10 years, it could be millions of kilometres off course. Space scientists continually check its path to keep it on target.

590 On the tiniest scale, velocity helps us to understand the world of atoms and their parts. These particles are smashed together with incredible force, such as in the world's largest machine, the LHC (Large Hadron Collider). The velocity of the resulting bits – their speed and direction – gives clues to their most basic make-up.

QUIZ

1. Rather than heading north, then the same distance east, what would be a quicker direction?

2. What is the name of the world's largest machine?

3. What is wrong with saying 'The car's velocity was 70 kilometres per hour'?

Answers:
1. Head north-east
2. Large Hadron Collider
3. You need to give the car's direction as well as its speed

◀ A US Air Force jet fighter watches space shuttle *Atlantis* on its final blast-off in 2011. The jet plane is capable of 2600 kilometres per hour. As the shuttle docks with the orbiting International Space Station, both the shuttle and the station will be travelling ten times faster. And both in the same direction – and so with the same velocity.

Speed and energy

591 Something that moves has not only speed, but also a form of energy — the ability to cause changes and make things happen. Energy due to movement or motion is called kinetic energy. You can see it at work everywhere – it is used to generate electricity from rushing river water and it is the reason that we have airbags and seatbelts in our cars.

592 Massively heavy things are more difficult to speed up. They have high inertia, which means they need lots of energy to give them motion. The heavy flywheel in an engine needs great force to get it going, but once it's spinning, it helps the engine run smoothly.

▶ One very strong human — Mikhail Sidorychev — can gradually overcome the inertia of a huge plane, giving it kinetic energy to get it moving.

593 Kinetic energy depends on two main features — an object's speed, and its mass (amount of matter). The faster something goes, the more kinetic energy it has, and the more mass it has, the more kinetic energy it has. So a very fast motorbike could have the same kinetic energy as a very slow truck.

HOW FAR?

You will need:

tennis ball   stiff card about 60 cm long   pen
measuring tape

1. Draw a scale on the card, marking every 2 cm. Prop up one end of the card at an angle of about 30° to make a ramp.

2. Release the ball from each mark in turn. Measure how far it rolls each time. The ball gains more speed from each higher mark, and so has more energy to roll farther.

594 Once an object is moving with speed, it has lots of kinetic energy, or high momentum. Then it resists losing speed – being slowed down. A huge, speedy ship such as an oil tanker has so much momentum that it may take 50 kilometres to slow down.

▼ Racing bikers have to learn how to slow down and lean into corners.

▼ On a 'Wall of Death', fast-circling riders produce enough outward force to overcome gravity and rise at right angles up the wall.

595 As an object goes around a bend or curve, it has different forces acting on it, and this affects its speed. A motorcycle can go fast in a straight line, but around a bend it must slow down as the rider leans to one side so that its tyres don't lose grip and skid.

596 Spinning at speed causes another set of forces. One is felt as a pull away from the centre of the spin. This is known as centrifugal force, and is used in machines called centrifuges. A medical centrifuge spins tubes of blood so fast, the heaviest parts sink to the bottom of the tube. This helps to separate blood into its different parts.

Natural speeds

597 The natural world has a huge range of speeds, from incredibly slow to ultra-fast. Some of the slowest movers are the world's landmasses or continents. They drift around the planet's surface by a few centimetres each year. Glaciers are thick 'rivers' of snow and ice. They slide slowly downhill, mostly by only a few metres each year. In Greenland, the Jakobshavn Glacier sped along at more than 12 kilometres per year, probably as a result of global warming.

598 Rivers have many different speeds, from 10-plus metres per second down steep rapids to less than one metre per minute in other places. The giant Amazon River's average flow speed is about 2 kilometres per hour. One of the fastest ocean currents is the Agulhas Current in the Indian Ocean, at 10 kilometres per hour.

▼ Where a river flows through a narrow gorge, it speeds up as rapids. The same amount of water passes every second as in places where the river is less restricted.

10 m/second

▼ A scientist using an instrument called a theodolite. This records the exact position of marker poles at certain times to determine a glacier's speed.

12 km/year

599 In 1980, the eruption of Mount St Helens, in the north-west USA, caused an avalanche and rockfall that travelled at more than 400 kilometres per hour. This was one of the fastest ever measured. Even a small avalanche can reach 120 kilometres per hour, which is much too fast to outrun.

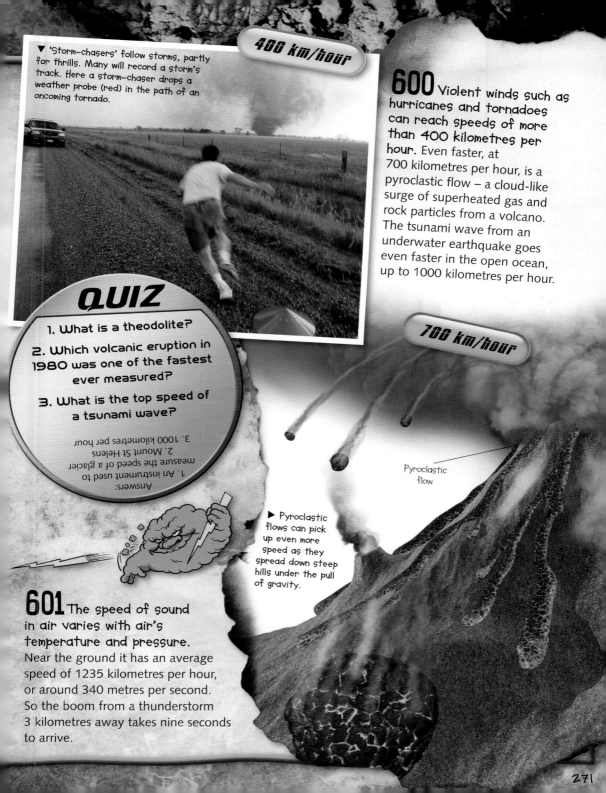

▼ 'Storm-chasers' follow storms, partly for thrills. Many will record a storm's track. Here a storm-chaser drops a weather probe (red) in the path of an oncoming tornado.

400 km/hour

600 Violent winds such as hurricanes and tornadoes can reach speeds of more than 400 kilometres per hour. Even faster, at 700 kilometres per hour, is a pyroclastic flow – a cloud-like surge of superheated gas and rock particles from a volcano. The tsunami wave from an underwater earthquake goes even faster in the open ocean, up to 1000 kilometres per hour.

700 km/hour

QUIZ

1. What is a theodolite?

2. Which volcanic eruption in 1980 was one of the fastest ever measured?

3. What is the top speed of a tsunami wave?

Answers:
1. An instrument used to measure the speed of a glacier
2. Mount St Helens
3. 1000 kilometres per hour

Pyroclastic flow

▶ Pyroclastic flows can pick up even more speed as they spread down steep hills under the pull of gravity.

601 The speed of sound in air varies with air's temperature and pressure. Near the ground it has an average speed of 1235 kilometres per hour, or around 340 metres per second. So the boom from a thunderstorm 3 kilometres away takes nine seconds to arrive.

Life in the fast lane

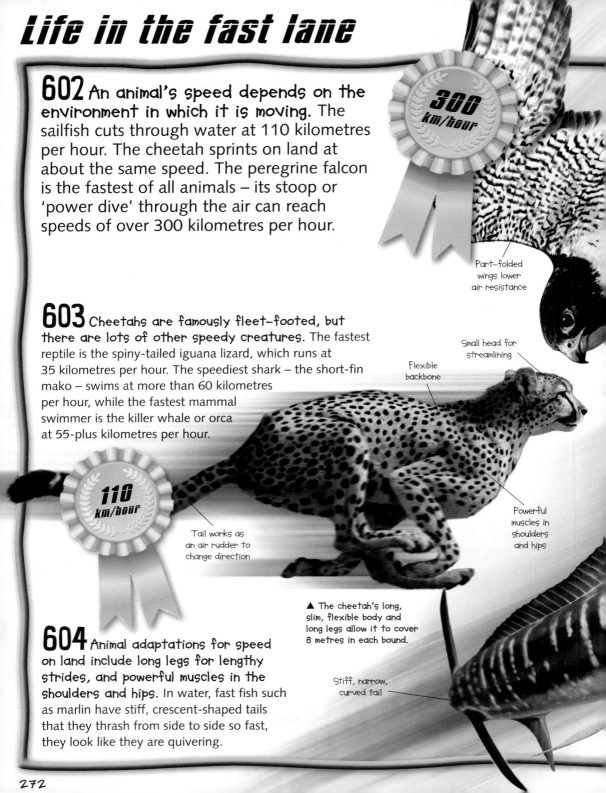

602 An animal's speed depends on the environment in which it is moving. The sailfish cuts through water at 110 kilometres per hour. The cheetah sprints on land at about the same speed. The peregrine falcon is the fastest of all animals – its stoop or 'power dive' through the air can reach speeds of over 300 kilometres per hour.

300 km/hour

Part-folded wings lower air resistance

603 Cheetahs are famously fleet-footed, but there are lots of other speedy creatures. The fastest reptile is the spiny-tailed iguana lizard, which runs at 35 kilometres per hour. The speediest shark – the short-fin mako – swims at more than 60 kilometres per hour, while the fastest mammal swimmer is the killer whale or orca at 55-plus kilometres per hour.

Small head for streamlining

Flexible backbone

110 km/hour

Tail works as an air rudder to change direction

Powerful muscles in shoulders and hips

▲ The cheetah's long, slim, flexible body and long legs allow it to cover 8 metres in each bound.

604 Animal adaptations for speed on land include long legs for lengthy strides, and powerful muscles in the shoulders and hips. In water, fast fish such as marlin have stiff, crescent-shaped tails that thrash from side to side so fast, they look like they are quivering.

Stiff, narrow, curved tail

605 One of the fastest muscle actions in the animal world is the mantis shrimp's club–like pincer or claw. It 'locks' in a bent position using a trigger-like part, builds up muscle force, and then 'unlocks' to throw a punch that lasts less than 1/200th of a second, moves at 22 metres per second, and strikes with the force of a rifle bullet.

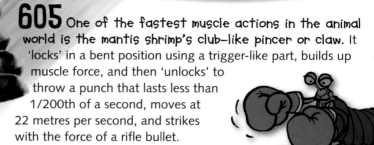

◀ The peregrine does not simply fall downwards in its stoop. It flaps its wings for even greater speed.

Wing feathers fanned for greater push

606 Inside living things, one of the fastest actions is the movement of nerve signals. They can travel at more than 100 metres per second, going from human toe to brain in less than 1/50th of one second.

607 Plants can be speedy too. The venus flytrap flicks its leaf shut around an insect victim in less than half a second. Plants such as giant kelp seaweed and some types of bamboo grow at great speed – up to one metre each day.

110 km/hour

Top (dorsal) fin folds down at speed

Pointed snout for less water resistance

▲ Blocks of powerful muscles along the sides of the sailfish's body swish its tail from side to side, and make up more than three–quarters of the fish's weight.

▶ If this fly touches the trigger hairs near the hinge of the venus flytrap's leaf, the trap at once snaps shut.

273

Breeding the best

608 People have held races to find the speediest animals and people for more than 5000 years. Early races involved horses, camels, dogs and humans. Running and chariot racing were among the most popular events at ancient Greece's Olympic Games, 2500 years ago.

609 Some of the biggest prizes are given for the fastest racehorses. Perhaps the quickest was Secretariat, an American thoroughbred that raced in the 1970s. He set records that still stand today, winning the 1973 Kentucky Derby at 16.8 metres per second (60 kilometres per hour).

610 People can select the fastest animals of each kind, and breed them together to produce even speedier ones. This process is called selective breeding. It has produced the fastest type of dog, the greyhound. It races at almost 20 metres per second (72 kilometres per hour) – nearly twice as fast as a human sprinter.

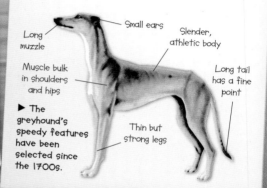

Long muzzle

Small ears

Slender, athletic body

Muscle bulk in shoulders and hips

Long tail has a fine point

▶ The greyhound's speedy features have been selected since the 1700s.

Thin but strong legs

▼ Fast-action photos show how a racehorse's leg-moving muscles are concentrated in the shoulder and buttock areas. Most of the leg is slim and easy to swing fast.

▲ The fastest camels are almost as rapid as racehorses, reaching speeds of over 55 kilometres per hour.

613 Training a champion animal speedster is a complicated business. Trainers pay great attention to diet and exercise, working out a series of activities that build gradually to the day of the big race. Some racehorses only run well if they have their 'best friend' stable companion with them on the day – which might be a donkey!

611 Many animals are raced for speed and stamina (endurance). Strange races include camels, ferrets, maggots, elephants, sled–pulling husky dogs, hamsters in wheeled cars, and pigs with pretend stuffed–toy 'jockeys'. Elephants weigh over 5 tonnes yet they can reach speeds of 6.6 metres per second (24 kilometres per hour).

612 Breeders look for several features in racing animals. These include a slim but muscular build, strong bones (especially in the legs), no spare fat, a strong heartbeat, and clear breathing to take in the oxygen in air needed by hard-working muscles.

WORM OLYMPICS

You will need:
earthworms   A4 paper   sticky tape

1. Roll and tape sheets of A4 paper into tubes about one centimetre wide.

2. Tape the paper rolls side by side.

3. Carefully gather garden earthworms and put each one into a tube at the 'Start' end.

4. The worm that is first to emerge completely at the 'Finish' end is the winner!

Note: After your race, put the worms back in the soil where you found them and wash your hands.

Out in front

614 Human speeds improve year by year. In 1912 the record time for the 100 metres sprint was 10.6 seconds. Today it is more than one second less. This is partly because people have generally become healthier, with better food and fewer illnesses, especially in childhood. We also understand more about exercise and how the body works.

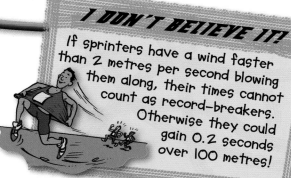

615 Human speeds have also increased for money reasons. Modern sport is big business that attracts the best brains to train athletes. Coaches devise incredibly detailed training programmes covering everything from building muscle and improving breathing, to planning their athlete's mental approach to each race.

► From 2008, Jamaica's Usain Bolt shattered sprint records and became World and Olympic champion at 100 and 200 metres, at speeds of up to 37.5 kilometres per hour.

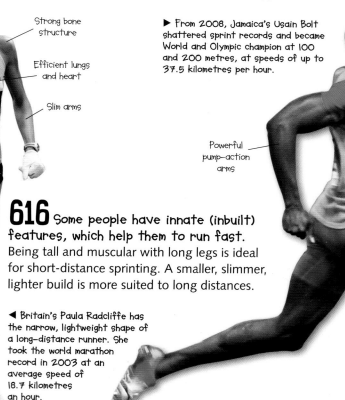

Strong bone structure

Efficient lungs and heart

Slim arms

Narrow hips and slim legs

Minimal body fat

616 Some people have innate (inbuilt) features, which help them to run fast. Being tall and muscular with long legs is ideal for short-distance sprinting. A smaller, slimmer, lighter build is more suited to long distances.

◄ Britain's Paula Radcliffe has the narrow, lightweight shape of a long-distance runner. She took the world marathon record in 2003 at an average speed of 18.7 kilometres an hour.

Powerful pump-action arms

Tall stature

Muscle bulk in hips and legs

Long legs for extended stride

617 Every so often, a great landmark or 'milestone' is reached in human speed. In 1954 English runner Roger Bannister was the first person to run a mile in less than four minutes – which many people said was impossible. In 1968 Jim Hines of the USA broke the '10-second barrier' and ran the 100 metres sprint in 9.9 seconds.

▶ When Bannister broke the four-minute mile, people doubted the time could reduce much more. Today's runners are 15 seconds faster.

▼ In 100 years, the record time for the 100 metres freestyle swim – here with modern French champion Alain Bernard – has reduced from 66 to 46 seconds.

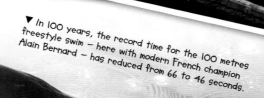

618 There are lots of different human speed records. These range from the 60-metre 'flying start' and sprints at 100, 200 and 400 metres, to middle-distance 800 and 1500 metres, and long-distance 5000 and the marathon (42,195 metres). If sprint swimmers in a 50 metres front crawl race could maintain their speed over 1500 metres, they would cut the record time for that race (currently 14 minutes and 30 seconds) by four minutes!

Designed for speed

619 The quest for speed has led people to design, build and operate all kinds of speed machines. From soap-box carts and penny-farthing bicycles to racing cars, powerboats, jet trucks, bullet trains and rocket planes – as with human speed, machine speed keeps improving through the years.

Contoured helmet

Arms and hands together

Slippery body suit fabric

Spokeless disc wheels

▲ Track cyclists use every design trick to reduce air resistance or drag.

620 One important feature of a speed machine is its overall size. Bigger is usually faster, but only up to a certain point. A larger machine can have a bigger, more powerful engine, but the weight of the machine itself, with its frame and working parts, increases greatly and speed becomes slower again.

Mirrors close to body

Bonnet 'flows' into windscreen

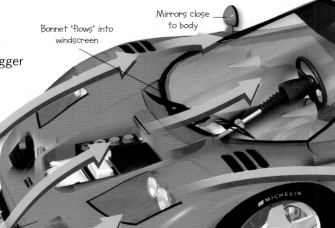

▶ Air is pushed over a car smoothly, rather than being allowed to go underneath and lift it at high speed.

Low sloping front

Rounded front wheel arches

◀ A hydrofoil lifts up at speed to reduce drag on its hull.

621 'Drag' is the enemy of speed. Drag is the resistance or pushing-back force from air or water, as an object shoves between its tiny particles or molecules. A speed machine is shaped to be streamlined or 'slippery' with a pointed front, smooth surfaces and curves, a tapering rear end, and no sticking-out parts.

622 Before building a speed machine, design models can be tested in wind tunnels or water tanks. This shows how the air or water flows past the vehicle. It reveals any swirls, eddies (circular movements) or vortexes (unsteady movements), which may increase drag and have a slowing effect.

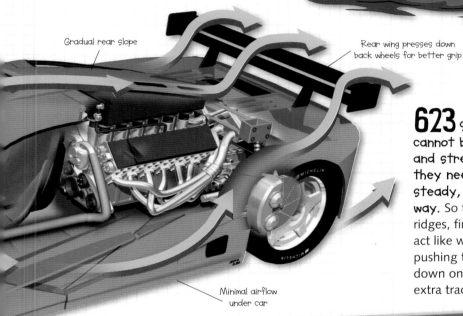

Gradual rear slope

Rear wing presses down back wheels for better grip

Minimal airflow under car

623 Speed machines cannot be totally smooth and streamlined, because they need to move in a steady, stable, safe way. So they may have ridges, fins or wings that act like wings in reverse, pushing the car's wheels down onto the ground for extra traction (grip).

624 Computers also help to design speed machines. A virtual design, existing only in the computer, can be put into a virtual wind tunnel or water tank, also in the computer, to see how it performs. By pressing a few keys the designers can redesign a part to try and improve performance.

▶ Computer modelling shows how swirling air currents are 'thrown off' the rear parts of a fast plane, slowing it down.

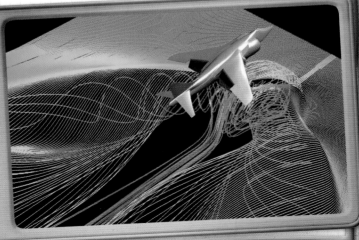

Making a breakthrough

625 Through history, different types of speed machines have got faster by small amounts. A big leap in performance is usually the result of a new invention or development, such as a new engine, better materials that save weight, or a new control method, such as a computer.

626 In the early 1950s a new kind of propeller-driven speedboat made a huge splash. *Slo-Mo-Shun IV* used a method called prop-riding, where the boat's hull rose at speed to lift the top parts of the propellers above the surface. This reduced their pushing force but reduced drag even more. It improved the water speed record by 60 kilometres per hour in two years, to 287 kilometres per hour.

▼ *Railton Mobil Special*, driven by John Cobb, was the last piston-engined vehicle to hold the world land speed record.

▼ *Spirit of America* became the first jet car to take the land speed record, powered by an old GE J47 engine from a Sabre jet fighter plane.

GOOD YEAR   SPIRIT OF AMERICA

627 In the late 1940s the world land speed record was held by John Cobb in *Railton Mobil Special*, at 634 kilometres per hour. This vehicle had piston engines that turned the wheels, like an ordinary car. By 1965 the record had shot up to almost 1000 kilometres per hour with Craig Breedlove in *Spirit of America*, due to the arrival of the jet engine.

FASTEST OR FARTHEST?

You will need:
computer   A4 paper

1. Make two paper planes of different designs – ask an adult to help you look online for instructions if you're not sure how.

2. Test your planes outdoors on a calm day. Which one is fastest? Which one flies farther? Dart-like designs are fast, but glider designs stay up longer and fly a greater distance. It's not always fastest that goes farthest.

628 In 1938 the steam locomotive *Mallard* set the speed record for railed vehicles, at 202.6 kilometres per hour. Then along came electric trains, which soon pushed the record higher, and by 2007 it was over 570 kilometres per hour. Maglev trains, which 'float' above rails, go even faster.

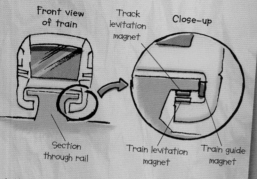

Front view of train

Track levitation magnet

Close-up

Section through rail

Train levitation magnet

Train guide magnet

▲ Maglev trains use magnetic levitation – magnetic forces that suspend the train over the track, removing the problem of wheels and friction.

▲ Concorde was the fastest-ever passenger aircraft. But fuel costs, noise and old age led to it being retired in 2003.

629 The invention of the jet engine had a huge effect on aircraft speed records. The fastest propeller plane was probably the Russian Tu-114 passenger aircraft of the 1960s, at 870 kilometres per hour. By 1969 jet-powered Concorde had more than doubled this to 2172 kilometres per hour. Today jet fighters reach 3300 kilometres per hour.

630 The fastest of all powered machines have rocket engines. In 1967 the USA's X-15 rocket plane reached 7273 kilometres per hour, which is still a record for any manned vehicle or craft – apart from in space. Returning from the Moon in 1969, Apollo astronauts reached 40,000 kilometres per hour.

▲ The X-15 was launched in mid air from a giant bomber aircraft. Two X-15 flights zoomed for a few seconds to the edge of space, over 100 kilometres high.

Modern speed machines

631 Apart from kitesurfers and windsurfers, the fastest sailing craft is *Hydroptère*. It has one main hull and two smaller outer hulls, and is a hydrofoil, rising up at speed on wing-like struts. The craft took the record in 2009 with a speed of 97.9 kilometres per hour.

632 In 1997 the UK's jet car *Thrust SSC* roared across Black Rock Desert, USA to set the land speed record of 1228 kilometres per hour. It was driven by fighter pilot Andy Green, with former record-holder Richard Noble as team boss. 'SSC' stands for Super-Sonic Car, because the vehicle also broke the sound barrier as it set the record.

▲ *Hydroptère* made several failed attempts on the water speed record – during one of which it almost sank – before its 2009 success.

▲ *Thrust SSC* caused a sonic boom as it scorched across Nevada's Black Rock Desert, on its record-breaking two-way run.

633 In 1978 the world water speed record of 511.1 kilometres per hour was set by Ken Warby in his home-made, jet-powered craft, *Spirit of Australia*. It was on Bowering Dam, Australia, with perfect conditions of wind and water surface. This record is one of the most dangerous, and two attempts to break it have killed the pilots. Warby's record still stands.

▲ Warby built *Spirit of Australia* in his garage, using a second-hand jet engine given by air force friends.

634 To design, build, test and run a new record-breaking speed machine costs huge amounts of money. This is one reason why main speed record attempts are rare. Teams hoping to take the land speed record include the UK's *Bloodhound*, the North American Eagle Project and Australia's *Invader 5R*.

Jet engine air intake

Stabilizer wing

Bloodhound aims to attempt the land speed record in 2017, depending on how much money is raised.

Nose wheel

Pointed nose

635 Apart from trains specially altered to break records, there are also records for the fastest regular or scheduled railway service. In 2011 a new type of train – called a 'bullet train' because of its shape and speed – linked the Chinese cities of Beijing and Shanghai. It carries 500 people and can reach 480 kilometres per hour.

636 To get away from the vast cost of breaking the all-out best speed, there is increasing interest in human-powered craft and vehicles. There are records in the air, on land and water, and even underwater. The human-powered submarine *Omer 5* set the underwater record in 2007, at 14.9 kilometres per hour.

Reaching the limit

637 Speeds cannot keep increasing forever. To break the land speed record, *Thrust SSC* needed an incredibly flat surface and a straight course of almost 20 kilometres. Faster cars will probably need longer courses, until the Earth's landscape is the limit.

◀ Skydivers move their arms, legs and body position to speed up or slow down. The belly-to-earth position gives a fall speed of 190 kilometres per hour.

638 As an object goes faster, the opposing drag or resistance rises too, at an ever-increasing rate. Eventually, resistance equals forward force, and the speed limit (terminal velocity) is reached. As parachutists free-fall to Earth, they are pulled by gravity but slowed by air resistance. When these forces balance the parachutist has terminal velocity, which is about 200 kilometres per hour.

639 Speeds are limited for safety reasons. On roads in built-up areas, the UK speed limit is usually 30 miles per hour. Accident information shows that at this speed, about one person in ten hit by a car dies. At just 10 miles per hour more, nine in ten die.

▼ Stopping distance increases in proportion. At 60 miles per hour, it is over three times more than 30 miles per hour, not twice.

SPEED	THINKING DISTANCE	BRAKING DISTANCE	STOPPING DISTANCE
20 mph	6 metres	6 metres	12 metres
30 mph	9 metres	14 metres	23 metres
40 mph	12 metres	24 metres	36 metres
50 mph	15 metres	38 metres	53 metres
60 mph	18 metres	55 metres	73 metres
70 mph	21 metres	75 metres	96 metres

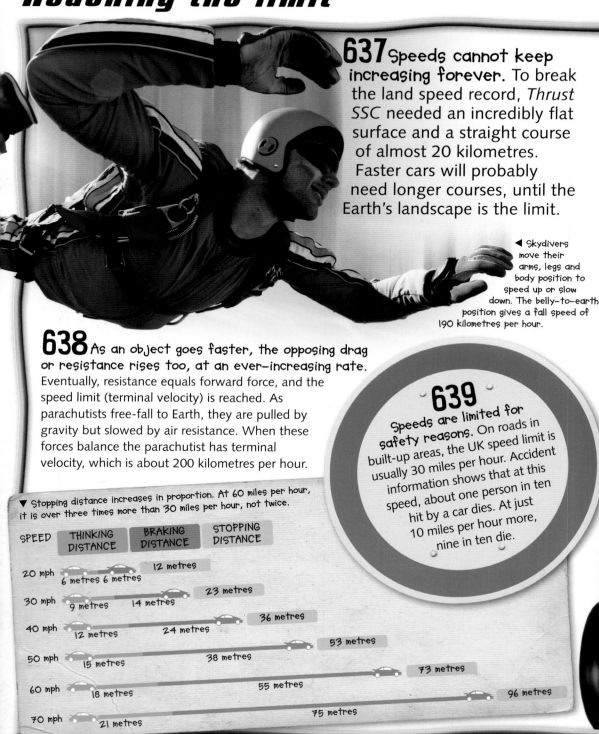

◀ A car's rev counter warns of danger above 7000 rpm. This is when the engine is turning more than 115 times each second.

640 Engines, motors and other machines have speed limits for their moving parts. Otherwise damage is likely as parts spin or move so fast that they crack and shatter. Many cars have a dial showing engine rpm – revolutions (turns) per minute. The high end of the dial is coloured to warn against making the engine turn so fast.

▼ Formula 1 car engines turn at up to 18,000 rpm. At this speed, if one tiny engine part fails, the whole engine may shatter and catch fire.

641 Computers may seem the fastest machines, but even they have their limits. They work by moving particles called electrons, which are pieces of atoms, in the form of tiny pulses of electricity. But electrons need energy to push them along, and they have a maximum travel speed. The upper limit may be reached in 15–20 years.

ROLLER SLIDE RACES

You will need:
children's play slide   string
pair of roller skates
objects of different weights

1. Choose two items of different weights and tie one to each skate.

2. Let both skates go from the top of the slide at the same time. Note which one reaches the bottom first.

3. Repeat for several objects. Does the heaviest one always win?

Speeding up, slowing down

642 Hardly anything goes at a steady speed — not even planets travelling around the Sun. The Earth's speed varies by more than 3600 kilometres per hour between the fastest and slowest part of its orbit. Movement always involves speeding up, called acceleration, and slowing down, or deceleration.

▼ Top Fuel dragsters are the fastest-accelerating cars. From standstill, they cover a one-quarter-mile track in five seconds, finishing at a top speed of over 500 kilometres per hour.

643 The rate of change for speed is measured by how the distance covered in a certain time changes with time. A car starts from standstill, goes one metre per second after one second, two metres per second after two seconds, and so on. Its rate of acceleration, or speeding up, is one metre per second per second. This is usually written as m/s^2.

▲ This car speeds up from standstill to 60 miles per hour in ten seconds. So its average rate of acceleration is 6 miles per second per second, or 6 miles/sec^2.

644 Speeding up and slowing down are caused by a change in force, such as an engine turning faster or wind blowing harder. A familiar example is when something falls to Earth's surface under the force of gravity. In theory, this causes an acceleration of 9.81 m/s^2, often known as the 'g force'. In reality, air resistance reduces this acceleration.

▶ Lieutenant Colonel John Paul Stapp experiences extreme g forces during a rocket-propelled acceleration and deceleration exercise in which he reached 1017 kilometres per hour in five seconds.

At standstill

Early acceleration

645 Bigger planets than Earth have much stronger forces of gravity, so their g forces are higher. On the largest planet, Jupiter, falling objects would accelerate at 25 m/s². On the Moon, which is much smaller, this would be 1.6 m/s².

646 Accelerometers measure how fast things speed up or slow down. Most contain small crystal-like parts that change shape slightly as their rate of movement alters, producing tiny amounts of electricity. Two of these devices at right angles can track the direction of a movement, as well as acceleration.

▲ If a micro-accelerometer (seen on the hand at the front of the image) detects a car's sudden slowdown, the safety airbag inflates in one tenth of one second.

647 Accelerometers are used in hundreds of everyday objects, from airbags in cars to the hand-held controllers for computer games and mobile phones. They are also used to detect motion in volcanoes and cliffs that might warn of eruptions, earthquakes and rockfalls.

Greatest acceleration

Top speed

Beginning to decelerate

Greatest deceleration

648 What speeds up, eventually slows down. Less speed, or deceleration, is a vital part of working machines, motors and engines. To save time and stay safe, many of them have specially designed ways of slowing down.

649 Some kinds of brakes use drag or resistance. Fast planes have air brakes – flaps on the wings or body that fold out into the passing air to increase drag. Very fast planes release a parachute at the rear when they need to slow down fast, for example when landing on an aircraft carrier.

▶ On a short runway, the F-117 Nighthawk stealth fighter uses a parachute as an airbrake, to help it slow down when landing. This saves wear on the wheels, tyres and brakes.

650 Brakes are a common way to slow down. Most use rubbing or friction, which converts kinetic energy (the energy of movement) into heat energy. Many cars have disc brakes, in which stationary pads on the car rub against a disc attached to the road wheel. In many types of electric saw the spinning blade is 'grabbed' by a friction device to slow it down fast when the motor is switched off.

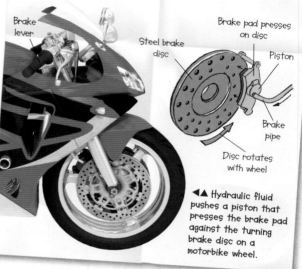

Brake lever

Steel brake disc

Brake pad presses on disc

Piston

Brake pipe

Disc rotates with wheel

◀◀ Hydraulic fluid pushes a piston that presses the brake pad against the turning brake disc on a motorbike wheel.

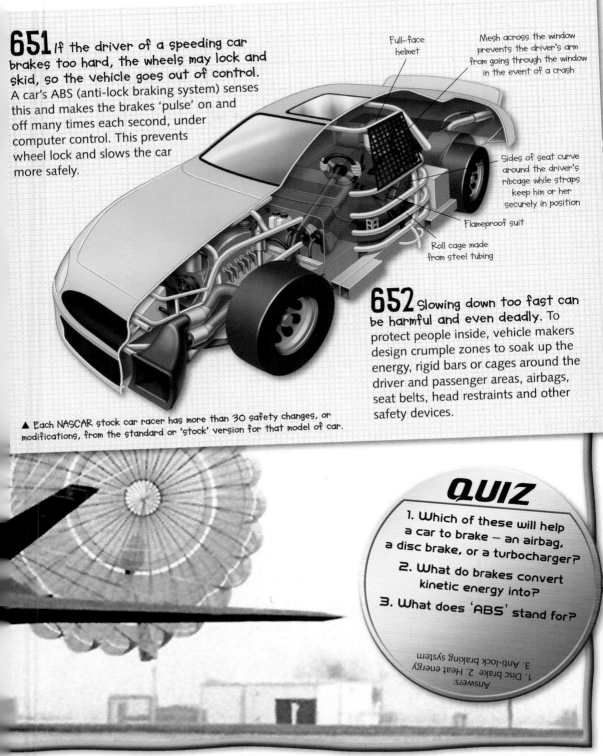

651 If the driver of a speeding car brakes too hard, the wheels may lock and skid, so the vehicle goes out of control. A car's ABS (anti-lock braking system) senses this and makes the brakes 'pulse' on and off many times each second, under computer control. This prevents wheel lock and slows the car more safely.

Full-face helmet

Mesh across the window prevents the driver's arm from going through the window in the event of a crash

Sides of seat curve around the driver's ribcage while straps keep him or her securely in position

Flameproof suit

Roll cage made from steel tubing

652 Slowing down too fast can be harmful and even deadly. To protect people inside, vehicle makers design crumple zones to soak up the energy, rigid bars or cages around the driver and passenger areas, airbags, seat belts, head restraints and other safety devices.

▲ Each NASCAR stock car racer has more than 30 safety changes, or modifications, from the standard or 'stock' version for that model of car.

QUIZ

1. Which of these will help a car to brake — an airbag, a disc brake, or a turbocharger?

2. What do brakes convert kinetic energy into?

3. What does 'ABS' stand for?

Answers:
1. Disc brake 2. Heat energy 3. Anti-lock braking system

Special speeds

653 Speed crops up where many people would not think about it. These special uses and examples of speed range from making music to catching people who are driving over the speed limit, to predicting the weather.

0 Calm Chimney smoke rises straight up

1 Light air Smoke drifts gently

3 Gentle breez Washing flutt

2 Light breeze Leaves rustle

4 Moderate breeze Paper blows around

654 Fast aircraft may measure their speed in Mach numbers. These compare the speed of an object to the speed of sound under the same conditions of air temperature and pressure. The speed of sound is always Mach 1. An aircraft flying at Mach 0.9 is travelling at nine tenths of the speed of sound. At sea level this is about 1110 kilometres per hour. Very high, in cold thin air, it is 995 kilometres per hour.

▶ A shock wave of air (area of very high pressure) forming around this F-18 Super Hornet shows it is close to going faster than sound.

655 Speed is part of how things vibrate, or move to and fro. This is known as frequency, measured in Hertz (Hz). Twenty Hz is 20 vibrations per second, the lowest or deepest sound human ears detect. A piano's highest or top note is 4186 Hz.

▼ High-pitched or high-frequency sounds have shorter waves than low or deep ones.

High pitch (short wave)

Low pitch (long wave)

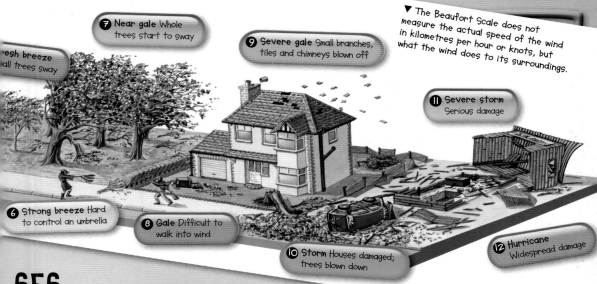

▼ The Beaufort Scale does not measure the actual speed of the wind in kilometres per hour or knots, but what the wind does to its surroundings.

7 Near gale Whole trees start to sway

9 Severe gale Small branches, tiles and chimneys blown off

11 Severe storm Serious damage

Fresh breeze all trees sway

6 Strong breeze Hard to control an umbrella

8 Gale Difficult to walk into wind

10 Storm Houses damaged; trees blown down

12 Hurricane Widespread damage

656 The Beaufort Scale for wind speed goes from 1, no wind, to 12, hurricane, and describes the wind's effects. For example, at 4 on the scale, dust and loose paper are raised and blown about, and small branches begin to move.

657 The speed of the shock or seismic waves from an earthquake or volcano shows its strength and how far damage will spread. These waves travel at 3–6 kilometres per second through rocks near the Earth's surface, but much faster – over 12 kilometres per second – through the middle of the planet.

658 'Speed guns' that check vehicle speeds use a feature of speed called the Doppler effect. The gun beams pulses of radio or similar waves and detects them as they bounce back off the vehicle. The faster the vehicle, the more it moves towards the gun between pulses, so the closer the bounced-back pulses are.

I DON'T BELIEVE IT!

Tornadoes on Earth have wind speeds of over 350 kilometres per hour. On planet Neptune, storm winds blow over six times faster, at 2200 kilometres per hour!

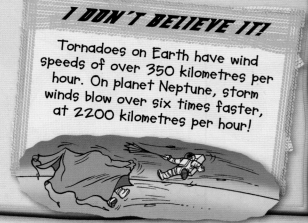

Ultimate speed

659 **Modern science tells us that the fastest possible speed is the speed of light.** It is about 300,000 kilometres per second (actually 299,792,458 metres per second). This means light could go around the Earth seven times in less than a second. As far as we know, nothing can travel faster.

660 **The speed of light is usually written as the symbol c.** It is so important that it is the only speed that is fixed or constant, everywhere at any time. In fact, it is more constant than time itself. Scientists explain weird events in deep space by saying that time can go faster or slower, but the speed of light cannot.

▼ The fastest-ever human-made objects, capable of reaching 252,792 kilometres per hour, were two *Helios* spacecraft sent to study the Sun in 1974.

661 **Light speed is not only for light waves.** It is for all similar kinds of waves, known as electromagnetic waves. These include radio waves, microwaves, infra-red and ultra-violet rays, X-rays and gamma rays. Also the speed of light is usually measured in a vacuum (a space empty of matter). It is slightly slower in air, and even slower in water.

▲ Like all forms of light, laser light beams – such as those seen here at a concert – go as fast as radio, X-rays and all other waves made of electrical and magnetic energy.

662 **Will it ever be possible to exceed light speed?** Some experts suggest ideas such as 'warp drive'. Instead of light passing through space, space is bent or warped to pass around the light beam.

663 **Going faster than the speed of light would lead to many strange events.** One idea is that as you approach light speed, time slows down. At light speed, time stops. So faster than light could allow you to travel back in time. Then you could read this book all over again and be just as amazed!

▲ In science fiction on TV and in movies, craft such as Star Trek's *Enterprise* sometimes go faster than light – perhaps when being pulled into a massive black hole.

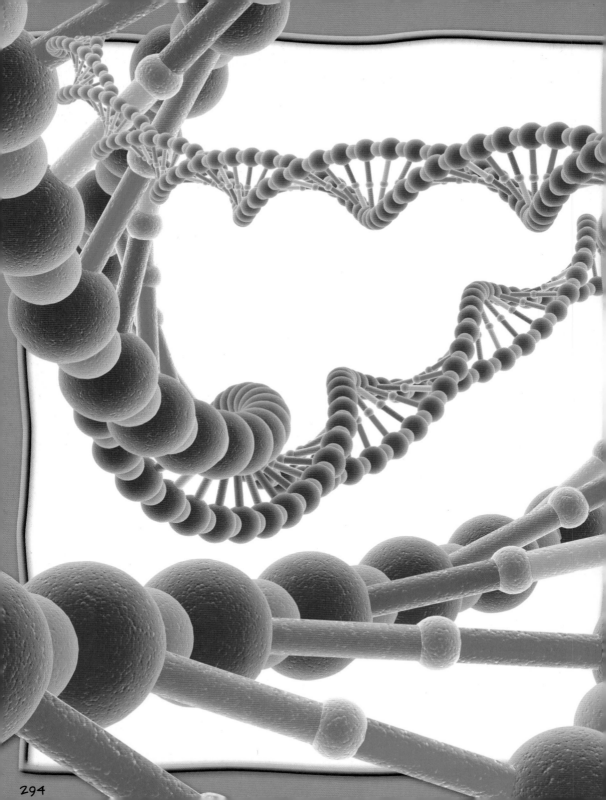

EVOLUTION

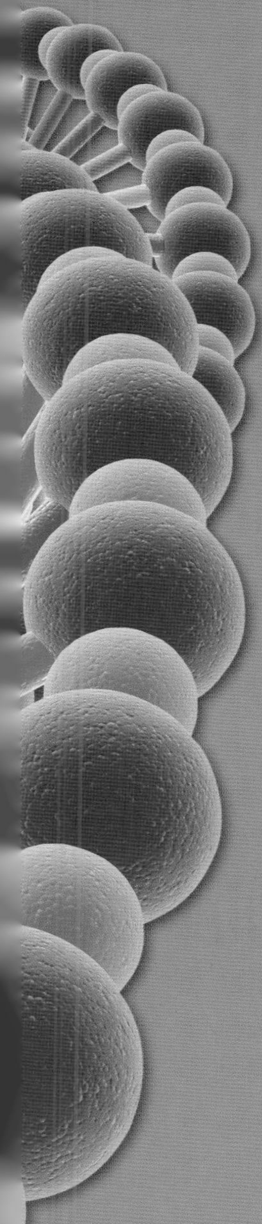

- Charles Darwin
- Classifying species
- Natural selection
- Studying fossils
- The evolutionary clock
- The first animals
- Reptiles and dinosaurs
- The rise of mammals
- Human evolution
- Artificial selection

How old was Darwin when he sailed around the world?

Where would you find a lemur?

What animal group do humans belong to?

How small were the smallest dinosaurs?

Life on Earth

664 Earth is about 4600 million years old. At first our planet could not support life. It was a mass of red-hot, liquid rock often battered by meteorites (rocks from space). Over millions of years Earth cooled down and conditions changed, making it possible for life to exist. The first organisms (life forms) appeared on Earth about 3500 million years ago.

▼ We don't know for certain what Earth looked like more than 3000 million years ago before life began. There were many volcanoes, but no oceans.

665 The first organisms were very simple – just a single cell. Cells are the tiny, basic building blocks of all living things. Over millions of years life has become incredibly varied and complex, adapting to Earth's ever-changing environments. For example, the animal kingdom includes birds, insects, fish, reptiles and mammals. This amazing development is called 'evolution'.

666 Evolution has been studied for more than one hundred years. In the 18th century, scientists such as Charles Darwin (1809–1882) started forming theories to explain the vast changes in life over time. Since then, scientists have continued to examine living things and fossils – the remains of once-living organisms preserved in rocks – to explain how evolution works.

Darwin's travels

667 **Charles Darwin was one of the world's greatest scientists.** His work on evolution changed people's ideas about life on Earth and it is still important today, influencing modern scientists.

▶ Charles Darwin joined HMS *Beagle* and sailed around the world when he was just 22 years old.

Despite its great weight, *Megatherium* could stand upright on two legs

668 **The young Charles Darwin was a keen collector of beetles and fossils.** He didn't do well in school and stopped studying medicine because he hated working on dead bodies. Darwin later went to Cambridge University to train to become a Christian priest, but some of his professors encouraged him to study living things instead.

▶ While at university, Darwin collected beetles, a popular craze of the time. These are some of the ones he gathered.

669 **In 1831, Darwin joined HMS *Beagle* as the ship's naturalist.** Naturalists are scientists that study animals and plants. Over the next five years, Darwin found many unknown species (types) of animals and plants. When HMS *Beagle* explored South America, Darwin saw volcanic eruptions, experienced earthquakes and discovered ancient animal remains.

▶ In Argentina, South America, Darwin found a complete fossil of an animal that he had never seen before. It was a giant ground sloth named *Megatherium*.

670 While on HMS *Beagle*, Darwin visited the Galápagos Islands off the coast of South America. Here he discovered animals that were found nowhere else on Earth, such as giant tortoises.

671 After Darwin returned to England he spent years working on his theory of evolution. He studied his notebooks and the examples (specimens) of animals and fossils he had gathered during his travels. Darwin also discussed his ideas with other scientists. Despite illness, he lived to 73 years old, a good age for the time.

◀ Darwin's notes show his idea that life is linked in an evolutionary tree.

299

The riddle of life

672 **A species is a type of living thing.** All the individuals of a species have a similar appearance. They can breed with each other to produce offspring (babies). There are millions of different species alive today, as well as millions that have become extinct (died out completely).

▼ Each of these butterflies is a different species. They do not breed with each other and look different.

Brown argus

Purple emperor

Clouded yellow

Adonis blue

Green hairstreak

673 **Darwin was not the first scientist to write about evolution.** French scientist Jean-Bapiste Lamarck (1744–1829) had a theory that if an animal adapted to its environment during its lifetime, the changes would be passed on to its offspring. Although not entirely correct, his ideas sparked interest. Other scientists also began to question whether God had created species as they now exist.

◄ Lamarck falsely believed that if a giraffe stretched its neck to reach the highest leaves on a tree, its neck would get longer — and its offspring would have longer necks too.

674 **For centuries, people thought that a species could not change.** Darwin examined mockingbirds from the Galápagos Islands and found differences between the specimens. He had an idea that the birds may have adapted to the islands' different environments. Darwin showed that a species could change over time and does not have a 'fixed' appearance.

► As Darwin explored the Galápagos Islands, he noticed small differences between the mockingbird species on each separate island.

675 In 1858, Alfred Russel Wallace (1823–1913), a fellow scientist, wrote to Darwin about his ideas on evolution. Darwin was horrified to discover that Wallace had similar theories to his own. This spurred Darwin into publishing his book, *On the Origin of Species* in 1859. Some people were very interested by its ideas, but others were outraged.

◄ This cartoon of Darwin with the body of an ape appeared in 1871 after he wrote that humans and apes had a common ancestor (relative from the past).

▼ Darwin's theories about humans being related to other apes, such as chimps, are now accepted by most scientists.

676 In 1871 Darwin published a second book entitled *The Descent of Man*. He wrote about the similarities and differences between humans and other apes, as well as the differences between humans from different cultures. Many people did not approve of the fact that Darwin had linked the evolution of people to that of chimpanzees.

677 Lots of people disagreed with Darwin, believing instead that God created all living things. This belief is called Creationism. Creationists believe that living organisms cannot produce new forms of life, and that only God can do this.

Classifying species

678 All living organisms are related and are linked in a huge web of life. To keep track of the vast number of species, living things can be classified (put into groups).

679 One method of classifying life is called cladistics. A clade is a group made up of an ancestor (a relative from the past) and all its living and extinct descendants, which developed from them.

680 A clade is based on features that have been inherited, or passed on, from the ancestor. Usually, only the descendants have the specific feature.

COMMON ANCESTOR

Animals with stalks attached to the sea floor. Crinoids have cup-shaped bodies and many feathery arms

Crinoids

Moving animals with mouths on the underside of their bodies

Star-shaped body with central disc and radiating arms

Large central disc and four or more radiating arms

Starfish

Smaller central disc than starfish and snake-like arms

Brittlestars

▲ ECHINODERM CLADE
Echinoderms are a unique group of animals, which have a spiny skin and five or more arms that radiate (branch) out from a body made up of five equal parts.

Round body shape with no arms

Body covered in long spines

Sea urchins

Elongated body with leathery skin

Sea cucumbers

CLASSIFYING SHOES

You will need:
pen   notepad   lots of shoes

1. Divide the shoes into groups such as trainers, boots, wellies.

2. Separate each group into smaller groups, using features such as heels, laces and so on.

3. Keep dividing the groups until each shoe has its own group. Draw a chart to show how you classified the shoes.

681 All humans are related to the very first human beings. These first humans shared an ancestor with chimpanzees. If we look back further still, all primates – the animal group that includes monkeys and apes such as chimps and humans – share the same shrew-like, mammalian ancestor.

682 The scientist Carolus Linnaeus (1707–1778) classified organisms in a clear, scientific way. He arranged species into groups according to their body features and gave each species a unique Latin name. Each name is made up of two words, for example, the tiger is *Panthera tigris*.

SPECIES Tiger
A species is a particular type of living thing. There are six living and three extinct sub-species of tiger, each with a unique appearance.

GENUS Panthera
Related species are placed together in a genus. The lion, tiger, leopard and Jaguar belong to this genus. They are the only cats that can roar.

Lion   Tiger

FAMILY Felidae
The members of a family are closely related. There are 41 members of the felidae cat family.

Caracal   Domestic cat   Tiger   Cheetah

ORDER Carnivora
In an order, species are grouped together due to shared characteristics. Animals in the carnivora order are all meat-eating mammals.

Red fox   Tiger   Sea lion   Wolf
Weasel

CLASS Mammals
There are five vertebrate classes — birds, amphibians, reptiles, fish and mammals. All mammals have hair, breathe air and feed their young milk.

Bat   Whale   Gorilla   Tiger   Koala   Rabbit   Polar bear

PHYLUM Chordates
Animals are grouped in different phylums depending on their body structure. Chordates have a spinal cord. Most are vertebrates (backboned animals).

Frog   Sailfish
Hummingbird   Tiger   Crocodile

683 Scientists used to classify different species purely by their appearance. For example plants were grouped according to leaf shape, or the colour and number of their petals. The study of DNA made scientists change their ideas about evolution and reclassify many species.

Dragonfly   Toad   Snail   Eagle
Tiger
Starfish   Jellyfish   Shark   Snake   Crab

KINGDOM Animalia
All living things are placed into five main groups, including animals, plants and fungi.

The struggle for survival

684 **Many things can affect an animal's survival.** For example, food supply, disease and climate. If there is a change, some individuals may survive the new conditions. The survivors pass on their favourable genes to their young – this is natural selection.

◀ Predators such as polar bears target their hunts at weak or sick animals. The healthier, fitter animals tend to survive and reproduce.

685 **Natural selection can cause changes within a species.** The ancestors of modern tigers may have had fewer stripes. Stripes give good camouflage as they help the animal blend in with its surroundings. The ancestors with the gene for more stripes may have been the most successful hunters, and so would have raised more offspring, passing on the genes for stripy coats.

▼▶ These are three of the different ways animals have evolved to ensure their genes are passed on.

APPEARANCE
A camouflaged appearance gives this tiger a natural advantage while hunting.

SEXUAL SELECTION
Stags with the biggest antlers and best fighting technique are more likely to win females and have young.

LOTS OF OFFSPRING
Some animals, such as toads, have to have lots of young as many won't survive to adulthood.

686 **When species change due to natural selection, evolution takes place.** This process of selection has led to all the different species alive today. It is also one reason species can become extinct, as the least successful animals die out.

QUIZ

1. Where are the Galápagos Islands?
2. Which shape of beak is good for feeding on nectar?
3. What does the word extinct mean?

Answers:
1. Off the coast of South America
2. Long and pointed
3. To have died out completely

687 If a species is separated and isolated this too can cause evolution. When a group of individuals is cut off from others of the same species, they can only breed with each other. As they adapt to the new local conditions they evolve into a new species, unable to breed with the original group they were separated from.

688 A group of animals can be isolated by a river, an ocean or a mountain range. The Galápagos Islands are isolated from South America by the Pacific Ocean. Thousands of years ago, a few finches were blown there by strong winds. They stayed on the islands and bred, evolving separately from the mainland birds.

▼▶ The Galápagos Islands provided a range of environments to which the finches adapted.

SOUTH AMERICA

Galápagos Islands

▼▶ There are about 14 different finch species on the Galápagos Islands. Each has a different beak shape suited to its particular diet.

Common cactus finch
Beak Long and pointed
Diet Nectar of cactus flowers

Large ground finch
Beak Large and thick
Diet Nuts, seeds and cactus fruits

Vegetarian tree finch
Beak Short, thick, parrot-like
Diet Plant buds, flowers, leaves

Woodpecker finch
Beak Pointed and narrow
Diet Insects and grubs

Looking for evidence

689 To show how species evolve, scientists look for evidence. They can examine and compare rocks, fossils and DNA (a substance inside most cells that carries all the genes for a living thing) for clues to back up their theories.

690 The study of rocks can tell us about the climate on Earth millions of years ago. Rocks that are rich in corals and the skeletons of other marine animals were formed when there were tropical oceans covering the land.

▼ Coelacanths (say 'seel-uh-kanths') were thought to be extinct until a living specimen was found in 1938. They are descended from the group of fish that evolved into amphibians.

Bony scales for protection not found on other live fish

Long, limb-like fins are used to 'walk' through the water

691 Fossils tell us what plants and animals looked like millions of years ago. Scientists compare living species with fossils of extinct species to see how much they have evolved over time.

692 Scientists can extract DNA from living cells to read their genetic code. The DNA of different organisms is compared to see how closely related they are. The most closely related have similar DNA.

◄ This fossil coelacanth shows that the fish has changed little over time.

Tenrecs are small, spiny animals found mostly in Madagascar. Their closest relatives are elephants and aardvarks

Prickly hedgehogs are found in Europe, Africa, parts of Asia and New Zealand

The echidna from Australia uses its long snout to find ants and termites

693 Some unrelated species have evolved similar traits. Animals in different parts of the world have evolved spines for protection, while hummingbirds, butterflies and possums all have long tongues for probing into flowers to reach nectar. This is called convergent evolution.

▲ Tenrecs, hedgehogs and echidnas are unrelated species, yet they have each evolved similar body features because they live in similar environments.

694 Where animals are found in the world tells us about how they evolved. When Madagascar became separated from Africa, lemurs (a type of primate) became isolated, and evolved separately from other African primates.

AFRICA

Madagascar

▲ Madagascar split from the coast of Africa about 165 million years ago.

▲ Lemurs, such as these ring-tailed lemurs, are found only in Madagascar.

307

Fossil clues

695 Fossils are the remains of living organisms that have been preserved in the ground. Most fossils are of animals, but plants can be fossilized too. The oldest fossils are of cyanobacteria (simple, single-celled organisms) that lived more than 3000 million years ago.

696 Fossil formation is a slow process. Some fossils can form in just 10,000 years, but most take much longer – usually hundreds of thousands, or even millions of years.

697 When an animal dies, its body might be buried under a layer of mud and sand. The soft body parts rot away but the hard parts, such as the bones, remain and become rock-like.

▼ The fossil magnolia (left) looks almost identical to the fruit from a living magnolia plant.

TRUE OR FALSE?

1. Fossils can be millions of years old.
2. The deeper the rock the younger the fossil.
3. Fossils helped Darwin work out his theory of evolution.

Answers:
1. True 2. False, usually the deeper the rock the older the fossil 3. True

▲ These palaeontologists (scientists who study the history of life on Earth) are working on an excavation or 'dig' in Wyoming in the United States, where dinosaur fossils have been found.

▶ These fossils were found in the La Brea Tar Pits near Los Angeles, United States. In the past, animals became trapped in the tar and died.

As we complete each piece, we fill it in. Keep checking back to watch our progress!

American lion cPanthera atroxs skeleton

698 Scientists can learn how an extinct species lived by studying its fossil. For example, the structure and joints of an animal's legs shows how the animal walked, and how its muscles were attached to its skeleton.

699 The study of fossils helped Darwin work out his theory of evolution. He noticed that animal fossils found on islands such as the Cape Verde Islands and Falkland Islands in the Atlantic Ocean looked different from those he found on the South American mainland, giving him ideas about separation and isolation.

700 Fossils can be dated to find out when they lived on Earth. One way is to work out of the age of the rock in which they were found. Usually, the deeper the rock, the older the fossil. To work out a fossil's absolute age, scientists make use of carbon-dating. All living things contain natural radioactivity, which leaks away at a steady rate. The amount remaining helps date the fossil.

Evolution through time

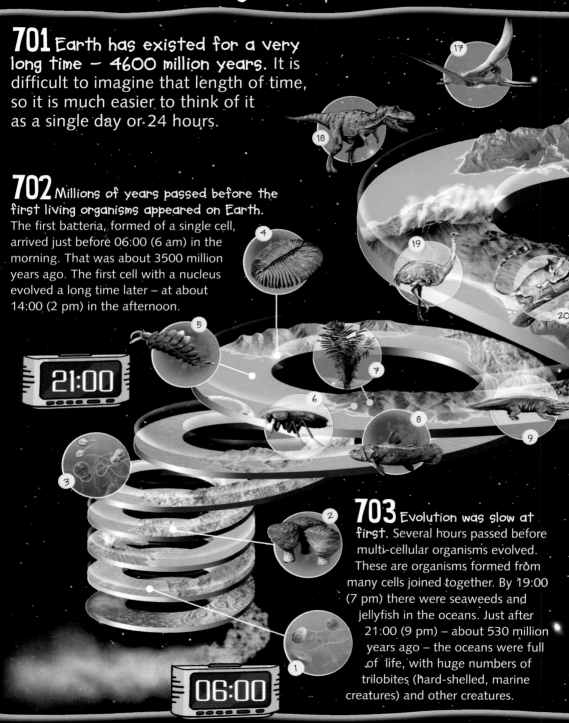

701 Earth has existed for a very long time – 4600 million years. It is difficult to imagine that length of time, so it is much easier to think of it as a single day or 24 hours.

702 Millions of years passed before the first living organisms appeared on Earth. The first bacteria, formed of a single cell, arrived just before 06:00 (6 am) in the morning. That was about 3500 million years ago. The first cell with a nucleus evolved a long time later – at about 14:00 (2 pm) in the afternoon.

703 Evolution was slow at first. Several hours passed before multi-cellular organisms evolved. These are organisms formed from many cells joined together. By 19:00 (7 pm) there were seaweeds and jellyfish in the oceans. Just after 21:00 (9 pm) – about 530 million years ago – the oceans were full of life, with huge numbers of trilobites (hard-shelled, marine creatures) and other creatures.

704 Animals moved onto land and by 22:00 (10 pm) there were insects flying in the sky. The dinosaurs ruled the Earth from about 23:00 (11 pm), while the first small, furry mammals appeared soon afterwards.

23:00

23:59

EVOLUTION THROUGH TIME KEY
1 Simple cells
2 Cyanobacteria
3 Cnidarians (soft-bodied animals)
4 Ediacaran (early marine animals)
5 *Anomalocaris* (arthropod – animals with segmented bodies and no backbone)
6 Cockroach (insect)
7 Cycad (cone-bearing plant)
8 Coelacanth (fish)
9 *Diadectes* (reptile-like amphibian)
10 *Dimetrodon* (small, early reptile)
11 Plesiosaur (marine reptile)
12 *Lilienstennus* (dinosaur)
13 *Pteranodon* (flying reptile)
14 Brachiosaur (large dinosaur)
15 Magnolia (flowering plant)
16 *Archaeopteryx* (early bird)
17 *Quetzalcoatlus* (pterosaur – flying reptile)
18 *Tyrannosaurus rex* (dinosaur)
19 Moa (flightless bird)
20 *Plesiadapis* (early mammal)
21 *Indricotheres* (rhinoceros-like mammal)
22 Sabre-tooth (carnivorous mammal)
23 *Macrauchenia* (hoofed mammal)
24 Wolf (carnivorous mammal)
25 *Homo sapiens* (modern man)

▲ This diagram shows the evolution of life from the very first organisms that appeared more than 3000 million years ago to modern humans.

705 It's difficult to believe that humans have been around for a relatively short time. Modern man arrived on Earth at just one minute to midnight, about 200,000 years ago.

706 Understanding the evolutionary clock helps scientists work out the speed at which evolution takes place. Over the last 4600 million years, species have appeared and then disappeared, to be replaced by other species more suited to the changing environments.

The start of life

Frequent volcanic activity

707 **For a few hundred million years, Earth was a hot mass of molten rock and gases.** The atmosphere – the layer of gases that surrounds the Earth – contained water vapour, carbon dioxide and nitrogen but no oxygen. Gradually, the surface cooled, clouds formed and water vapour fell as rain. Rain poured onto the land to create the oceans.

◀ The Earth looked very different 3000 million years ago, during a period known as the Archaean. Much of the planet was covered by oceans.

Deep sea vents

708 Once there were oceans, conditions became more suited to the evolution of living things. The first building blocks of life appeared – amino acids, proteins and DNA. There are many theories about how these chemicals were created and how they joined up to form cells, but nobody knows for sure. It is one of the greatest mysteries.

Stromatolites

709 The cooling continued and by about 3500 million years ago the first cells had evolved. These first cells were cyanobacteria. They grew in the sunny parts of the ocean and used sunlight to make food. During this process, cyanobacteria released oxygen into the atmosphere.

▼ Stromatolites, a type of cyanobacteria, are among the earliest fossils. They can still be seen at Shark Bay, Australia.

710 For the next 2500 to 3000 million years, life was very simple. There was bacteria, simple animals and plants, but no animals with a head, body and tail.

▶ The first animals were soft bodied like Jellyfish. *Charnia* was a strange animal that looked more like a plant.

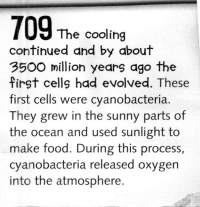

Jellyfish

Charnia

711 About 570 to 600 million years ago, evolution took off. Within a hundred million years or so, there were thousands of new species. There were seaweeds in the oceans, which – like the cyanobacteria – used light to make food, and there was an abundance of animals in the oceans.

Early animals

712 Fossils show that there were some very unusual animals living in the oceans about 500 million years ago. Some had several heads, trunks like elephants, backward-facing mouths, and many other odd features.

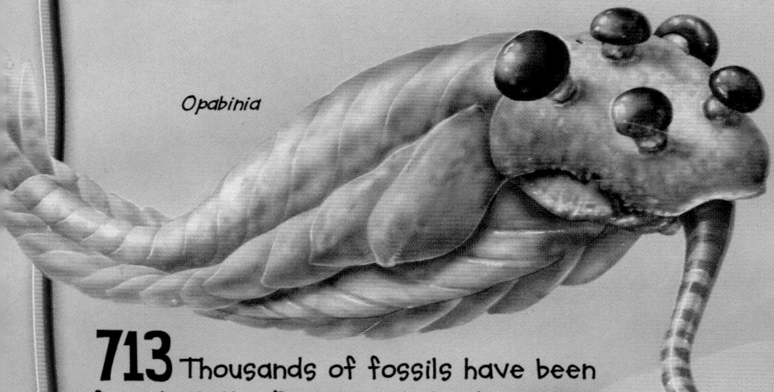

Opabinia

▼ Animals from the Cambrian Period died out when conditions on Earth changed. There are no living relatives.

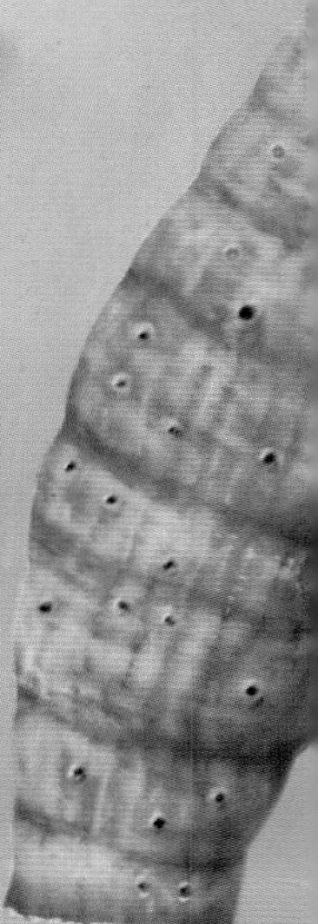

713 Thousands of fossils have been found at the Burgess Shale deposits in Canada. The site was discovered in 1909 by Charles Walcott (1850–1927). He dug up more than 65,000 fossils. Amazingly, some were of soft-bodied animals such as jellyfish.

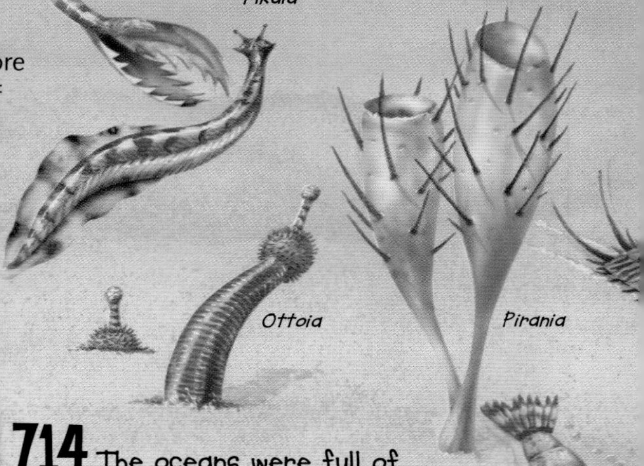

Pikaia

Ottoia

Pirania

▼ These scientists are working on a dig in the famous Walcott Quarry in the Burgess Shale deposits, Canada.

714 The oceans were full of life during the Cambrian Period (545–495 million years ago). There were molluscs, echinoderms, trilobites, worms, jellyfish and some early fish. Fish were different from the other animals as they had backbones – they were the first vertebrate animals.

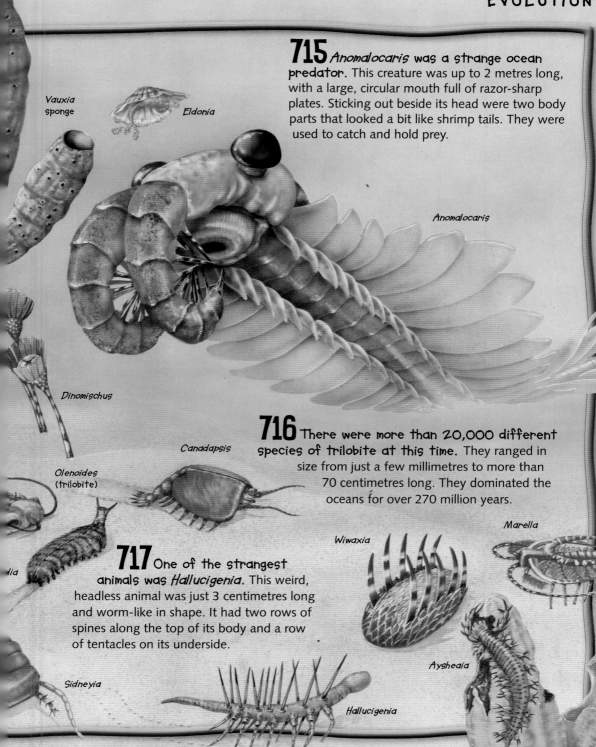

715 *Anomalocaris* was a strange ocean predator. This creature was up to 2 metres long, with a large, circular mouth full of razor-sharp plates. Sticking out beside its head were two body parts that looked a bit like shrimp tails. They were used to catch and hold prey.

Vauxia sponge

Eldonia

Anomalocaris

Dinomischus

716 There were more than 20,000 different species of trilobite at this time. They ranged in size from just a few millimetres to more than 70 centimetres long. They dominated the oceans for over 270 million years.

Canadapsis

Olenoides (trilobite)

Marella

Wiwaxia

717 One of the strangest animals was *Hallucigenia*. This weird, headless animal was just 3 centimetres long and worm-like in shape. It had two rows of spines along the top of its body and a row of tentacles on its underside.

...ia

Aysheaia

Sidneyia

Hallucigenia

Moving onto land

718 Simple plants first appeared about 400 million years ago. Mosses are primitive plants that can only grow in damp areas. Ferns are more highly evolved – they appeared 350 million years ago. By around 300 million years ago much of the land was covered by conifer forests and swamps.

▲ This scene shows some early tree and plant species in a flooded forest during the Carboniferous Period (359–299 million years ago).

719 Most of the first land animals were plant eaters. One was *Arthropleura*, the largest ever millipede-like animal. Although it was related to arthropods such as insects and crabs, it grew to the size of a crocodile, with a body up to 2 metres in length.

720 Imagine a scorpion larger than you! This was *Pterygotus*, a fearsome predator that hunted fish more than 400 million years ago. Some of its relatives were among the first animals to crawl onto land. Sea scorpions are extinct, but they were the ancestors of the arachnid animal group that includes spiders and scorpions.

EVOLVING ANIMALS

You will need:
pencil   notepad   tracing paper
1. Draw a simple outine of an animal.
2. Make a copy using tracing paper, but change one body part.
3. Trace the second picture. This time change something else.
4. Do this ten times, then look at your drawings to see how the animal evolved.

▼ Fossil footprints of *Arthropleura* have been found in rocks, showing the animals moved quickly over the ground.

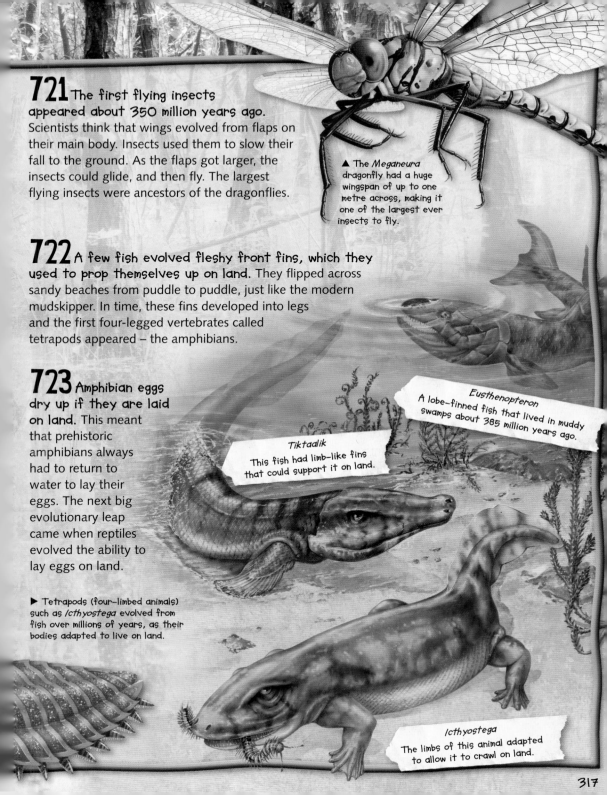

721 The first flying insects appeared about 350 million years ago. Scientists think that wings evolved from flaps on their main body. Insects used them to slow their fall to the ground. As the flaps got larger, the insects could glide, and then fly. The largest flying insects were ancestors of the dragonflies.

▲ The *Meganeura* dragonfly had a huge wingspan of up to one metre across, making it one of the largest ever insects to fly.

722 A few fish evolved fleshy front fins, which they used to prop themselves up on land. They flipped across sandy beaches from puddle to puddle, just like the modern mudskipper. In time, these fins developed into legs and the first four-legged vertebrates called tetrapods appeared – the amphibians.

723 Amphibian eggs dry up if they are laid on land. This meant that prehistoric amphibians always had to return to water to lay their eggs. The next big evolutionary leap came when reptiles evolved the ability to lay eggs on land.

Eusthenopteron
A lobe-finned fish that lived in muddy swamps about 385 million years ago.

Tiktaalik
This fish had limb-like fins that could support it on land.

▶ Tetrapods (four-limbed animals) such as *Icthyostega* evolved from fish over millions of years, as their bodies adapted to live on land.

Icthyostega
The limbs of this animal adapted to allow it to crawl on land.

Reptiles and dinosaurs

724 The very first reptiles developed from amphibians around 315 million years ago. They were small, lizard-like animals that laid eggs with a leathery shell. This adaption meant that they could live in dry habitats. They moved onto land where few animals had ventured before.

▲ One of the first reptiles was *Hylonomus*, a small, lizard-like animal. It laid eggs on land.

▲ Over millions of years, more than 1000 different dinosaur species evolved as they adapted to Earth's changing environments.

725 Dinosaurs evolved about 230 million years ago from a group of crawling reptiles. Dinosaurs ruled the Earth for about 170 million years, outnumbering the many other backboned creatures that lived at the same time.

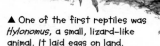

726 The first dinosaurs, such as *Eoraptor*, were small, upright and ran on their back legs. Their upright posture was possible because they developed different hips from other reptiles. They could place their legs directly under their body to raise it off the ground. This allowed them to move faster.

727 The smallest dinosaurs weighed just a few kilograms, but there were some giants too. One of the largest was *Argentinosaurus*, which scientists think was about 40 metres long and weighed up to 50 tonnes. It is difficult to be sure as complete skeletons are rarely found.

▶ *Giganotosaurus* was one of the largest carnivorous dinosaurs. Like *Argentinosaurus*, it lived in South America.

▼ For about 100 million years enormous dinosaurs called sauropods, including *Argentinosaurus*, roamed the planet.

728 One of the most well known dinosaurs is *T rex*. It was one of the largest land carnivores that ever existed. *T rex* stood up on its hind legs and used its long tail to balance. It was 4 metres high at the hips and about 13 metres long. Despite its size, it was not quite as large as its relative *Giganotosaurus*.

▲ Near the end of the dinosaur's reign, sauropods were replaced by the plant-eating *Triceratops* (1), *Ankylosaurus* (2) and the duck-billed dinosaurs (3).

QUIZ

1. When did the first reptiles appear?
2. Was *Triceratops* a plant or meat eater?
3. For how long did dinosaurs rule the land?

Answers:
1. 315 million years ago
2. A plant eater 3. About 170 million years

729 About 65 million years ago a huge number of living things died out in a short time. This was probably caused by a meteor smashing into Earth, throwing up vast amounts of dust into the atmosphere and causing a global winter. More than half of the world's species could not survive the sudden changes and became extinct, including nearly all large land animals.

The first birds

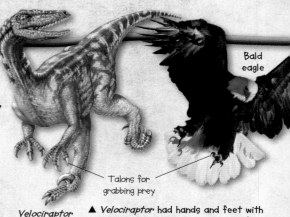

Bald eagle

730 About 150 million years ago a small type of dinosaur evolved feathers and the ability to fly. Many scientists believe this dinosaur became the first bird. Birds are more closely related to the dinosaurs than dinosaurs are to modern-day crocodiles because they share a common ancestor.

Talons for grabbing prey

Velociraptor

▲ *Velociraptor* had hands and feet with curved claws, similar to the talons of modern-day birds of prey.

Long tail

▶ Scientists are not sure whether *Archaeopteryx* could flap its wings or just glide from tree to tree.

731 Darwin suspected that birds and dinosaurs were linked. In 1861, just two years after *On the Origin of Species* was published, the fossil skeleton of a bird-like creature, *Archaeopteryx*, was discovered. It had features of both dinosaurs, such as teeth and a bony tail, and birds, such as wings.

732 Birds share many features with reptiles. Reptiles have scaly skin, and scales can still be seen on the legs of birds. Both birds and reptiles lay eggs with a shell. Birds are thought to be descended from small, raptor-like dinosaurs called 'maniraptorans', which includes the *Velociraptor*.

Long flight feathers

Wing claws

Lightweight body

Toothed beak

◀ The feathers, claws and skull of *Archaeopteryx* can be seen clearly on fossils of this prehistoric creature.

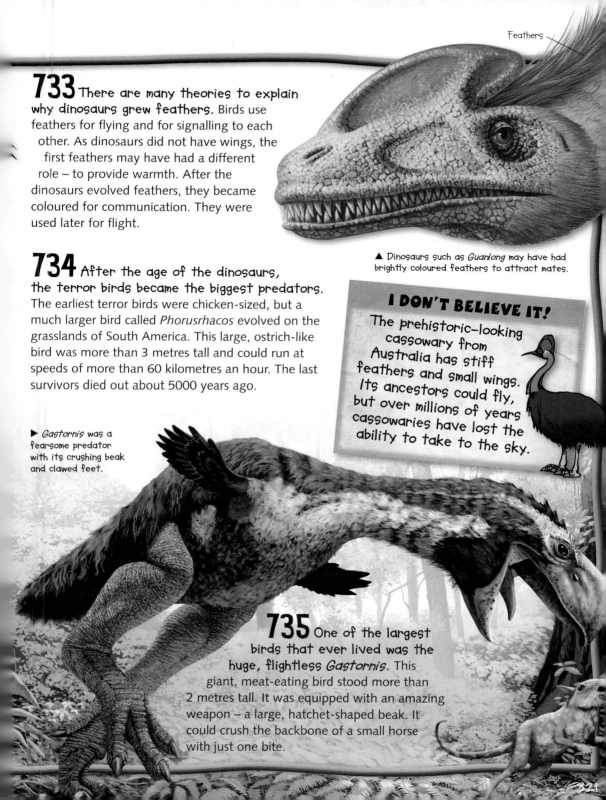

Feathers

733 There are many theories to explain why dinosaurs grew feathers. Birds use feathers for flying and for signalling to each other. As dinosaurs did not have wings, the first feathers may have had a different role – to provide warmth. After the dinosaurs evolved feathers, they became coloured for communication. They were used later for flight.

▲ Dinosaurs such as *Guanlong* may have had brightly coloured feathers to attract mates.

734 After the age of the dinosaurs, the terror birds became the biggest predators. The earliest terror birds were chicken-sized, but a much larger bird called *Phorusrhacos* evolved on the grasslands of South America. This large, ostrich-like bird was more than 3 metres tall and could run at speeds of more than 60 kilometres an hour. The last survivors died out about 5000 years ago.

I DON'T BELIEVE IT!
The prehistoric-looking cassowary from Australia has stiff feathers and small wings. Its ancestors could fly, but over millions of years cassowaries have lost the ability to take to the sky.

▶ *Gastornis* was a fearsome predator with its crushing beak and clawed feet.

735 One of the largest birds that ever lived was the huge, flightless *Gastornis*. This giant, meat-eating bird stood more than 2 metres tall. It was equipped with an amazing weapon – a large, hatchet-shaped beak. It could crush the backbone of a small horse with just one bite.

Mammals take over

736 The first mammals evolved about 220 million years ago, and existed alongside the dinosaurs. They evolved from a different group of reptiles to dinosaurs and birds, called therapsids. The first mammals were small and weasel-like, and they probably hunted insects.

▶ The small, early mammal *Leptictidium* used its long snout to sniff out prey such as this cicada.

737 The rise of mammals was not quick — it took millions of years for them to develop and become more varied. Just like the dinosaurs before them, mammals evolved to suit many different habitats. Some returned to the sea in the form of whales and dolphins, others evolved long legs and roamed the grasslands, while bats developed wings and took to the air.

738 All mammals have the same arrangement of bones in their limbs. This is called the pentadactyl limb. The basic plan in the arm is a single bone in the upper limb (the humerus), which is jointed to two bones in the lower limb (the radius and the ulna). Each limb ends in five digits.

▼ The pentadactyl limb in each of these mammals has evolved so that it is adapted to suit their lifestyle.

Human   Cat   Whale

Humerus

Radius

Ulna   Bat

Digits   Horse

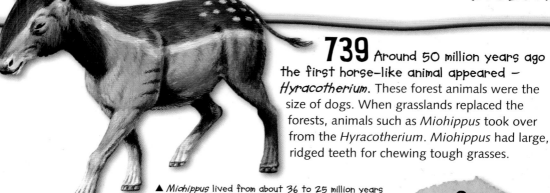

739 Around 50 million years ago the first horse-like animal appeared – *Hyracotherium*. These forest animals were the size of dogs. When grasslands replaced the forests, animals such as *Miohippus* took over from the *Hyracotherium*. *Miohippus* had large, ridged teeth for chewing tough grasses.

▲ *Miohippus* lived from about 36 to 25 million years ago. Its fossils have been found in North America.

740 Some amazing mammals lived during the last Ice Age, about 70,000 years ago. They adapted to survive in the extreme cold, as much of the land was covered in ice. Woolly mammoths lived alongside the sabre-tooth. This big cat was more like a bear in size and hunted bison and small mammoths.

QUIZ

Which of the following mammals is the odd one out?

Tiger Seal Horse Echidna Bat Whale Dog

Answer:
Echidna, the rest are placental mammals

741 There are almost 5500 species of mammal alive today. The most primitive are the egg-laying monotremes, such as the echidna, which share many characteristics with their reptilian ancestors. Marsupials such as the kangaroo and koala give birth to tiny babies that they care for in their pouch. The biggest group is the placental mammals, which give birth to well-developed young.

▶ Seals are placental mammals. The females are pregnant for one year and feed their young on milk.

▶ There are only two monotreme mammals, the echidna (right) and the duck-billed platypus.

▶ Marsupial mammals such as kangaroos carry their young around in a pouch.

The human story

742 Humans belong to the primate mammal group. All primates have a large brain for their size, with forward-facing eyes that give 3D vision. Most primates have fingers with nails that are used for manipulating and grasping objects.

Forward-facing eyes

Large brain

▶ Primates include lemurs, monkeys and apes such as gibbons, chimps and gorillas (shown here).

Fingers with nails

Ardipithecus ramidus
4.4 million years ago

Australopithecus afarensis
3.9–2.9 million years ago

Australopithecus africanus
2–3 million years ago

743 The first primates appeared about 75 million years ago. Humans have a common ancestor with chimps that lived in Africa about six million years ago. Then the line splits, with chimps evolving separately to humans. Four million years ago, our human ancestors were still tree dwellers that tottered on two legs.

▶ This timeline shows how various human groups have evolved, from very early kinds that lived in Africa over four million years ago, to modern humans.

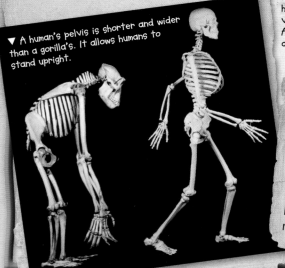

▼ A human's pelvis is shorter and wider than a gorilla's. It allows humans to stand upright.

744 Two-and-a-half million years ago, the first human ancestor to use tools appeared. *Homo habilis* had a large brain and was very adaptable. It ate a varied diet, scavenging meat rather than eating grasses and learnt to use stone tools to smash bones to get at the rich marrow inside.

745 Two million years ago, one group of early humans moved out of Africa, and populated other regions of the world. This ancestor was *Homo erectus*, and it had a more human-like appearance. It lived in a variety of different habitats and learnt how to use fire and cook food.

I DON'T BELIEVE IT!

In 1974, scientists found fossilized bones in Ethiopia, Africa. The bones were 3.2 million years old and belonged to a small female creature. Scientists called her Lucy but her Latin name is *Australopithecus afarensis*.

746 Neanderthal people lived in Europe about 130,000 years ago. Europe was still in an Ice Age at this time. The Neanderthals had a short, stocky body, which was adapted for living in the cold. They hunted animals and ate a mostly meat diet. Then about 30,000 years ago, the climate got warmer, humans from Africa arrived and the Neanderthals died out.

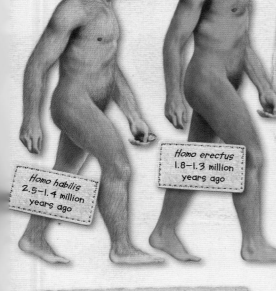

Homo habilis
2.5–1.4 million
years ago

Homo erectus
1.8–1.3 million
years ago

747 The modern human, with a highly developed brain, originated in Africa about 200,000 years ago. Like many other early humans, modern humans proved to be highly adaptable. They developed a culture and language, and learnt to depend on tools to alter their environment.

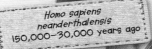

Homo sapiens
neanderthalensis
150,000–30,000 years ago

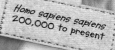

Homo sapiens sapiens
200,000 to present

325

Designer evolution

748 People can alter evolution through artificial selection. This is similar to natural selection, but it involves people selecting the parents of the next generation. Over time, artificial selection can lead to new types of plants and animals.

749 The pet dog is related to the wolf. About 15,000 years ago, people started to tame the wolves that were found around their settlements. Over time, the appearences of the tamed animals changed as people selected parent dogs with particular features.

▼ Dogs can be grouped according to their appearance and the purpose for which they were bred.

GUNDOG
Irish setter

HOUND
Irish wolfhound

TERRIER
Jack Russell

TOY
Chihuahua

UTILITY
Bulldog

WORKING
Old English sheepdog

▲ Wolves are ancestors of all dog breeds. Wolves and dogs still have many features in common such as howling and barking.

750 The many different dog breeds look very different, but they are all the same species. This means they can breed with each other. There are different breeds of pet cats too, each bred for a particular appearance.

751 Artificial selection has developed crops and livestock too. By choosing parent plants with high yields or disease resistance, scientists have changed crop plants, such as wheat and rice. Dairy cows are now producing more milk, as farmers breed from cows that produce the most milk.

▲ Plant breeding can produce crop plants with more flavour, greater yields and more resistance to disease.

752 The most beneficial characteristics are chosen during artificial selection. Because most living things have two parents, they show variation – new features that have developed as a result of their parental genes being shuffled. This gives some individuals an advantage. For example, some plants' genes make them grow taller, allowing them to reach sunlight more easily than other plants.

753 Clones – individuals that are genetically identical to each other – can also be made by artificial selection. They are at an evolutionary disadvantage, however, because there is no variation between the individuals. If a group of cloned animals or plants are affected by disease, they could all be wiped out.

▼ Modern varieties of rice have greater yields. The latest types have been genetically altered so they survive in drought and salt water conditions.

329

Evolution in action

754 **Evolution never stops — it is taking place around us right now.** Usually, it occurs slowly, over millions of years. It took modern humans six million years to evolve from forest-dwelling animals. But sometimes evolution can happen in just a few years — or even less.

755 **By understanding evolution, scientists have a better chance of fighting diseases.** Humans can be vaccinated against influenza ('flu), a disease caused by a virus. The virus can evolve quickly, meaning scientists must keep developing new vaccines to keep up.

◄ Influenza vaccines no longer work when mutations change the surface of the influenza virus.

756 **Farmers use weedkillers on their crops, but some weeds are becoming resistant.** When a crop is sprayed, any weed that has a gene for resistance to the weedkiller survives, while the others die. This survivor produces seeds and soon there are more resistant weeds.

► The excessive use of weedkillers can cause some weeds to evolve a resistance to the chemicals.

▲ Mosquitoes carry parasites that cause malaria. The rise in global temperatures means they can now survive in more places.

757 **The world's climate is changing and this is affecting evolution.** Species with more variation can adapt to the changes and survive, while those that can't keep up are in danger of dying out. Climate change is also affecting the arrival of the seasons – in many places, spring is starting earlier. This is causing problems for plants and animals that depend on each other for survival.

758 **Some lizards are changing their appearance to escape ants.** Fire ants are small but aggressive and can kill the small fence lizard. Lizards that live close to these ants have longer legs than those that live in areas without the ants. Genes for long legs have been inherited to help the lizards escape.

▲ Long-legged fence lizards are more likely to survive and breed than the short-legged ones.

759 **Humans have evolved over the last few thousand years.** Many adults cannot drink milk due to the lactose (sugar) it contains. About 5000 years ago, Europeans began keeping cattle. A mutation occured that allowed adults to digest the lactose. Human beings are an adaptable species – our ability to change may help us to survive in an ever-changing world.

▼ The Hadza tribe of Africa are one of the few remaining hunter-gather tribes living in a way similar to our ancient ancestors.

HUMAN BODY

- Babies and children
- Skin, hair and nails
- Skeletons and muscles
- Lungs and breathing
- Food and digestion
- Circulation
- The heart
- Senses and nerves
- The brain
- Keeping healthy

Why do we sweat?

How many bones do I have?

What is hair made from?

How fast do nerve signals travel?

Where is my windpipe?

How do I learn new things?

Outside, inside

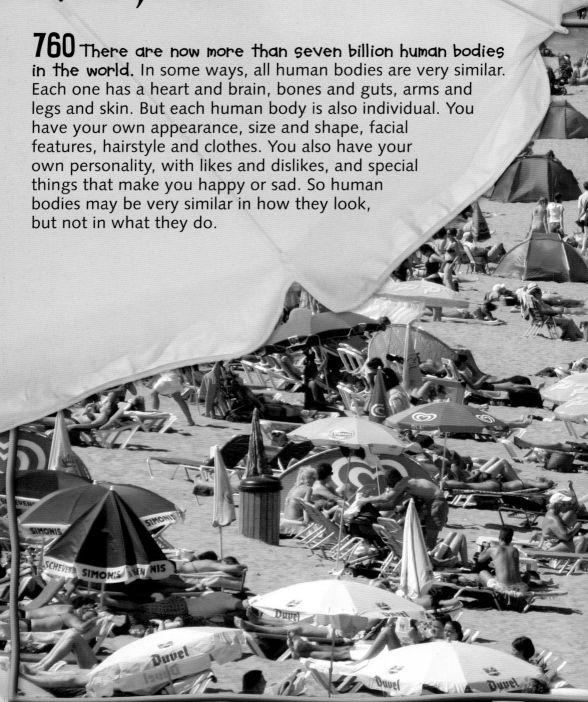

760 **There are now more than seven billion human bodies in the world.** In some ways, all human bodies are very similar. Each one has a heart and brain, bones and guts, arms and legs and skin. But each human body is also individual. You have your own appearance, size and shape, facial features, hairstyle and clothes. You also have your own personality, with likes and dislikes, and special things that make you happy or sad. So human bodies may be very similar in how they look, but not in what they do.

▲ We tend to notice small differences on the outside of human bodies, such as height, width, hair colour and clothes. This allows us to recognize our family and friends.

Baby body

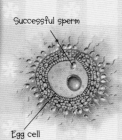

Successful sperm

Egg cell

761 A full-grown human body is made of billions of microscopic parts, called cells. But in the beginning, the body is a single cell, smaller than this full stop. Yet it contains all the instructions, known as genes, for the whole body to grow and develop.

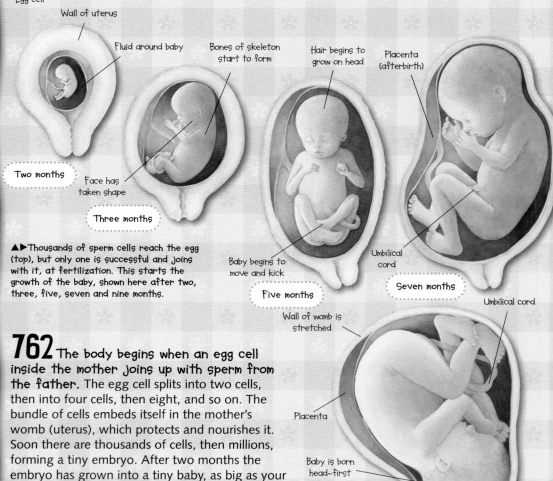

Wall of uterus

Fluid around baby

Bones of skeleton start to form

Hair begins to grow on head

Placenta (afterbirth)

Two months

Face has taken shape

Three months

▲▶Thousands of sperm cells reach the egg (top), but only one is successful and joins with it, at fertilization. This starts the growth of the baby, shown here after two, three, five, seven and nine months.

Baby begins to move and kick

Umbilical cord

Five months

Seven months

Umbilical cord

Wall of womb is stretched

762 The body begins when an egg cell inside the mother joins up with sperm from the father. The egg cell splits into two cells, then into four cells, then eight, and so on. The bundle of cells embeds itself in the mother's womb (uterus), which protects and nourishes it. Soon there are thousands of cells, then millions, forming a tiny embryo. After two months the embryo has grown into a tiny baby, as big as your thumb, with arms, legs, eyes, ears and a mouth.

Placenta

Baby is born head-first

Nine months

Cervix (neck of womb)

763 After nine months in the womb, the baby is ready to be born. Strong muscles in the walls of the womb tighten, or contract. They push the baby through the opening, or neck of the womb, called the cervix, and along the birth canal. The baby enters the outside world.

764 A newborn baby may be frightened and usually starts to cry. Inside the womb it was warm, wet, dark, quiet and cramped. Outside there are lights, noises, voices, fresh air and room to stretch. The crying is also helpful to start the baby breathing, using its own lungs.

765 Being born can take an hour or two – or a whole day or two. It is very tiring for both the baby and its mother. After birth, the baby starts to feel hungry and it feeds on its mother's milk. Finally, mother and baby settle down for a rest and some sleep.

▲ Once the baby is settled it is time for its mother to admire her newborn and rest.

The growing body

766 A new baby just seems to eat, sleep and cry. It feeds on milk when hungry and sleeps when tired. Also, it cries when it is too hot, too cold, or when its nappy needs changing.

767 A new baby is not totally helpless. It can do simple actions called reflexes, to help it survive. If something touches the baby's cheek, it turns its head to that side and tries to suck. If the baby hears a loud noise, it opens its eyes wide, throws out its arms and cries for help. If something touches the baby's hand and fingers, it grasps tightly.

768 A new baby looks, listens, touches and quickly learns. Gradually it starts to recognize voices, faces and places. After about six weeks, it begins to smile. Inside the body, the baby's brain is learning very quickly. The baby soon knows that if it laughs, people will laugh back and if it cries, someone will come to look after it.

WHAT HAPPENS WHEN?

Most babies learn to do certain actions in the same order. The order is mixed up here. Can you put it right?

walk, crawl, roll over, sit up, smile, stand

Answers:
smile, roll over, sit up,
crawl, stand, walk

▼ In the grasping reflex, the baby tightly holds anything that touches its hand or fingers. Its grip is surprisingly strong!

▼ Most babies crawl before they walk, but some go straight from sitting or 'bottom-shuffling' to walking.

770 As a baby grows into a child, at around 18 months, it learns ten new words every day, from 'cat' and 'dog' to 'sun' and 'moon'. There are new games such as piling up bricks, new actions such as throwing and kicking, and new skills such as using a spoon at mealtimes and scribbling on paper.

769 At about three months old, most babies can reach out to hold something, and roll over when lying down. By the age of six months, most babies can sit up and hold food in their fingers. At nine months, many babies are crawling well and perhaps standing up. By their first birthday, many babies are learning to walk and starting to talk.

771 At the age of five, when most children start school, they continue to learn an amazing amount. This includes thinking or mental skills such as counting and reading, and precise movements such as writing and drawing. They learn out of the classroom too – how to play with friends and share.

▼ Playing is lots of fun, but it's learning too, as children develop control over the muscles in their fast-growing bodies.

On the body's outside

772 Skin's surface is made of tiny cells that have filled up with a hard, tough substance called keratin, and then died. So when you look at a human body, most of what you see is 'dead'! The cells get rubbed off as you move, have a wash and get dry.

773 Skin rubs off all the time, and grows all the time too. Just under the surface, living cells make more new cells that gradually fill with keratin, die and move up to the surface. It takes about four weeks from a new skin cell being made to when it reaches the surface and is rubbed off. This upper layer of skin is called the epidermis.

Hair

Oil gland

Epidermis

Dermis

Hair follicle

▲ This view shows skin magnified (enlarged) about 50 times.

▲ Lots of dead skin is removed without you realizing when you dry yourself after a shower.

774 Skin's lower layer, the dermis, is thicker than the epidermis. It is made of tiny, bendy, thread-like fibres of the substance collagen. The dermis also contains small blood vessels, tiny sweat glands, and micro-sensors that detect touch.

775 One of skin's important jobs is to protect the body. It stops the delicate inner parts from being rubbed, knocked or scraped. Skin also prevents body fluids from leaking away and it keeps out dirt and germs.

776 Skin helps to keep the body at the same temperature. If you become too hot, sweat oozes onto your skin and, as it dries, draws heat from the body. Also, the blood vessels in the lower layer of skin widen, to lose more heat through the skin. This is why a hot person looks sweaty and red in the face.

Safety helmet protects head and brain

Elbow-pads cushion fall

777 Skin gives us our sense of touch. Millions of microscopic sensors in the lower layer of skin, the dermis, are joined by nerves to the brain. These sensors detect different kinds of touch, from a light stroke to heavy pressure, heat or cold, and movement. Pain sensors detect when skin is damaged. Ouch!

Gloves save fingers from scrapes and breaks

Knee-pads prevent hard bumps

▲ Skin is tough, but it sometimes needs help to protect the body. Otherwise it, and the body parts beneath, may get damaged.

SENSITIVE SKIN

You will need:
friend   sticky-tack
two used matchsticks   ruler

1. Press some sticky-tack on the end of the ruler. Press two matchsticks into the sticky-tack, standing upright, about 1 centimetre apart.

2. Make your friend look away. Touch the back of their hand with both matchstick ends. Ask your friend: 'Is that one matchstick or two?' Sensitive skin can detect both ends.

3. Try this at several places, such as on the finger, wrist, forearm, neck and cheek.

Hair and nails

778 There are about 120,000 hairs on the head, called scalp hairs. There are also eyebrow hairs and eyelash hairs. Grown-ups have hairs in the armpits and between the legs, and men have hairs on the face. And everyone, even a baby, has tiny hairs all over the body – 5 to 10 million of them!

Blonde wavy hair is the result of carotene from an oval hair follicle

Black curly hair is the result of black melanin from a flat hair follicle

◀ Hair contains pigments (coloured substances) – mainly melanin (dark brown) and some carotene (yellowish). Different amounts of pigments, and the way their tiny particles are spread out, cause different hair colours.

Straight red hair is the result of red melanin from a round hair follicle

779 Each hair grows from a deep pit in the skin, called a follicle. The hair is only alive where it gets longer, at its base or root, in the bottom of the follicle. The rest of the hair, called the shaft, is like the surface of the skin – hard, tough, dead and made of keratin. Hair helps to protect the body, especially where it is thicker and longer on the head. It also helps to keep the body warm in cold conditions.

Straight black hair is the result of black melanin from a round follicle

780 Scalp hairs get longer by about 3 millimetres each week, on average. Eyebrow hairs grow more slowly. No hairs live forever. Each one grows for a time, then it falls out, and its follicle has a 'rest' before a new hair sprouts. This is happening all the time, so the body always has some hairs on each part.

781 Nails, like hairs, grow at their base (the nail root) and are made of keratin. Also like hairs, nails grow faster in summer than in winter, and faster at night than by day. Nails lengthen by about half a millimetre, on average, each week.

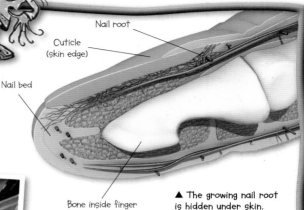

Nail root

Cuticle (skin edge)

Nail bed

Bone inside finger

▲ The growing nail root is hidden under skin. The nail slides slowly along the nail bed.

▲ Nails make the fingertips stronger and more rigid for pressing hard on guitar strings. Slightly longer nails pluck the strings.

782 Nails have many uses, from peeling off sticky labels to plucking guitar strings or scratching an itch. They protect and stiffen the ends of the fingers, where there are nerves that give us our sense of touch.

I DON'T BELIEVE IT!

A scalp hair grows for up to five years before it falls out and gets replaced. Left uncut during this time, it would be about one metre long. But some people have unusual hair that grows faster and for longer. Each hair can reach more than 5 metres in length before dropping out.

► Keeping your nails clean is very important. If you don't, germs can build up under your nails and make you ill.

The bony body

783 Without bones, the body would be as floppy as a jellyfish! Bones do many jobs. The long bones in the arms work like levers to reach out the hands. The finger bones grasp and grip. Bones protect softer body parts. The dome-like skull protects the brain. The ribs shield the lungs and heart. Bones also produce blood cells, as explained on the opposite page.

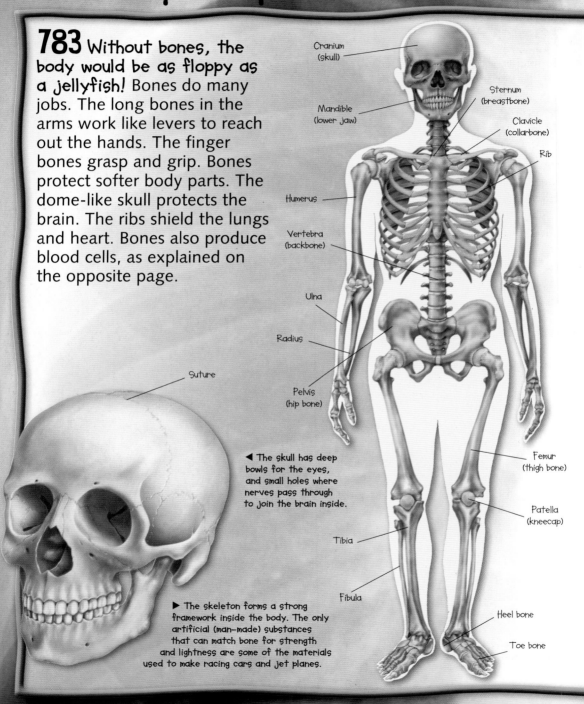

Cranium (skull)

Sternum (breastbone)

Mandible (lower jaw)

Clavicle (collarbone)

Rib

Humerus

Vertebra (backbone)

Ulna

Radius

Pelvis (hip bone)

Suture

Femur (thigh bone)

Patella (kneecap)

Tibia

Fibula

Heel bone

Toe bone

◄ The skull has deep bowls for the eyes, and small holes where nerves pass through to join the brain inside.

► The skeleton forms a strong framework inside the body. The only artificial (man-made) substances that can match bone for strength and lightness are some of the materials used to make racing cars and jet planes.

784
All the bones together make up the skeleton. Most people have 206 bones, from head to toe as follows:

- 8 in the upper part of the skull, the cranium or braincase
- 14 in the face
- 6 tiny ear bones, 3 deep in each ear
- 1 in the neck, which is floating and not directly connected to any other bone
- 26 in the spinal column or backbone
- 25 in the chest, being 24 ribs and the breastbone
- 32 in each arm, from shoulder to fingertips (8 in each wrist)
- 31 in each leg, from hip to toetips (7 in each ankle)

785
Bone contains threads of the tough, slightly bendy substance called collagen. It also has hard minerals such as calcium and phosphate. Together, the collagen and minerals make a bone strong and rigid, yet able to bend slightly under stress. Bones have blood vessels for nourishment and nerves to feel pressure and pain. Also, some bones are not solid. They contain a jelly-like substance called marrow. This makes tiny parts for the blood, called red and white blood cells.

Spongy bone

Marrow

Nerves and blood vessels

Compact (hard) bone

'Skin' of bone (periosteum)

End or head of bone

▲ Bone has a hard layer outside, a spongy layer next, and soft marrow in the middle.

NAME THE BONE!
Every bone has a scientific or medical name, and many have ordinary names too. Can you match up these ordinary and scientific names for various bones?

1. Mandible 2. Femur 3. Clavicle
4. Pelvis 5. Patella 6. Sternum

a. Thigh bone b. Breastbone
c. Kneecap d. Hip bone
e. Collarbone f. Lower jaw bone

Answers:
1f 2a 3e 4d 5c 6b

The flexible body

786 Without joints, almost the only parts of your body that could move would be your tongue and eyebrows! Joints between bones allow the skeleton to bend. You have more than 200 joints. The largest are in the hips and knees. The smallest are in the fingers, toes, and between the tiny bones inside each ear which help you hear.

787 There are several kinds of joints, depending on the shapes of the bone ends, and how much the bones can move. Bend your knee and your lower leg moves forwards and backwards, but not sideways. This is a hinge-type joint. Bend your hip and your leg can move forwards, backwards, and also from side to side. This is a ball-and-socket joint.

Collarbone

Shoulder blade

▶ This X-ray shows a dislocated (out of place) shoulder. The shoulder joint has the biggest range of movement, so this injury is common.

Head of upper arm bone

TEST YOUR JOINTS
Try using these different joints carefully, and see how much movement they allow. Can you guess the type of joint used in each one – hinge or ball-and-socket?

1. Fingertip joint (smallest knuckle)
2. Elbow
3. Hip
4. Shoulder

Answers:
1. hinge 2. hinge
3. ball-and-socket 4. ball-and-socket

788 Inside a joint where the bones come together, each bone end is covered with a smooth, shiny, slippery, slightly springy substance, known as cartilage. This is smeared with a thick liquid called synovial fluid. The fluid works like the oil in a car, to smooth the movements and reduce rubbing and wear between the cartilage surfaces.

789 The bones in a joint are linked together by a bag-like part, the capsule, and strong, stretchy, strap-like ligaments. The ligaments let the bones move but stop them coming apart or moving too far. The shoulder has seven strong ligaments.

790 In some joints, there are cartilage coverings over the bone ends and also pads of cartilage between the cartilage! These extra pads are called articular discs. There is one in each joint in the backbone, between the spinal bones, which are called vertebrae. There are also two of these extra cartilages, known as menisci, in each knee joint. They help the knee to 'lock' straight so that we can stand up without too much effort.

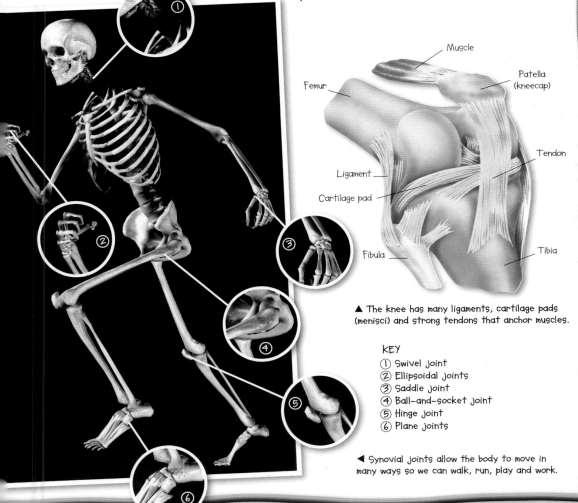

Muscle

Femur

Patella (kneecap)

Ligament

Tendon

Cartilage pad

Fibula

Tibia

▲ The knee has many ligaments, cartilage pads (menisci) and strong tendons that anchor muscles.

KEY
① Swivel joint
② Ellipsoidal joints
③ Saddle joint
④ Ball-and-socket joint
⑤ Hinge joint
⑥ Plane joints

◄ Synovial joints allow the body to move in many ways so we can walk, run, play and work.

When muscles pull

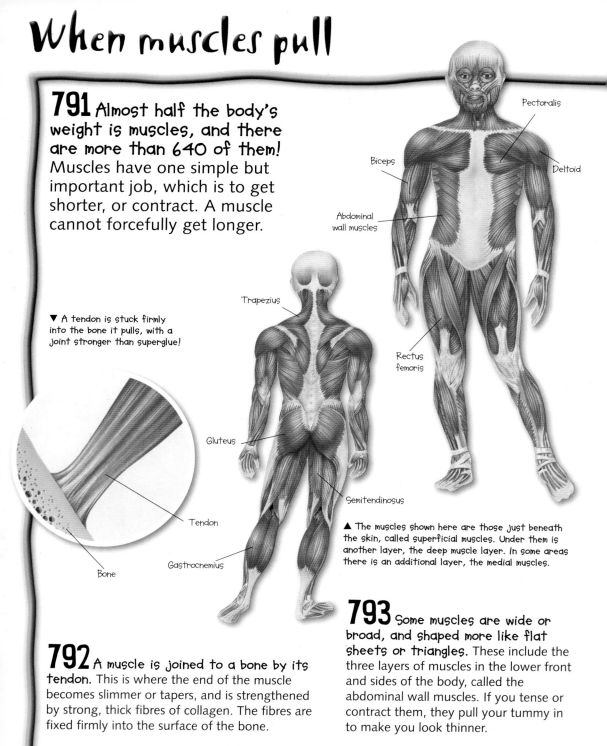

791 Almost half the body's weight is muscles, and there are more than 640 of them! Muscles have one simple but important job, which is to get shorter, or contract. A muscle cannot forcefully get longer.

▼ A tendon is stuck firmly into the bone it pulls, with a joint stronger than superglue!

Pectoralis

Biceps

Deltoid

Abdominal wall muscles

Trapezius

Rectus femoris

Gluteus

Semitendinosus

Tendon

Bone

Gastrocnemius

▲ The muscles shown here are those just beneath the skin, called superficial muscles. Under them is another layer, the deep muscle layer. In some areas there is an additional layer, the medial muscles.

792 A muscle is joined to a bone by its tendon. This is where the end of the muscle becomes slimmer or tapers, and is strengthened by strong, thick fibres of collagen. The fibres are fixed firmly into the surface of the bone.

793 Some muscles are wide or broad, and shaped more like flat sheets or triangles. These include the three layers of muscles in the lower front and sides of the body, called the abdominal wall muscles. If you tense or contract them, they pull your tummy in to make you look thinner.

794 Most muscles are long and slim, and joined to bones at each end. As they contract they pull on the bones and move them. As this happens, the muscle becomes wider, or more bulging in the middle. To move the bone back again, a muscle on the other side of it contracts, while the first muscle relaxes and is pulled longer.

795 Every muscle in the body has a scientific or medical name, which is often quite long and complicated. Some of these names are familiar to people who do exercise and sports. The 'pecs' are the pectoralis major muscles across the chest. The 'biceps' are the biceps brachii muscles in the upper arms, which bulge when you bend your elbow.

▶ A breakdancer needs endurance, strength and control over their muscles to carry out moves such as this.

796 If you take plenty of exercise or play sport, you do not gain new muscles. But the muscles you have become larger and stronger. This keeps them fit and healthy. Muscles which are not used much may become weak and floppy.

Biceps gets shorter and bends the elbow

To move the forearm back down, the triceps shorten and the biceps get longer

▶ Muscles work in two-way pairs, like the biceps and triceps, which bend and straighten the elbow.

Biceps

Triceps

Muscle power

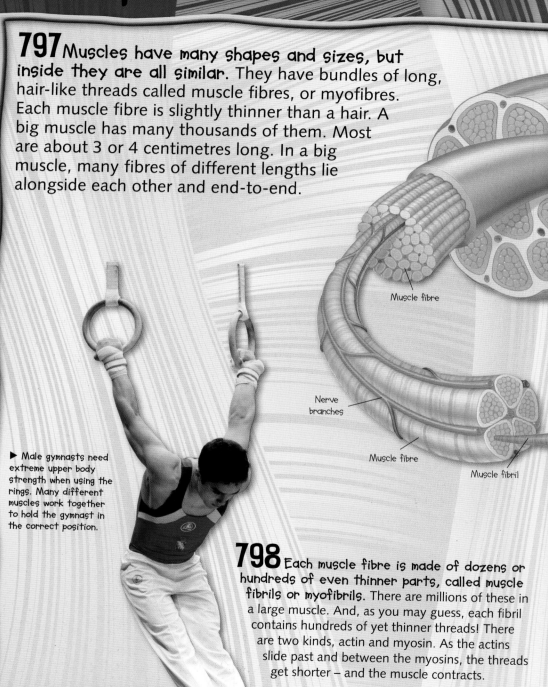

797 Muscles have many shapes and sizes, but inside they are all similar. They have bundles of long, hair-like threads called muscle fibres, or myofibres. Each muscle fibre is slightly thinner than a hair. A big muscle has many thousands of them. Most are about 3 or 4 centimetres long. In a big muscle, many fibres of different lengths lie alongside each other and end-to-end.

Muscle fibre

Nerve branches

Muscle fibre

Muscle fibril

▶ Male gymnasts need extreme upper body strength when using the rings. Many different muscles work together to hold the gymnast in the correct position.

798 Each muscle fibre is made of dozens or hundreds of even thinner parts, called muscle fibrils or myofibrils. There are millions of these in a large muscle. And, as you may guess, each fibril contains hundreds of yet thinner threads! There are two kinds, actin and myosin. As the actins slide past and between the myosins, the threads get shorter – and the muscle contracts.

Body of muscle

◄ The main part of a muscle is the body or belly, with hundreds of muscle fibres inside.

Actin

Myosin

► Dozens of arm and hand muscles move a pen precisely, a tiny amount each time.

799 Muscles are controlled by the brain, which sends messages to them along string-like nerves. When a muscle contracts for a long time, its fibres 'take turns'. Some of them shorten powerfully while others relax, then the contracted ones relax while others shorten, and so on.

WHICH MUSCLES?

Can you match the names of these muscles with different parts of the body?

a. Gluteus maximus b. Masseter
c. Sartorius d. Cardiac muscle
e. Pectoralis major

1. Heart 2. Chest 3. Front of thigh
4. Buttock 5. Mouth

Answers:
a4 b5 c3 d1 e2

800 The body's biggest muscles are the ones you sit on — the gluteus maximus muscles in the buttocks. The longest muscle is the sartorius, across the front of the thigh. Some of its fibres are more than 30 centimetres in length. The most powerful muscle, for its size, is the masseter in the lower cheek, which closes the jaws when you chew.

The breathing body

801 The body cannot survive more than a few minutes **without breathing.** This action is so important, we do it all the time without thinking. We breathe to take air into the body. Air contains the gas oxygen, which is needed to get energy from food to power all of the body's vital life processes.

▶ Body parts make up the respiratory system in the head, neck and chest. These carry out the process of breathing air to take oxygen into the body.

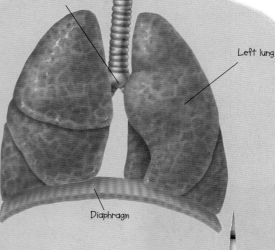

Nasal chamber

Nose

Voice-box (larynx)

Windpipe

Bronchus

Left lung

Diaphragm

▲ Scuba divers wear special breathing apparatus called 'aqua lungs'. They control their breathing to make their oxygen supply last as long as possible.

802 Parts of the body that work together to carry out a main task are called a system — so the parts that carry out breathing are the **respiratory system.** These parts are the nose, throat, windpipe, the air tubes or bronchi in the chest, and the lungs.

803 The nose is the entrance for fresh air to the lungs — and the exit for stale air from the lungs. The soft, moist lining inside the nose makes air warmer and damper, which is better for the lungs. Tiny bits of floating dust and germs stick to the lining or the hairs in the nose, making the air cleaner.

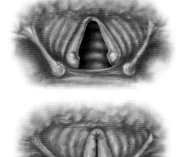

▼ When playing the trumpet, the diaphragm and chest control the air flowing in and out of the lungs.

804 The windpipe, or trachea, is a tube leading from the back of the nose and mouth, down to the lungs. It has about 20 C-shaped hoops of cartilage in its wall to keep it open, like a vacuum cleaner hose. Otherwise the pressure of body parts in the neck and chest would squash it shut.

805 At the top of the windpipe, making a bulge at the front of the neck, is the voice-box or larynx. It has two stiff flaps, vocal cords, which stick out from its sides. Normally these flaps are apart for easy breathing. But muscles in the voice-box can pull the flaps almost together. As air passes through the narrow slit between them it makes the flaps shake or vibrate – and this is the sound of your voice.

HUMMMMMM!

You will need:

stopwatch

Do you think making sounds with your voice-box uses more air than breathing? Find out by following this experiment.

1. Take a deep breath in, then breathe out at your normal rate, for as long as you can. Time the out-breath.

2. Take a similar deep breath in, then hum as you breathe out, again for as long as you can. Time the hum.

3. Try the same while whispering your favourite song, then again when singing.

▲ The vocal cords are held apart for breathing (top) and pulled together for speech (bottom).

351

Breathing parts

806 The main parts of the respiratory (breathing) system are the two lungs in the chest. Each one is shaped like a tall cone, with the pointed end at shoulder level.

807 Air comes in and out of the lungs along the windpipe, which branches at its base to form two main air tubes, the bronchi. One goes to each lung. Inside the lung, each bronchus divides again and again, becoming narrower each time. Finally the air tubes, thinner than hairs, end at groups of tiny 'bubbles' called alveoli.

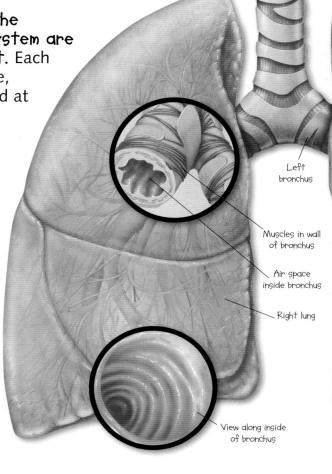

Left bronchus

Muscles in wall of bronchus

Air space inside bronchus

Right lung

View along inside of bronchus

I DON'T BELIEVE IT!

On average, the air breathed in and out through the night by a sleeping person, would fill an average-sized bedroom. This is why some people like to sleep with the door or window open!

808 There are more than 200 million tiny air bubbles, or alveoli, in each lung. Inside, oxygen from breathed-in air passes through the very thin linings of the alveoli to equally tiny blood vessels on the other side. The blood carries the oxygen away, around the body. At the same time a waste substance, carbon dioxide, seeps through the blood vessel, into the alveoli. As you breathe out, the lungs blow out the carbon dioxide.

809 Breathing needs muscle power!

The main breathing muscle is the dome-shaped diaphragm at the base of the chest. To breathe in, it becomes flatter, making the lungs bigger, so they suck in air down the windpipe. At the same time, rib muscles lift the ribs, also making the lungs bigger. To breathe out, the diaphragm and rib muscles relax. The stretched lungs spring back to their smaller size and blow out stale air.

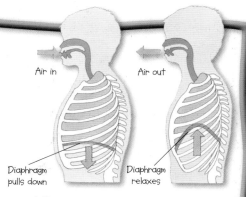

Air in

Air out

Diaphragm pulls down

Diaphragm relaxes

▲ Breathing uses two main sets of muscles, the diaphragm and those between the ribs.

▶ After great activity, the body breathes faster and deeper, to replace the oxygen used by the muscles for energy.

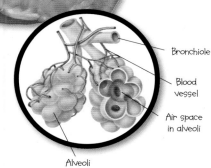

Bronchiole

Blood vessel

Air space in alveoli

Alveoli

▲ Inside each lung, the main bronchus divides again and again, into thousands of narrower airways called bronchioles.

810 As you rest or sleep, each breath

sends about half a litre of air in and out, 15 to 20 times each minute. After great activity, such as running a race, you need more oxygen. So you take deeper breaths faster – 3 litres or more of air, 50 times or more each minute.

The hungry body

811 All machines need fuel to make them go, and the body is like a living machine whose fuel is food. Food gives us energy for our body processes inside, and for breathing, moving, talking and every other action we make. Food also provides raw materials that the body uses to grow, maintain itself and repair daily wear-and-tear.

812 We would not put the wrong fuel into a car engine, so we should not put unsuitable foods into the body. A healthy diet needs a wide variety of foods, which have lots of vital nutrients. Too much of one single food may be unhealthy, especially if that food is very fatty or greasy. Too much of all foods is also unhealthy, making the body overweight and increasing the risk of illnesses.

▶ It is important for children to learn how to cook healthily. Grilling or barbecuing food is much healthier than frying it.

▲ Fresh fruits such as bananas, and vegetables such as carrots, have lots of vitamins, minerals and fibre, and are good for the body in lots of ways.

▼ Foods such as bread, pasta and rice contain lots of starch, which is a useful energy source.

813 There are six main kinds of nutrients in foods, and the body needs balanced amounts of all of them.

- Proteins are needed for growth and repair, and for strong muscles and other parts.
- Carbohydrates, such as sugars and starches, give plenty of energy.
- Some fats are important for general health and energy.
- Vitamins help the body to fight germs and disease.
- Minerals are needed for strong bones and teeth and also healthy blood.
- Fibre is important for good digestion and to prevent certain bowel disorders.

◀ Fish, low-fat meats such as chicken, and dairy produce such as cheese all contain plenty of valuable proteins.

FOOD FOR THOUGHT

Which of these meals do you think is healthier?

Meal A
Burger, sausage and lots of chips, followed by ice cream with cream and chocolate.

Meal B
Chicken, tomato and a few chips, followed by fresh fruit salad with apple, banana, pear and melon.

Answer:
Meal B

▲ Fats and oily foods are needed in moderate amounts. Plant oils are healthier than fats and oils from animal sources.

Bite, chew, gulp

814 The hardest parts of your whole body are the ones that make holes in your food — teeth. They have a covering of whitish or yellowish enamel, which is stronger than most kinds of rocks! Teeth need to last a lifetime of biting, nibbling, gnashing, munching and chewing. They are your own food processors.

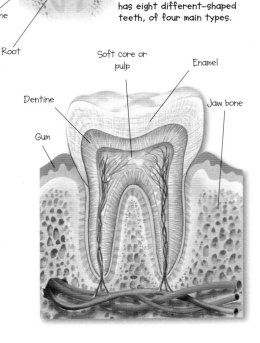

Incisor

Canine

Premolar

Molar

Jaw bone

Root

▲ In an adult, each side (left and right) of each jaw (upper and lower) usually has eight different-shaped teeth, of four main types.

815 There are four main shapes of teeth. The front ones are incisors, and each has a straight, sharp edge, like a spade or chisel, to cut through food. Next are canines, which are taller and more pointed, used mainly for tearing and pulling. Behind them are premolars and molars, which are lower and flatter with small bumps, for crushing and grinding.

Soft core or pulp

Enamel

Dentine

Jaw bone

Gum

► At the centre of a tooth is living pulp, with many blood vessels and nerve endings that pass into the jaw bone.

816 A tooth may look almost dead, but it is very much alive. Under the enamel is slightly softer dentine. In the middle of the tooth is the dental pulp. This has blood vessels to nourish the whole tooth, and nerves that feel pressure, heat, cold and pain. The lower part of the tooth, strongly fixed in the jaw bone, is the root. The enamel-covered part above the gum is the crown.

817 Teeth are very strong and tough, but they do need to be cleaned properly and regularly. Germs called bacteria live on old bits of food in the mouth. They make waste products which are acid and eat into the enamel and dentine, causing holes called cavities. Which do you prefer – cleaning your teeth after main meals and before bedtime, or the agony of toothache?

▶ Clean your teeth by brushing in different directions and then flossing between them. They will look better and stay healthier for longer.

▼ The first set of teeth lasts about ten years, while the second set can last ten times longer.

First set
(milk or deciduous teeth)

Second set
(adult or permanent set)

818 Teeth are designed to last a lifetime. Well, not quite, because the body has two sets. There are 20 small teeth in the first or baby set. The first ones usually appear above the gum by about six months of age, the last ones at three years old. As you and your mouth grow, the baby teeth fall out from about seven years old. They are replaced by 32 larger teeth in the adult set.

819 After chewing, food is swallowed into the gullet (oesophagus). This pushes the food powerfully down through the chest, past the heart and lungs, into the stomach.

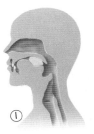

① Tongue pushes food to the back of the throat

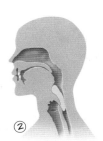

② Throat muscles squeeze the food downwards

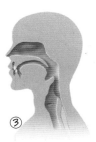

③ The oesophagus pushes food to the stomach

Food's long journey

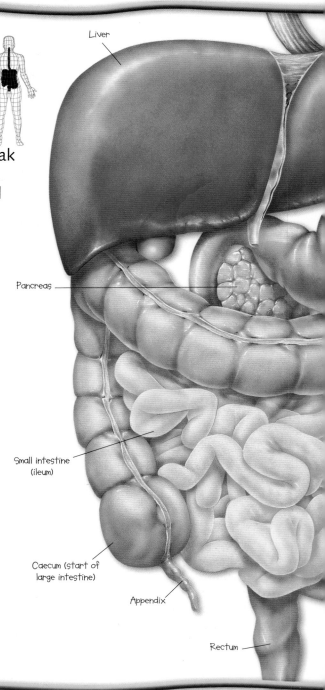

820 The digestive system is like a tunnel about 9 metres long, through the body. It includes parts of the body that bite food, chew it, swallow it, churn it up and break it down with natural juices and acids, take in its goodness, and then get rid of the leftovers.

821 The stomach is a bag with strong, muscular walls. It stretches as it fills with food and drink, and its lining makes powerful digestive acids and juices called enzymes, to attack the food. The muscles in its walls squirm and squeeze to mix the food and juices.

822 The stomach digests food for a few hours into a thick mush, which oozes into the small intestine. This is only 4 centimetres wide, but more than 5 metres long. It takes nutrients and useful substances through its lining, into the body.

Liver

Pancreas

Small intestine (ileum)

Caecum (start of large intestine)

Appendix

Rectum

823 The large intestine follows the small one, and it is certainly wider, at about 6 centimetres, but much shorter, only 1.5 metres. It takes in fluids and a few more nutrients from the food, and then squashes what's left into brown lumps, ready to leave the body.

Stomach

Large intestine

Villus

Vessels inside villus

Vessels in intestine lining

▶ The lining of the small intestine has thousands of tiny finger-like parts called the villi, which take nutrients from food, into the blood and lymph system.

◀ The digestive parts almost fill the lower part of the main body, called the abdomen.

I DON'T BELIEVE IT!

What's in the leftovers? The brown lumps called bowel motions or faeces are only about one-half undigested or leftover food. Some of the rest is rubbed-off parts of the stomach and intestine lining. The rest is millions of 'friendly' but dead microbes (bacteria) from the intestine. They help to digest our food for us, and in return we give them a warm, food-filled place to live.

824 The liver and pancreas are also parts of the digestive system. The liver sorts out and changes the many nutrients from digestion, and stores some of them. The pancreas makes powerful digestive juices that pass to the small intestine to work on the food there.

Blood in the body

825 The heart beats to pump the blood all around the body and pass its vital oxygen and nutrients to every part. The same blood goes round and round, or circulates, in its network of blood vessels. So the heart, blood vessels and blood are known as the circulatory system.

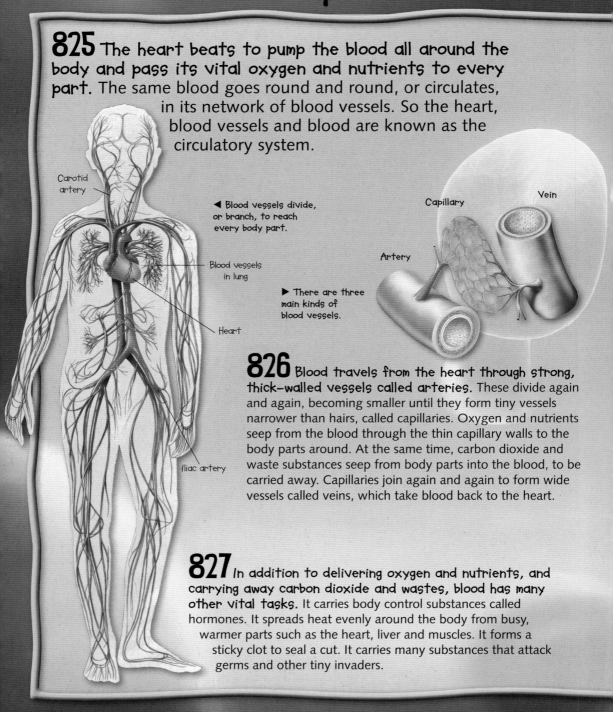

Carotid artery

◀ Blood vessels divide, or branch, to reach every body part.

Capillary

Vein

Blood vessels in lung

Artery

▶ There are three main kinds of blood vessels.

Heart

Iliac artery

826 Blood travels from the heart through strong, thick–walled vessels called arteries. These divide again and again, becoming smaller until they form tiny vessels narrower than hairs, called capillaries. Oxygen and nutrients seep from the blood through the thin capillary walls to the body parts around. At the same time, carbon dioxide and waste substances seep from body parts into the blood, to be carried away. Capillaries join again and again to form wide vessels called veins, which take blood back to the heart.

827 In addition to delivering oxygen and nutrients, and carrying away carbon dioxide and wastes, blood has many other vital tasks. It carries body control substances called hormones. It spreads heat evenly around the body from busy, warmer parts such as the heart, liver and muscles. It forms a sticky clot to seal a cut. It carries many substances that attack germs and other tiny invaders.

828 Blood has four main parts. The largest is billions of tiny, saucer-shaped red cells, which make up almost half of the total volume of blood and carry oxygen. Second is the white cells, which clean the blood, prevent disease and fight germs. The third part is billions of tiny platelets, which help blood to clot. Fourth is watery plasma, in which the other parts float.

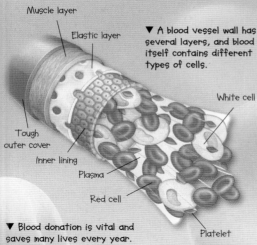

Muscle layer
Elastic layer
Tough outer cover
Inner lining
Plasma
Red cell
White cell
Platelet

▼ A blood vessel wall has several layers, and blood itself contains different types of cells.

▶ Each kidney has about one million tiny filters, called nephrons, in its outer layer, or cortex.

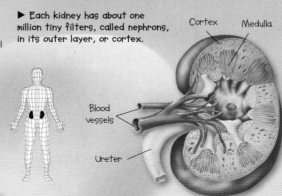

Cortex
Medulla
Blood vessels
Ureter

A Positive

▼ Blood donation is vital and saves many lives every year.

829 Blood is cleaned by two kidneys, situated in the middle of your back. They filter the blood and make a liquid called urine, which contains unwanted and waste substances, plus excess or 'spare' water. The urine trickles from each kidney down a tube, the ureter, into a stretchy bag, the bladder. It's stored here until you can get rid of it – at your convenience.

The beating body

830 **The heart is about as big as its owner's clenched fist.** It is a hollow bag of very strong muscle, called cardiac muscle or myocardium. This muscle never tires. It contracts once every second or more often, all through life. The contraction, or heartbeat, squeezes blood inside the heart out into the arteries. As the heart relaxes it fills again with blood from the veins.

831 Inside, the heart is not one bag-like pump, but two pumps side by side. The left pump sends blood all around the body, from head to toe, to deliver its oxygen (systemic circulation). The blood comes back to the right pump and is sent to the lungs, to collect more oxygen (pulmonary circulation). The blood returns to the left pump and starts the whole journey again.

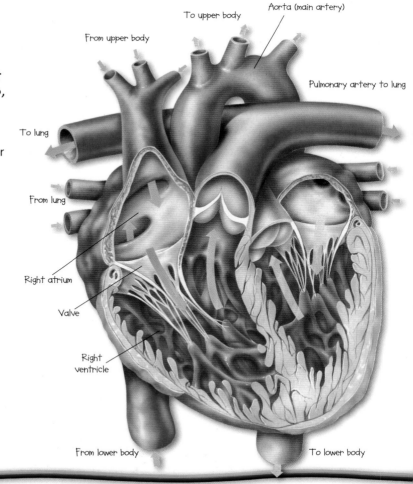

From upper body

To upper body

Aorta (main artery)

Pulmonary artery to lung

To lung

From lung

Right atrium

Valve

Right ventricle

From lower body

To lower body

▶ The heart is two pumps side by side, and each pump has two chambers, the upper atrium and the lower ventricle.

832 Inside the heart are four sets of bendy flaps called valves. These open to let blood flow the right way. If the blood tries to move the wrong way, it pushes the flaps together and the valve closes. Valves make sure the blood flows the correct way, rather than sloshing to and fro, in and out of the heart, with each beat.

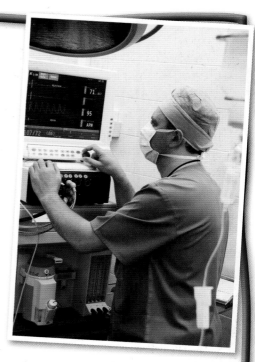

▲ Doctors use ECG machines to monitor the electrical activity of the heart.

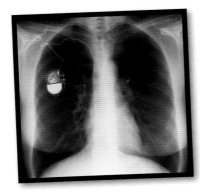

▶ This X-ray of a chest shows a pacemaker that has been implanted to control an irregular heartbeat.

833 The heart is the body's most active part, and it needs plenty of energy brought by the blood. The blood flows through small vessels, which branch across its surface and down into its thick walls. These are called the coronary vessels.

834 The heart beats at different rates, depending on what the body is doing. When the muscles are active they need more energy and oxygen, brought by the blood. So the heart beats faster, 120 times each minute or more. At rest, the heart slows to 60 to 80 beats per minute.

HOW FAST IS YOUR HEARTBEAT?

You will need:
plastic funnel   tracing paper
plastic tube (like hosepipe)   sticky-tape

You can hear your heart and count its beats with a sound-funnel device called a stethoscope.

1. Stretch the tracing paper over the funnel's wide end and tape in place. Push a short length of tube over the funnel's narrow end.

2. Place the funnel's wide end over your heart, on your chest, just to the left, and put the tube end to your ear. Listen to and count your heartbeat.

Looking and listening

835 The body finds out about the world around it by its senses — and the main sense is eyesight. The eyes detect the brightness, colours and patterns of light rays, and change these into patterns of nerve signals that they send to the brain. More than half of the knowledge, information and memories stored in the brain come into the body through the eyes.

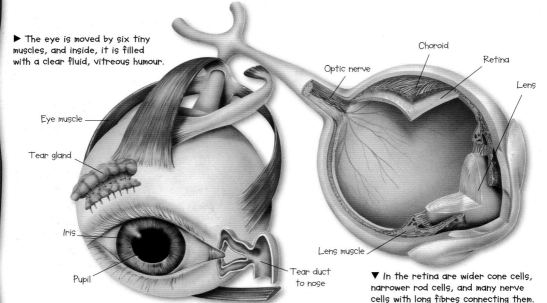

▶ The eye is moved by six tiny muscles, and inside, it is filled with a clear fluid, vitreous humour.

Optic nerve

Choroid

Retina

Lens

Eye muscle

Tear gland

Iris

Pupil

Lens muscle

Tear duct to nose

▼ In the retina are wider cone cells, narrower rod cells, and many nerve cells with long fibres connecting them.

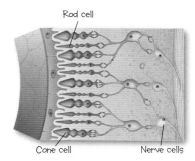

Rod cell

Cone cell

Nerve cells

836 Each eye is a ball about 2.5 centimetres across. At the front is a clear dome, the cornea, which lets light through a small, dark-looking hole just behind it, the pupil. The light then passes through a pea-shaped lens, which bends the rays so they shine a clear picture onto the inside back of the eye, the retina. This has 125 million tiny cells, rods and cones, which detect the light and make nerve signals to send along the optic nerve to the brain.

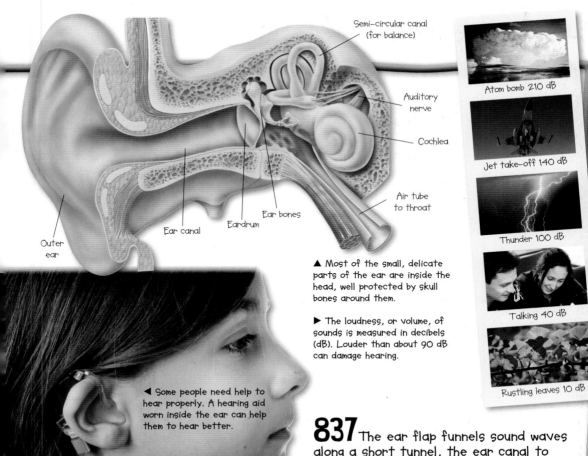

Semi-circular canal
(for balance)

Auditory
nerve

Cochlea

Air tube
to throat

Ear bones

Eardrum

Ear canal

Outer
ear

▲ Most of the small, delicate parts of the ear are inside the head, well protected by skull bones around them.

▶ The loudness, or volume, of sounds is measured in decibels (dB). Louder than about 90 dB can damage hearing.

Atom bomb 210 dB

Jet take-off 140 dB

Thunder 100 dB

Talking 40 dB

Rustling leaves 10 dB

◀ Some people need help to hear properly. A hearing aid worn inside the ear can help them to hear better.

BRIGHT AND DIM

Look at your eyes in a mirror. See how the dark hole which lets in light, the pupil, is quite small. The coloured part around the pupil, the iris, is a ring of muscle.

Close your eyes for a minute, then open them and look carefully. Does the pupil quickly get smaller?

While the eyes were closed, the iris made the pupil bigger, to try and let in more light, so you could try to see in the darkness. As you open your eyes, the iris makes the pupil smaller again, to prevent too much light from dazzling you.

837 The ear flap funnels sound waves along a short tunnel, the ear canal to the eardrum. As sound waves hit the eardrum it shakes or vibrates, and passes the vibrations to a row of three tiny bones. These are the ear ossicles, the smallest bones in the body. They also vibrate and pass on the vibrations to another part, the cochlea.

838 Inside the cochlea, the vibrations pass through fluid and shake rows of thousands of tiny hairs that grow from specialized hair cells. As the hairs vibrate, the hair cells make nerve signals, which flash along the auditory nerve to the brain.

smelling and tasting

▼ The parts that carry out smelling are in the roof of the large chamber inside the nose.

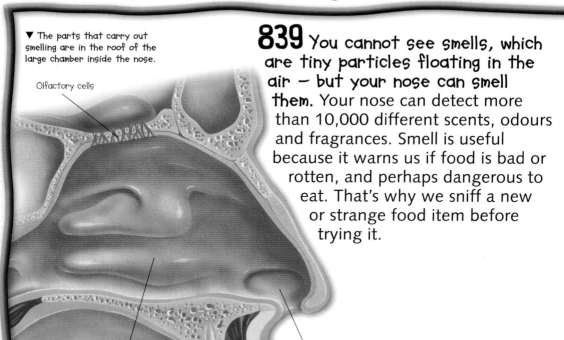

Olfactory cells

Nasal cavity

Mucus lining

839 You cannot see smells, which are tiny particles floating in the air – but your nose can smell them. Your nose can detect more than 10,000 different scents, odours and fragrances. Smell is useful because it warns us if food is bad or rotten, and perhaps dangerous to eat. That's why we sniff a new or strange food item before trying it.

840 Smell particles drift with breathed-in air into the nose and through the nasal chamber behind it. At the top of the chamber are two patches of lining, each about the area of a thumbnail and with 5 million olfactory cells. The particles land on their sticky hairs, and if they fit into landing sites called receptors there, like a key into a lock, then nerve signals flash along the olfactory nerve to the brain.

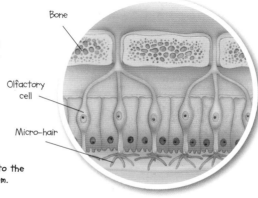

Bone

Olfactory cell

Micro-hair

▶ Olfactory (smell) cells have micro-hairs facing down into the nasal chamber, which detect smell particles landing on them.

841 The body's most flexible muscle is also the one which is coated with 10,000 micro-sensors for taste — the tongue. Each micro-sensor is a taste bud shaped like a tiny onion. Most taste buds are along the tip, sides and rear upper surface of the tongue. They are scattered around the much larger flaps and lumps on the tongue, which are called papillae.

◄ The tongue is sensitive to flavours, texture and temperature.

842 Taste works in a similar way to smell, but it detects flavour particles in foods and drinks. The particles touch tiny hairs sticking up from hair cells in the taste buds. If the particles fit into receptors there, then the hair cell makes nerve signals, which go along the facial and other nerves to the brain.

SWEET AND SOUR

The tongue detects five basic flavours.

Which of these foods is sweet, salty, savoury (umami), bitter or sour?

1. Coffee 2. Lemon 3. Bacon
4. Ice cream 5. Mushroom

Answers:
1. bitter 2. sour 3. salty
4. sweet 5. savoury

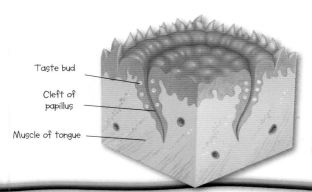

Taste bud

Cleft of papillus

Muscle of tongue

◄ The large pimple-like lumps at the back of the tongue, called papillae, have tiny taste buds in their deep clefts.

The nervous body

Brain

Spinal cord

843 The body is not quite a 'bag of nerves', but it does contain thousands of kilometres of these pale, shiny threads. Nerves carry tiny electrical pulses known as nerve signals or neural messages. They form a vast information-sending network that reaches every part, almost like the body's own Internet.

844 Each nerve is a bundle of much thinner parts called nerve fibres. Like wires in a telephone cable, these carry their own tiny electrical nerve signals. A typical nerve signal has a strength of 0.1 volts (one-fifteenth as strong as a torch battery). The slowest nerve signals travel about half a metre each second, the fastest at more than 100 metres per second.

Sciatic nerve

Tibial nerve

Axon

◀ Nerves branch from the brain and spinal cord to every body part.

Dendrites

Synapse (junction between nerve cells)

845 All nerve signals are similar, but there are two main kinds, depending on where they are going. Sensory nerve signals travel from the sensory parts (eyes, ears, nose, tongue and skin) to the brain. Motor nerve signals travel from the brain out to the muscles, to make the body move about.

▶ The brain and nerves are made of billions of specialized cells, nerve cells or neurons. Each has many tiny branches, dendrites, to collect nerve messages, and a longer, thicker branch, the axon or fibre, to pass on the messages.

846 Hormones are part of the body's inner control system. A hormone is a chemical made by a gland. It travels in the blood and affects other body parts, for example, making them work faster or release more of their product.

847 The main hormonal gland, the pituitary, is also the smallest. Just under the brain, it has close links with the nervous system. It mainly controls other hormonal glands. One is the thyroid in the neck, which affects the body's growth and how fast its chemical processes work. The pancreas controls how the body uses energy by its hormone, insulin. The adrenal glands are involved in the body's balance of water, minerals and salts, and how we react to stress and fear.

▲ Sports such as snowboarding cause us to produce more adrenaline due to excitement and fear.

◄ Female and male bodies have much the same hormone-making glands, except for the reproductive parts – ovaries in the female (left) and testes in the male (right).

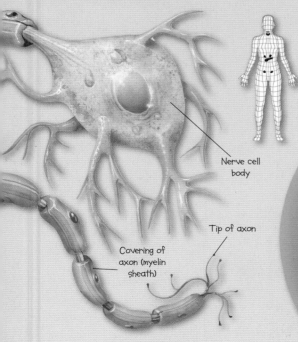

Nerve cell body

Tip of axon

Covering of axon (myelin sheath)

TIME TO REACT!

You will need:

friend   ruler

1. Ask a friend to hold a ruler by the highest measurement so it hangs down. Put your thumb and fingers level with the other end, ready to grab.

2. When your friend lets go grasp it and measure where your thumb is on the ruler. Swap places so your friend has a go.

3. The person who grabs the ruler nearest its lower end has the fastest reactions. To grab the ruler, nerve signals travel from the eye, to the brain, and back to the muscles in the arm and hand.

The brainy body

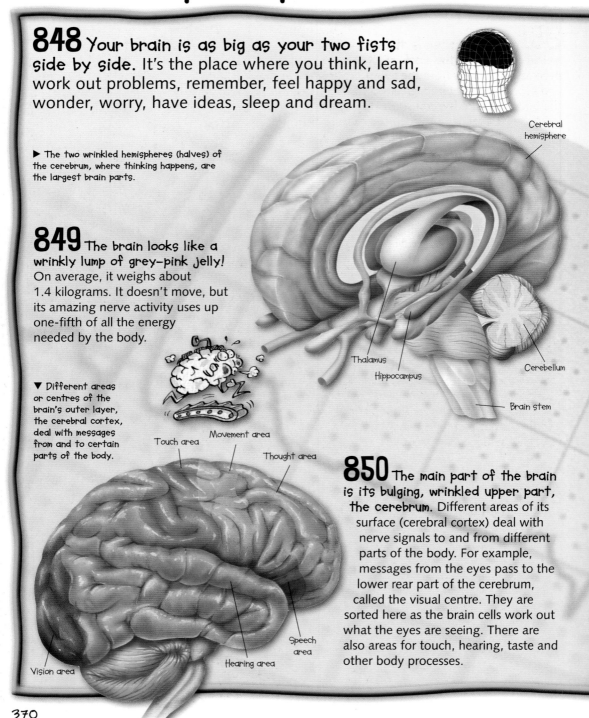

848 Your brain is as big as your two fists side by side. It's the place where you think, learn, work out problems, remember, feel happy and sad, wonder, worry, have ideas, sleep and dream.

Cerebral hemisphere

▶ The two wrinkled hemispheres (halves) of the cerebrum, where thinking happens, are the largest brain parts.

849 The brain looks like a wrinkly lump of grey–pink jelly! On average, it weighs about 1.4 kilograms. It doesn't move, but its amazing nerve activity uses up one-fifth of all the energy needed by the body.

Thalamus

Hippocampus

Cerebellum

Brain stem

▼ Different areas or centres of the brain's outer layer, the cerebral cortex, deal with messages from and to certain parts of the body.

Touch area

Movement area

Thought area

Vision area

Hearing area

Speech area

850 The main part of the brain is its bulging, wrinkled upper part, the cerebrum. Different areas of its surface (cerebral cortex) deal with nerve signals to and from different parts of the body. For example, messages from the eyes pass to the lower rear part of the cerebrum, called the visual centre. They are sorted here as the brain cells work out what the eyes are seeing. There are also areas for touch, hearing, taste and other body processes.

851 The cerebellum is the rounded, wrinkled part at the back of the brain. It processes messages from the motor centre, sorting and coordinating them in great detail, to send to the body's hundreds of muscles. This is how we learn skilled, precise movements such as writing, skateboarding or playing music (or all three), almost without thinking.

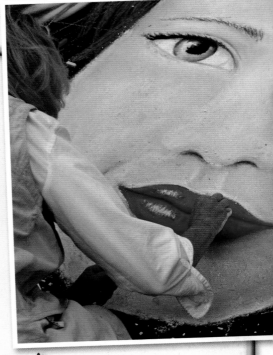

▲ Our brains allow us to draw from memory, expressing emotions.

852 The brain stem is the lower part of the brain, where it joins the body's main nerve, the spinal cord. The brain stem controls basic processes vital for life, like breathing, heartbeat, digesting food and removing wastes.

853 The brain really does have 'brain waves'. Every second it receives, sorts and sends millions of nerve signals. Special pads attached to the head can detect these tiny electrical pulses. They are shown on a screen or paper strip as wavy lines called an EEG, electro-encephalogram.

▼ The brain's 'waves' or EEG recordings change, depending on whether the person is alert and thinking hard, resting, falling asleep or deeply asleep.

I DON'T BELIEVE IT!

The brain never sleeps! EEG waves show that it is almost as busy at night as when we are awake. It still controls heartbeat, breathing and digestion. It also sifts through the day's events and stores memories.

Index

Page numbers in **bold** refer to main subject entries; page numbers in *italics* refer to illustrations

A

abacuses 117, *117*
ABS (anti-lock braking system) 289
acceleration **286–287**, *286–287*
accelerometers 287
acid rain 54
acids 43, *43, 63*
acoustics **24–25**
adrenal glands 369
aerobatics *246*, 247
agriculture *see* farming
Agulhas Current 270
ailerons 223, 226, 227, 233
air 72, 350
airbags 287, *287*
air brakes 288
Airbus A380 *220–221*, *230–231*, 233
Airbus Super Transporter Beluga 254, *254*
aircraft carriers 248, *248*, 288
air currents *279*
airliners 214, 219, *219*, 220, *220–221*, 221, 231, **232–233**, *232–233*, 251, *251*, 261, 281, *281*
airports 22, 23, **234–235**, *234–235*
airships 44, 218, *218*, 239, *239*
air traffic controllers 23, 229, *229*, 235
alchemy 69
Alcock, John 217
Aldrin, Buzz 176
al-Fazari, Muhammad 62
algebra 63
algorithms 63
alien life 210
alkalis *43*
alkaloids 43
al-Khwarizmi 63
alloys *40*
aluminium 45, *45, 73*

alveoli 352
AM (amplitude modulation) 34
Amazon River 270
ambulances 245
amino acids 312
amphibians 317
anatomy 65, *65*
  see also humans, body
Andromeda galaxy 84, *84*
anemometers 66
animals
  extinction 304
  natural selection 304
  selective breeding 274
  species 300, **302–303**, 304–305
  speed **272–275**, *272–275*
  tracking 51
  see also evolution, *and individual entries*
Ankylosaurus 319
Anning, Mary 71
Anomalocaris 315
anthrax 77
antibiotics 77
antiseptics 76
Antonov AN-225 228, 244, *244*
apes 301, *301*, 302
Apollo missions **164–165**, **176–177**, 199, 281
aqua lungs *350*
Arabic numerals 63
arachnids 316
Arber, Werner 87
Archaeopteryx 320, *320*
Archimedes 60, 61
Ardipithecus ramidus 324
Ares rocket 253
Argentinosaurus 319, *319*
Ariane 5 rockets *181*, 252
Armstrong, Neil 164, 176
ARPANET 38
arrows 92, 102
arteries 65, 360, *360*, 362
Arthropleura 316, *316*
arthropods 316
articular discs 345
artificial selection **326–327**
aspen trees 327
asphalts 42

asteroid belt *134, 147*, 202, *202–230*
asteroids 135, 147, *147*, **202–203**, *202–203*
astrolabe 62
astronauts 130, *130*, 137, 139, 158, 159, 160, 161, 164, 165, 175, 177, 253
astronomy 59, 62, 67, **84–85**, 163, 172
Atlantis space shuttle *267*
atmosphere 312
atomic science **80–81**
atomic theory 73
atomic weight 73
atoms 30, 32, *32*, 44, 45, **46–47**, *46–47*, 59, 73, 79, 80, 81, 88, 267
Australopithecus afarensis 324
Australopithecus africanus 324, 325
automatic pilot 231
avalanches 270
Avery, Oswald 86
axes 95, *95, 104*
axles 16, *16, 40, 47*

B

B2 Stealth Bomber 254, *255*
babies
  animal 323
  human 334, *334*, 335, *335*, **336–337**, *336–337*, 340
backbone *272*, 314, *342*, 343, 345
bacteria 67, 77, 87, 118, 308, 310, 313, 357, 359
bagpipes 121, *121*
Baird, John Logie 123
ball-and-socket joints 344, *345*
ballistas 112
bamboo 273
Bannister, Roger 277, *277*
bases 43
bats *25*
batteries 21, 32, *32*, 43, 74, *74*, 75
battering rams 113
battleships *113*
Beagle 2 lander *191, 197*

Beagle, HMS 298, *298*, 299
Beaufort Scale 291, *291*
Becquerel, Henri 79
Behaim, Martin 110
Bell, Alexander Graham 122
bellows 104
Bell XI plane 251
BepiColombo mission 209, *209*
Berliner, Emile 124
Bernard, Alain *277*
Berners-Lee, Tim 38, 88
bicycles 17, *17*, 99, *99*, 278, *278*
Big Bang 85, 88, 154, *155*
Big Crunch *155*
binary code 35
biplanes 218
birds 24, *50*, 51, **320–321**, *320–321*
   see also *individual entries*
bitumens 42
Black Hawk helicopters *237*
black holes 88, 151, *151*, 163, 211
bladder 361
blood 65, *65*, 269, **360–361**, 362, 363
blood cells 342, 343, 361, *361*
Bloodhound 283, *283*
blood vessels 339, 343, *343*, 352, 356, 360, *360*, 361, 363
body temperature 19, 339
Boeing 747 jumbo jet 220, 223, *232–233*, 244, 251
Bohr, Niels 80
Bolt, Usain *276*
bomber planes 219, 242, *242*
bones **342–343**, *342–343*, 345, 346, 347
boneshakers 99, *99*
books 116, *116*
boomerangs 95
Booth, Hubert Cecil 126
Bose-Einstein Condensate (BEC) 88
bosons 89
botany 59
box guitar *25*
Boyle, Robert 72
Boyle's Law 72

brains 53, 324, 325, 336, 349, 364, 365, 367, **370–371**, *370–371*
brakes 288, *288*, 289
breakdancing *347*
breathing **350–353**, *350–353*
Breedlove, Craig 280
Breitling Orbiter 3 239, *239*
bricks 109
bronchi 350, *350*, 352, *352*
bronchioles *353*
bronze 104, *104*
Brown, Arthur 217
Buckland, William 71
buckyballs *47*
Bullet Cluster 153
bullet trains 283
buoyancy 61, *61*
Burgess Shale 314
Burj Khalifa *105*
Burnell, Jocelyn Bell 85
burning 19, *19*, 72
butterflies *300*
butterfly nebula *149*

C

C-5 Galaxy cargo plane *244*
cables 29
Calcar, Jan van 65
calcium 343
calculus 67
camels *275*
cameras *123*, 125, *125*, 184, 193
camouflage *304*
cannons 112, 113
capillaries 360, *360*
caravels *107*
carbohydrates 355
carbon 45
carbon-dating 309
carbon dioxide 43, 312, 352, 360
carbon fibre *40*
cardiac muscle 362
cargo planes 231, 243, 244, *244*, 254, *254*
car jacks 16
cars 22, 64, 99, 258, 268, 278, *278–279*, 285, 286, *286*, 288, 289, *289*

cars *(cont.)*
   electric *21*
   engines 20, 40, 285
   jet cars *280*, 282, *282*, 284
   racing cars *40*, 260, *285*
   stopping distances *284*
cartilage 344, 345, *345*
Cassini-Huygens mission 172, 180, *183*, 189, 190, 207
cassowaries 321
catalysts 54
catamarans 258
catapults 103, *103*, 112
cathode rays 78, 80
cats 326
CD players 125
CDs 29, *29*, 37, 125
cells 66, *66*, 87, 296, 310, 334, *334*, 338, 343
Celsius 19
centrifugal force 269
cepheids 84
ceramics *41*
cerebellum *370*, 371
cerebral cortex 370, *370*
cerebrum 370, *370*
Ceres *202*, 203
CERN 38, *89*
Chadwick, James 81
Chain, Ernest 77
Chandrayaan 1 spacecraft 177
Chappe, Claude 122
charcoal 105
chariots 98, *98*, 274
Charnia 313
Charon 140, *140*
cheetahs 261, 272, *272*
chemicals 32, **42–43**
chemistry 59, **72–73**
chimpanzees 301, *301*, 302, 324
Chinook helicopters 237, *237*
chromosomes 86, *86*
chronometers 111, *111*
circuits 32, 33
circulatory system 65, *65*, **360–363**, *360–363*
citric acid 43, *43*
cladistics 302
classification 70, **302–303**

INDEX

clay 41, **108–109**, *108–109*
Clementine orbiter 177
climate change 54, 325, 329
clocks 66, 264, 265
cloning 87, 327
clothes 92
clouds 138, *138*, 139, 142, 145, 312
coal 33
Cobb, John 280, *280*
cochlea 365, *365*
cockpits 220, *220*, 230, 231, 232, 246
coelacanth *306*
Cohen, Stanley 87
collagen 338, 343, 346
colours 28, 69
  spectrum 26
combine harvesters 101, *101*
combustion *see* burning
Comet airliner 219, *219*
comets 135, 146, *146*, 147, 187, *191*, 200, **204–205**, *204–205*, 261
communication, long-distance **122–123**, *122–123*
communications satellites 162, *162*
compasses 110, *110*, 111
composite materials 41, *41*
compressors 224, *224*
computer modelling 279, *279*
computers **36–37**, *36–37*, 38, 63, 88, 117, 230, 279, 285
Concorde 251, *251*, 281, *281*
condensation 42
conduction 18, 32, 40
cone cells 364, *364*
constellations 110, *110*
contact lenses 27
continents 270
convection 19, *19*
cooking 97, *97*, 325
copper *73*, 104
coronal mass ejections (CMEs) *200*
corrosion 43
Cosmic Microwave Background 85
CPUs (Central Processing Units) 36

cranes 17
craters 137, 141, *141*
Creationism 301
cricket 265
Crick, Francis 86
Crookes, William 78
Crossbow catamaran 258
crossbows 103, *103*
crumple zones 289
cuneiform writing 116
Curie, Pierre and Marie 79, *79*
Curiosity rover 197, *197*
cyanobacteria 308, 313
cylinders 20, *20*

D

Dalton, John 73
dams 55, 115, *115*
dark matter 154, *154*
Darwin, Charles 297, **298–299**, 301, 309, 320
Dawn spacecraft 156, 203, *203*
day and night 136
deceleration **286–289**, *286–289*
decibels 24, *24*, 365
Deep Impact spacecraft *191*, 205
Deep Space 1 spacecraft 182, 187, *187*
Deep Space Network (DSN) 182, *183*
dentine 356, *356*, 357
dermis 338, *338*
Descartes, René 67
Descent of Man, The (Darwin) 301
diamonds 45, *45*
diaphragm 353, *353*
digestive system **358–359**, *358–359*
digital cameras *125*
digital music players *124*
digital radio 35
dinosaurs 71, 311, **318–319**, *318–319*, 320, 321
Dirac, Paul 83
disc brakes 288, *288*
diseases 45, 76, 77, 328, *329*
distillation 63
distribution grids 33

DNA 83, **86–87**, 89, 306, 312
dogs 274, *274*, 326, *326*
dolphins 322
Doppler effect 291
dragsters *286*
drums 122
duck-billed platypuses 323
DVDs 29, 37

E

ears 24, 365, *365*
Earth 70, 132, *134*, 135, **136–137**, *136–137*, 138, 150, 262
  age 296
  atmosphere 312
  day and night 136
  first life forms 296, 310
  magnetic field 51, *174*, 199
  orbital speed 263, 286
  seasons 136, 329
earthquakes 29, 271, 287, 291
earth sciences 59
Eastman, George 125
ECG (electro-cardiograph) 53, *363*
echidnas *307*, 323, *323*
echinoderms 302
echoes 25
ecology **50–51**, *50*
Edison, Thomas 124, *124*, 125, 127
EEG (electro-encephalograph) 53, 371
eggs 317, 318, *318*, 323, 334, *334*
Ehrlich, Paul 77
Einstein, Albert 82, *82*, 83
ejection seats 243
electric currents *32*, 74, 75, *75*, 78
electricity 21, 25, 26, 31, **32–33**, 38, 53, 55, **74–75**, *74–75*, 127
  hydroelectricity 55, *115*
electric motors 21, *21*, 23, 75, *193*
electric trains 281
electromagnetic radiation 89
electromagnetic spectrum *34*
electromagnetic waves 34, 78, *78*, 293

electromagnetism *30*, 31, 74, 75, *75*, 115
electron microscopes 119, *119*
electrons 30, 32, *32*, 46, *47*, 80, *80*, *83*, 285
elements **44–45**, *44–45*, 72, 73, *73*
elephants 275
elevators 221, *226*, 228, *233*, 251
ellipsoidal joints *345*
email 38
embryos 334
enamel 356, *356*, 357
endoscope 53, *53*
Endurance robot submarine 179
energy 28, 89, 148, 350, 354
  chemical 20
  clean 55
  electrical 28, 32, *32*, 34
  kinetic *21*, 268, 269, 288
  light 26, 28, *32*
  magnetic 34
engines **20–21**, *20–21*, 40, 268
  diesel 20
  jet *20*, 21, 219, 223, *223*, 224, *224*, *233*, *236*, 251, 252, 280, *280*, 281
  petrol 20
  piston 280, *280*
  propeller engines 223, *223*, 246
  rockets 181, 242, 252, 281
  rpm 285
  spacecraft 182
  steam 115
  turbofan 224, *224*, 225
  turbojet 224, *224*
  turboprop 225, *225*
Enterprise (Star Trek) *293*
enzymes 358
Eoraptor 318
epidermis 338, *338*
Equator *262*
Eris *145*
Eros NEA 202
escape velocity 180, 261
Euclid 60
Eurofighter Typhoon *214*
Europa 166, *166*
Eusthenopteron 317

evolution **296–329**
  artificial selection **326–327**
  convergent 307
  natural selection 304
exhaust gases 21, 54
ExoMars mission 209, *209*
exoplanets 167, *167*
experiments 48–49
explosions 19, 20, 21, *24*, 44
extinction 300, 304, 319
eyes and eyesight 324, **364**, *364*, 365
eye surgery 53, *53*

F
F-18 Super Hornet *290–291*
F-26 Fighting Falcon *250–251*
F-35B plane *240–241*, 241
F-117 Nighthawk *288*
Fahrenheit 19
Faraday, Michael 75, 115
Faraday cage *75*
farming 54, 60, **100–101**, *100–101*, 163, 327, 328
fats 355, *355*
Fermi, Enrico 81
ferns 316
fertilization *334*
fibre 355
fighter planes *214*, 218, *218*, 219, *219*, *221*, 231, 242, *242*, 267, *288*
finches 305, *305*
fire **96–97**, *96–97*, 325
fire ants 329
fire-fighting planes 245, *245*
fireworks *18*, 112
fish *50*, 272, *306*, 314, 317
Fleming, Alexander 77
flight decks **230–231**, *230–231*
flint tools 94, *94*, 95, *95*, 100
floating *see* buoyancy
floats 249
Florey, Howard 77
flowering plants *70*
flutes 120
flyby missions 178, 183, **186–187**, 201, 206, 207, 208
Flying Bedstead 241

flying boats 219
flying saucers 210
flywheels 268
FM (frequency modulation) 34
follicles 340
food **354–355**, *354–355*
  digestion **358–359**, *358–359*
forces 68, 222, *222*, 284, 286
fossils 70, 71, *71*, 297, *298*, 306, *306*, **308–309**, *308–309*, 314
four-minute mile 277, *277*
Franklin, Benjamin 74, *74*
Franklin, Rosalind 86
freon 126
frequency 24, 34, 290
friction 96, 288
Friedmann, Alexander 85
frowning 347
fuels 20, 21, 33, 42, *42*, 45
fuselage 220, *220*, 221, *233*

G
Gagarin, Yuri 175
Galápagos Islands 299, 300, 305, *305*
galaxies 59, 84, *84*, 85, **152–153**, *152–153*, 155, 263
  clusters 153, *153*
  elliptical 152, *153*
  irregular 152, *153*
  spiral 152, *153*
Galen 65
Galileo Galilei 67, 118
Galileo spacecraft *179*, 206, *206*
Galvani, Luigi 74
gamma rays 293
gases 72, *72*, 73, 148, 149, 312
gas giants 134, 135, 142, 144, **206–207**
Gastornis 321, *321*
Gatling, Richard 113
Gatling guns 113, *113*
gears 17, *17*, 20, *47*, 107, 114, *114*
generators 32, *33*, 115, *115*
genes, genetics 59, **86–87**, *86–87*, 304, 306, 327, 329, 334
Genesis spacecraft 198, *199*
genetically modified organisms 87

INDEX

geology 59, 71
germs 76, 77, 339, 351, 357, 360, 361
g forces 286, *286*, 287
Giganotosaurus 319, *319*
Giotto space probe 205
giraffes *300*
glaciers 270, *270*
glass 27, *27*, 41, 43, 55, 118
gliders 216, *216*, 246, *246*, 247
Global Hawk spy planes *243*
global warming 54, 270
globes 110
gold 104, *104*
'Goldilocks' planets 167, 211
gorillas *324*
Gossamer Albatross 255
GPS (Global Positioning System) 111, 265, 266
graphs 67
grasping reflex 336, *336*
gravity 51, 68, 83, 88, 134, 148, 156, 183, 185, 269, 284, 286, 287
gravity assist 183, 186, 208
Great Red Spot 142, *142*
Greek fire 113
Green, Andy 282
Greene, Brian 89
greenhouse effect 54
greyhounds 274, *274*
GRP (glass-reinforced plastic) 41
Guanlong 321
gunpowder 112, 113
guns 112, 113, *113*, 218
Gutenberg, Johannes 117
gymnasts *348*

H
habitats 166
Hadza tribe *329*
hair **340**, *340*, 341
hair cells 365, 367
Halley's Comet 146, 205
Hallucigenia 315
hang-gliders 64, 247
harps 120, *120*
Harrier jump jets 241, *241*
Harrison, John *111*

Harvey, William 65
Hato, Sahachiro 77
Hau, Lene Vestergaard 88
Hawk-Eye system 265, *265*
Hawking, Stephen 88
Hayabusa spacecraft 173, *173*, 203, *203*
head-up displays 231
hearing 365
hearing aids 66
heart 342, 360, *360*, **362–363**, *362–363*
heartbeats 53, 363
heat **18–19**, 20, 82, 96
Heathrow Airport 235
heat waves 34
hedgehogs *307*
helicopters 64, 217, **236–237**, *236–237*, 245, 247, 249
Helios 2 spacecraft 200, *200*, 201, 292
Helios airplane 255, *255*
helipads 249
helium 46, *46*, 239
helmets 242, 278, 289, 339
Henry, Joseph 75
Hertz, Heinrich 78
Hertz (Hz) 24, 290
hieroglyphs 116
Higgs, Peter 89
Higgs boson 89, *89*
Himilco 106
Hindenburg 218, *218*
Hines, Jim 277
hinge joints 344, *345*
hobby horses 99, *99*
Holley, Robert 87
Homo erectus 325, *325*
Homo habilis 324, *325*
Homo sapiens neanderthalensis 325, *325*
Homo sapiens sapiens 325, *325*
Hooke, Robert 66, *118*
hormones 360, 369
horses 98, *98*, 99, 274, *274*, 275, 323
hot air balloons 216, *216*, **238–239**, *238–239*
Houbolt, John *178*

household cleaners *43*
Houston, Peter 125
hovering 237, *237*, 240, 241
Hubble, Edwin 84, *84*
human-powered vehicles 283
humans
  body **332–371**
  evolution 311, **324–325**, *324–325*, 329
  speeds **276–277**, *276–277*
  see also Stone Age people
hunter-gatherers *329*
hurricanes 271
Hutton, James 70, *70*
Huygens, Christiaan 66, *66*, 67
hydroelectricity 55, *115*
hydrofoils *278*, 282
hydrogen 44, *44*, 46, *46*, 72, 73, 81, 218
Hydroptère 282, *282*
Hylonomus 318
hypotheses 48
Hyracotherium 323

I
Ibn Sina 62
Ice Ages 323, 325
ichthyosaurs 71
Icthyostega 317
impactors 191, *191*, 205
inertia 68, 268, *268*
influenza ('flu) 328, *328*
infrared waves 18, 184, 293
insects 311, 317
insulators 32
International Space Station (ISS) **160–161**, *160–161*
Internet 37, **38–39**, 88, 117
Io 142, 143
ion thrusters 182, *182*
iPads 37, 125
iPhones 39
iron 30, *30*, 31, 40, 105, *105*, 137
Irwin, James *177*
Islamic science **62–63**, 64
Iso-Hollo, Vomma *264*

J
Jabir ibn Hayyan 63, *63*

Jakobshavn Glacier 270
Janssen, Zacharias 118
jellyfish *313*, 314
Jenner, Edward 76, *76*
Jessop, William 99
jet cars *280*, 282, *282*, 284
jet planes *21*, 24, *24*, 219, *219*, 224, *224*, **232–233**, *232–233*, 240, 241, 258, 260, *261*, *267*, 281, *281*
jetways 23
joints **344–345**, *344–345*
Jones, Brian 239
jump jets 240, 241, *241*
Jupiter *134*, 142, *142*, 143, 186, 206, 207, 287

K

Kaku, Michio 89
kangaroos 323, *323*
kelp 273
keratin 338, 340, 341
kerosene 21, *42*
keyboards 36, *37*
Khorana, Har Gobind 87
kidneys 361, *361*
killer whales 272
kilns 108, *108*, 109
kilometres per hour 258, 260, 261, 262
kinetic energy *21*, 268, 269, 288
kitesurfing 258
knots (sailing speeds) 260
koalas 323
Koch, Robert 77
Kornberg, Arthur 87
Kuiper Belt 140, *204*

L

Lamarck, Jean-Baptiste 300
lamps 97
landers (spacecraft) 173, 178, **190–191**, *190–191*, 194, 195, *195*, 196, *197*, *207*, 209
large intestine 359, *359*
larynx 350, *350*, 351
lasers **28–29**, *28–29*, 38, 53, *53*, *293*
Lavoisier, Antoine 72, *72*, 73

Laws of Motion 68
LCD (liquid crystal display) *37*
lead 46, 105
Leavitt, Henrietta *84*
Leeuwenhoek, Anton von 66, 67
Leibnitz, Gottfried 67
Lemaître, Georges 85
lemurs 307, *307*
lenses 27, *27*, 118
Leonardo da Vinci 64–65, *64*
Leptictidium 322
levers 16, *16*, 60, 61, *61*
LHC (Large Hadron Collider) 267
life forms, earliest 296, 310
life sciences 59
lift (in flight) 222, *222*, 223, *232*
ligaments 345
light 19, **26–27**, *26–27*, 82, 88
    speed of 27, 34, 82, **292–293**
    white 26, *28*
    see also lasers
light bulbs 127, *127*
lightning 74, 75, *75*
light rays *27*, 83
light waves 26, 28, 34, 189
light years 292
Lilienthal, Otto 216, *216*
Linnaeus, Carolus 70, *70*, 303
Lippershey, Hans 118
Lister, Joseph 76
liver 359
lizards 272, 329, *329*
Lodge, Oliver *122*
longbows 102, *102*
loudspeakers 25
Lumière brothers 125, *125*
Lunar Rover 165, 176
Luna spacecraft 174
lungs 335, 342, 350, *350*, 351, 352, *352–353*, 353, 362
Lunokhod rovers *192*
Lyell, Charles 71

M

machine guns 113, 218
machines **16–17**, *16–17*
Mach numbers 290
Madagascar 307, *307*
Magellan spacecraft 201

Maglev trains 30, 281, *281*
magnetic fields 30, 31, *31*, 74, 75, *75*, *174*, 185, *199*
magnetic levitation *281*
magnetometers 185
magnets, magnetism 21, *21*, 25, 26, **30–31**, *30–31*, 33, 51, 74, 75, 80, 115, 182, 193
magnification **118–119**
malaria *329*
Mallard 281
mammals 303, 311, **322–323**, *322–323*, 324
mantis shrimp 273
maps 110, 245, 265
marathons *276*, 277
Marconi, Guglielmo 123
Mariner space probes 139, *139*, 196, 201
marlin 272
marrow 343, *343*
Mars *134*, 135, 138, 139, *139*, 167, 173, 182, 192, 193, 195, **196–197**, *196–197*, 209
Mars Express 182
Mars Global Surveyor 188, *189*, 197
Mars Pathfinder 191, 196
Mars Reconnaissance Orbiter 184, *185*, *197*
marsupials 323, *323*
mass 83, 268
materials **40–41**, *40–41*
mathematics **60–61**, 63, 67
matter 89, 154, *267*, 268
medicine **52–53**, 59, 62, **76–77**
Megalosaurus 71, *71*
Meganeura 317
Megatherium 298
melanin *340*
Mendeleyev, Dmitri 73
Mendel, Gregor 86
men-of-war ships 107
mercury (element) *73*
Mercury (planet) *134*, 135, 138, 141, *141*, 150, 201, 209
Messenger spacecraft 201, *201*
Messerschmitt 262 *219*
metals 18, *18*, 27, *30*, 32, 40, 73

metalworking **104–105**, *104–105*
meteorites 296
meteorology 59
meteors 147, 319
meteor showers *147*
methane *207*
microbes 77
microbiologists 59
microchips 36, 37
microlights 246, *246*
microscopes 66, *66*, 83, 118, *118*, 119, *119*, 193, 195
microwaves 34, 123, 127, 189, 293
MiG fighter plane *221*
miles per hour 261
military planes 240, **242–243**, *242–243*, **248–249**, *248–249*, 250
   see also bomber planes; fighter planes
Milky Way 59, 152, *152*, 263
minerals *73*, 355
Miohippus 323, *323*
Miranda 144
mirrors 26, *26*, 27
missiles 242, *251*, 255
mission control centres **198–199**, *198–199*
mobile phones *39*, 123, *123*
mockingbirds 300, *300*
molecules 45, 47
momentum 269
monotremes 323, *323*
Montgolfier brothers 216
Moon 118, 133, 137, *137*, 174, 192, 287
Moon missions **164–165**, 175, **176–177**
moons 67, 135, 140, *142*, 143, 144, *144*, 166, 189, 207, *207*
Morgan, Thomas Hunt 86
Morse, Samuel 122
Morse code 122, *122*
mortars 112
mosquitoes *329*
mosses 316
motorcycles 24, 269, *269*
Mount St Helens 270

movie projectors 125
movies 125
Muhammad 62
muscles 272, 273, *274*, 275, 335, *337*, *345*, **346–349**, *346–349*, 351, 358, 362, 367, 371
musical instruments 92, **120–121**, *120–121*, 290
myocardium 362

N

nails **341**, *341*
nanotechnology 47, 77
nanotubes *47*
NASA *198*, 255
NASCAR stock cars 289, *289*
natural philosophy 59
natural selection 304
navigation **110–111**, *110–111*
Neanderthals 325, *325*
near-Earth Asteroids (NEAs) 202
NEAR-Shoemaker space probe 202
nebulae 84, 148, *148*, 149, *149*, 150
Neptune *134*, 144, *144–145*, 145, 186, 187, 206, 207, 291
nerves, nervous system 53, 273, 343, *343*, 367, **368–369**, *368–369*
neurons 368
neutrons 46, *46*, 81
New Horizons space probes 140, *178–179*, 183, 208, *208*
Newton, Isaac 67, **68–69**
Niépce, Joseph Nicéphore 125
Nirenberg, Marshall 87
nitrogen 72, 81, 312
Noble, Richard 282
nose 351, 366, *366*
nuclear bombs 79, *80*, 81
nuclear chain reactions 81, *81*
nuclear fission 81
nuclear power stations 45
numerals 63, 117
nutrients 355, 358, 359, 360

O

ocean currents 270

oceanography 59
oceans 136, 310, 312, 314–315
Oersted, Hans 74
oesophagus 357, *357*
oil 33
   see also petroleum (crude oil)
oil refineries 42
oil rigs *42*, 249
oil spills and leaks 51, 54
olfactory cells 366, *366*
Olympic Games 264, 274
Olympus Mons 139, *139*
Omer 5 283
On the Origin of Species (Darwin) 301, 320
Oort cloud *204*
opaque materials 27
Oppenheimer, Robert 81
Opportunity rover 193, *193*, *194*, 197, *197*, 198
optic nerve 364, *364*
optics **26–27**
orbiters 177, 178, *184*, *185*, **188–189**, *188–189*, 207
orbits 188, 263
orcas 272
orchestras 120–121
ores 104
Orion spacecraft 253
oxygen 19, *46*, 72, *72*, 73, 233, *233*, 313, 350, 353, 360, 361, 362
ozone layer 54

P

pacemakers *363*
packet switching 38
palaeontology 59, *308*
pancreas *358*, 359, 369
pâpier maché 41
papillae 367, *367*
parachutes *157*, *178*, *190*, 243, 253, 284, 288
paragliders 247
particle physics 59
Pasteur, Louis 77
payloads 180
pendulums 66, *66*
penicillin 77, *77*

pentadactyl limb 322, *322*
Penzias, Arno 85
percussion 120
peregrine falcons 272, *272–273*
Periodic Table 44, *44–45*, 73, *73*
petrol 20
petroleum (crude oil) 40, 42, *42*, 55
pH *43*
phlogiston 72
Phoenix lander 173, 195, *195*, 196, *197*
Phorusrhacos 321
phosphate 343
photo finishes 264
photography 125
  see also cameras
photovoltaic cells *32*, 55
physical sciences 59
physics 59
pianos 121, *121*, 290
Piccard, Bertrand 239
picture writing 116, *116*
pigments *340*
pilots 226, 230, *230*, 231, 242, *242*, 243, 246, 247, 251, 266
Pioneer spacecraft 182, 186, 207
Pioneer Venus spacecraft 201
piston engines 280, *280*
pitch (acoustics) 24
pitch (flight) 226, *227*
pituitary gland 369
pivots (fulcrums) 16, *16*, 60, *61*, *110*
placental mammals 323, *323*
Planck, Max 82
plane joints *345*
planes *45*, 266, *266*, 279, 288, 290, *290–291*
  earliest 217
  engines 221, **224–225**, *224–225*
  flight **222–223**
  manoeuvres **226–227**, *226–227*
  parts of **220–221**, *220–221*
  taking off and landing **228–229**, *228–229*, 234, 235, 248, 251
  vertical take-off planes **240–241**, *240–241*, 248

see also airliners; jet planes; military planes
planets **134–135**
  dwarf planets 140, *145*
  exoplanets 167, *167*
  gas giants 134, 135, 142, 144, **206–207**
  'Goldilocks' planets 167, 211
  see also individual planets
plant evolution 316, 327
plasma 200, 361, *361*
plasma screens *35*
plasmids 87
plastics 27, 32, 40, 42
platelets 361
play 337, *337*
plesiosaurs 71, *71*
ploughs 100, *100*
Pluto 140, *140*, 145, *145*, 208
polar bears *304*
Pole Star 110
pollution 22, *50*, *51*, *54*, 55, 163
polonium 79
potters' wheels 109, *109*
pottery 96, **108–109**, *108–109*
power stations 33, *50*, *54*, *54*
Predator spy plane 255
primates 302, 324
printers *117*
printing presses 117, *117*
prisms 26, *26*, 69
prominences 132, *132*
propeller engines 223, *223*, 246
propellers 225, *225*, 240, 255, *255*, 280
prop-riding 280
proteins 312, 355, *355*
protons 46, *46*, 81
Proxima Centauri 211
pterosaurs 71
Pterygotus 316
Ptolemy 110
pulleys 17, *17*, 61
pulmonary circulation 362
pulsars 85
pulse 53
pylons 33, *33*
pyramids 60
pyroclastic flow 271, *271*

Q
quantum mechanics 82, 83
querns 100

R
racehorses 274, *274*, 275
radar 23, *23*, 51, 185, 189, *239*, 254
Radcliffe, Paula 276
radiation 79, 82
radio 23, 34, *34*, 35, 123, 163, 195
radioactivity 45, 79, 80, 309
radio beacons 266
radio telescopes 119, *119*
radio waves 34, *34*, 35, 38, 78, 123, 184, 189, 254, 293
radium 78, 79
Railton Mobil Special 280, *280*
railway lines 99, *99*
rainbows 26, 69
ramps 17
Random Access Memory 37
rapids *270*
Read Only Memory 37
Reber, Grote 119
record players 124, *124*
recycling 55, *55*
Red Arrows *246–247*
red shift 84
reflection 25, 26, *26*
reflexes 336, *336*
refraction 27, *27*
refrigerators 100, 126, *126*
relativity, theories of 82, 83
reptiles 71, 317, **318–319**, *318–319*, 320
resistance (drag) 222, 223, *223*, 228, 252, 278, *278*, 280, 284, 288
respiratory system **350–353**, *350–353*
retina 53, 364, *364*
retro-thrusters 190, *191*
rev counters *285*
rice *327*
rivers 270, *270*
robotics 49, 77, 161, 192, 194, *194*, 195

rocket planes 281, *281*
rockets **156–157**, *156–157*, 164,
180–181, *180–181*, 211, 242,
243, 252, *252*, 261
booster rockets 252, 253
rockfalls 270, 287
rocks 71, 134, 135, 136, 306,
309, 312
lunar 165, 176, 199, *199*
space rocks 137, *141*, 147
rods and poles (measurements)
264
roll (flight) 226, *227*
Roman numerals 63
Röntgen, Wilhelm 79
Rosetta spacecraft 202
rotors 236, *236*, 237
rovers **192–193**, *192–193*, 194,
194, 195, *196*, 197, *197*, 209
rudders 226, 227, 233, 239, 251
running 276, 277, *277*
runways 234, 246, 248
Ruska, Ernst 119
Rutherford, Ernest 80, 81

S

sabre-tooths 323
saddle joints *345*
sailfish 272, *273*
sailing ships 107, *107*, 114
sails 106, *107*, 114
Sakigake space probe 205
salts 43
satellites 34, 38, 111, *111*, 123,
123, **162–163**, *162–163*, 170–
171, 174, *174*, 265
satellite telescopes 163, *163*
satnav *101*, 111, 265, 266
Saturn 67, *67*, 134, 142, 143,
143, 172, 186, 189, 206, 207
Saturn 5 rockets 164, *180–181*
sauropods *319*
Savery, Thomas 115
saws 95, *95*, 114
scanners 22
scanning tunnelling microscopes
83
Schmitt, Jack 199
science fiction **210–211**

scientific method **48–49**
scientists **58–59**, *58–59*
scorpions 316
Scott, David *177*
screws 16, *16*
scuba divers *72*, *350*
seals *323*
seaplanes 249, *249*
search engines 38
seasons *136*, 329
Secretariat 274
seed-drills 101, *101*
see-saws 16, *16–17*, 61
selective breeding 274
semaphore 122, *122*
Semmelweiss, Ignaz 76
senses **364–367**, *364–367*
sextants 111, *111*
Shard 60
sharks 266, 272
ships and boats **106–107**, *106–
107*, 114, *258–259*, 260, 269,
278, 279, 280, 282, *282*
shock waves 250, *290*, 291
shooting stars 147, *147*
Sidorychev, Mikhail *268*
simulators 242
single-celled organisms 308, 310
singularities 88
skeleton 342, *342*, 343
skin **338–339**, *338–339*
skull 342, *342*
skydiving *284*
Skylab 160
sledges 98
slings 103
Slo-Mo-Shun IV 280
small intestine 358, *358*, 359, *359*
smallpox 76
smart bombs 242
smartphones *123*
smell, sense of **366**, *366*
smelting 104, 105, *105*
smiling 347
smoke signals 122
SMS (Short Message Service) 39
snowboarding *369*
social networking 39
sodium chloride 43

SOHO spacecraft 200
Sojourner rover *196*
Solar Challenger plane 255
solar eclipses 133, *133*
solar flares 132, *132*
solar power *32*, 55, 161, 191,
193, 255, *255*
Solar Probe Plus 200
Solar System 134, 263
solar wind 198, *199*, 206
sonar *24*, 51
sonic boom 250, *250*
Sopwith Camel 218, *218*
sound **24–25**, 250, 271, 290
sound barrier 250, *250*, 282
sound recording **124–125**, *124–
125*
sound waves 24, *24*, 25, 250, 365
Soyuz spacecraft 161
space 82, 130
living in **158–161**
space exploration **172–175**
launch **180–181**, *180–181*
launch windows 178
mission control centres **198–199**,
198–199
mission planning **178–179**
space probes 119, 267
see also individual probes
SpaceShip Two 211
space shuttles 157, *157*, 244, *244*,
252, 253, *253*, 267
space stations **160–161**, *160–161*
spacesuits *130*, 137, 158, *158*
space-time 82, 83
space travel **156–157**, *156–157*
spears 94, 102, *102*
spear throwers 102, *102*
species 300, 304–305
classification **302–303**
spectacles 27, 118, *118*
spectrometers *185*, 189
spectrum 26
speech recognition technology 36
speed 82, **258–259**, 268, 269
acceleration **286–287**, *286–287*
animals **272–275**, *272–275*
deceleration **286–289**, *286–289*
humans **276–277**, *276–277*

speed *(cont.)*
  of light 27, 34, 82, **292–293**
  limits 284
  measuring **264–265**, *264–265*
  natural speeds **270–271**, *270–271*
  records 280, *280*, 281, 282, 283
  relative speeds **262–263**, *262–263*
  of sound 271, 290
  speed machines **278–283**, *278–283*
  units **260–261**, *260–261*
  velocity **266–267**, *266–267*, 284
speedboats *258–259*, 280
speed guns 291
Spencer, Percy L. 127
sperm cells *334*
spiders 316
spinnakers *107*
spinning 269
Spirit of America 280, *280*
Spirit of Australia 282, *282*
spirit levels *28–29*
Spirit rover 193, *193*, 194, 197, *197*
sprinting *264*, 276, *276*, 277
Sputnik 174, *174*
spy planes 243, *243*, 255
spy satellites 163
stags *304*
Stapp, John Paul *286–287*
starch *355*
Stardust space probe 205, *205*
stars *44*, 84, 110, *110*, 132, **148–149**, *148–149*, 167, *263*
  birth of 148, *148*
  clusters 149
  death of **150–151**, *150–151*, 155
  pulsars 85
  red giant stars *149*, 150, *150*
  white dwarf stars 150, *151*
  see also galaxies
steam engines 115
steam trains *99*, 281
steam turbines 33
steel 30, *41*, 43, *95*, 105
steelworks 105

STEREO-*craft 188*
stomachs 358, *359*
Stone Age people 92, 94–95, *94–95*, 100, 108, 120, *325*
stone tools 94, 104, 324
stopping distances *284*
stopwatches 264, *264*
storm-chasers *271*
stromatolites *313*
sub-atomic particles 46
submarines 179, 243, 283
substances **42–43**, 44, 59
Suisei space probe 205
sulphuric acid 43
Sun 18, **132–133**, 134, 135, *141*, 146, 147, 149, 150, 152, *188*, 200, *200*, *263*
sunlight 26, 69, 137
sunspots 132, *132*
supernovae 151, *151*
supersonic planes 241, **250–251**, *250–251*
superstrings 89
surgery 53, *53*, *76*
Surveyor landers 175, *175*, 195
sweat 338, 339
swimming 277, *277*
swimsuits 279
swivel joints *345*
synovial fluid 344
synovial joints *345*
syphilis 77
systemic circulation 362

T

tanker planes *242*, 243
tanks 65
tape measures 264
tars 42
taste buds 367
taste, sense of **367**
taxiways 235
teeth **356–357**, *356–357*
telephones 29, 122, *122*, 162
telescopes 67, *84*, 118, *172*
  radio 119, *119*
  satellite 163, *163*
  X-ray 163
television 29, 34, 35, 123, 162

temperatures 19, *19*
  body temperature 19, 339
tendons *345*, 346, *346*
tennis 265
tenrecs *307*
terminals 234, *235*
terminal velocity 284
terror birds 321
tetrapods 317, *317*
texting 39
theodolites *270*
therapsids 322
thermal radiation 18
thermals 247
thermometers *19*
Thomson, JJ 80
thrust 222, *222*, 223
Thrust SSC 282, *282*, 284
thunder 24, 271
thyroid 369
tidal power 55
tigers *51*, *303*, 304, *304*
Tiktaalik 317
tilt-rotor planes 240
time 82, 292, 293
Titania 144
titanium *40*, 193
Titan (moon) 67, 189, 190, *207*
Titan rockets 180
toads *304*
toilets 127
tongue 367, *367*
tornadoes 271, *271*, 291
touch 339, 341
traction 279
tractors 20, 99
traffic lights 23
trains 23, *23*, 24, *30*, 262, 281, *281*, 283
train signals 23, *23*
transparent materials 27
trebuchets 112, *112*
Trevithick, Richard 115
T rex 319
Triceratops 319
trilobites 310, 314, 315
trucks 24, 99, *99*
trumpets 121, *121*, *351*
tsunamis 271

INDEX

Tu-114 passenger plane 281
Tull, Jethro 101
turbines *20*, 33, 55, *55*, 115, *115*
twins *87*
Twyford, Thomas 127
tyres *40*, 99, 269

U

UFOs 210
ultrasonic 25
ultraviolet rays 184, 293
Ulysses space probe 200
Universe 59, 89, **154–155**
  expansion 85, 155, 263
uranium 45, 79, 81
Uranus *134*, 144, *144*, 186, 187,
  206, 207
urine 361

V

V-22 Osprey 240, *240*
vaccines 328
vacuum cleaners 126, *126*
valves *362*, 363
Van Allen Belts 174, *174*
Vega space probes 205
veins 65, 360, *360*
Velociraptor 320, *320*
velocity **266–267**, *266–267*, 284
Venera program 190, 201
Venter, Craig 89
Venus *134*, 135, 138, *138*, 150,
  179, 193, 201
Venus Express spacecraft 201
venus flytraps 273, *273*
vertebrates 303, 314, 317
vertical take-off planes **240–241**,
  240–241, 248
Vesalius, Andreas 65
Vesta *202*, 203
Vickers Vimy 217
Viking landers 194, 196, *196*
Vikings 106, *106*
villi 359, *359*
vitamins 355
vocal cords 25, 351, *351*
volcanoes 29, *58*, *70*, 136, *138*,
  139, 270, 271, 287, 291, 296
volcanologists *58*

Volta, Alessandro 74
volts 32, 33
Vostok spacecraft 175, *175*
Voyager space probes 186, *187*,
  206, 207, 209, *209*

W

Walcott, Charles 314
Wallace, Alfred Russel 301
Wall of Death *269*
Warby, Ken 282
warp drive 293
water 19, 32, 73, 136, 166
water-bombing planes 245
water pipes 105
water vapour 312
waterwheels 114, *114*
Watson, James 86
weapons 92, *94*, 95, *95*, **102–103**,
  102–103, 104, 105, **112–113**,
  112–113
weather balloons 239
weather satellites 162, *162*
web pages and websites 38, 88
weedkillers 328, *328*
weightlessness 159
whales 51, 322
wheels 16, *16*, 98, *98*, 99, 194,
  220, 221, 229, *229*, 288, *288*,
  289
Wilmut, Ian 87
Wilson, Robert 85
windmills 114, *114*
windpipe 350, *350*, 351, 352,
  i353
wind power 55, *55*, **114–115**,
  114–115
winds 139, 206, 271, 291, *291*
wind speeds 66, 291
wind tunnels 279
wind turbines 115, *115*
wolves 326, *326*
womb (uterus) 334, *334*, 335
woolly mammoths *95*, 323
World War I 218
World War II 219
World Wide Web 38, 39, 88
wormholes 211
Wright Flyer 217, *217*

Wright, Wilbur and Orville 217
writing 116, *116*, 117

X

X-15 rocket plane 281, *281*
X-rays 34, 79, *79*, 163, 184, 293,
  344, *363*
X-ray telescopes 163

Y

yachts *107*
yaw 226, *227*
Yeager, Chuck 251
years 138

Z

zoology 59

Acknowledgements

All artworks are from the Miles Kelly Artwork Bank

The publishers would like to thank the following sources for the use of their photographs:
(t = top, b = bottom, l = left, r = right, c = centre, bg = background)

Front cover Shutterstock.com (tl) MCarter, (tr) Johan Swanepoel, (bl) Natursports, (br) Kjpargeter, (c) XYZ
Back cover Shutterstock.com (tl) Marcel Jancovic, (cr) ifong, (bl) Shilova Ekaterina
Spine Shutterstock.com (t) Sashkin

Alamy 60(bl) Guy Bell; 79(bg) Photo Researchers; 84(bl) Pictorial Press Ltd; 193(tr) Keith Morris
Ardea.com 324(bl) Jean Michel Labat
Corbis 62(bl) Blue Lantern Studio; 179(br) Roger Ressmeye; 198(t) Bill Ingalls/NASA/Handout/CNP; 199(tr) Roger Ressmeyer; 229(tr) Ron Watts; 230–231(bg) Arne Dedart/dpa; 237(tr) Michel Setboun; 239(br) Lowell Georgia; 241(bg); 244(t), (b) George Hall; 245(c) Charles O'Rear; 260–261(tc) Steve Bardens; 270–271(bg) Thilo Brunner; 276(bl) PCN Photography/PCN; 277(tr) Hulton-Deutsch Collection; 280(c) Bettmann; 286–287(bg) Leo Mason; 290–291(bg) Christopher Pasatieri/Reuters; 308–309(bg) Louie Psihoyos
Dreamstime 26(c) Silverstore; 27(br) Adam1975; 29(t) Paha_l; 303(c) Mailthepic; 335(b) Alan Heartfield; 336(b) Mykola Velychko; 351(tr) Tobkatrina; 357(tr) Kati1313; 369(br) Barsik
European Space Agency (ESA) 168(bg) NASA/D. Ducros 2003; 182(cl) D. Ducros; 201(bl) 2007 MPS/DLR-PF/IDA; 209(cr) AOES Medialab; 198–199(cb); 208–209(tc) C.Carreau
FLPA 14(t) Rob Reijnen/Minden Pictures; 304(t); 305(bc), (br) Tui De Roy/Minden Pictures; 307(b) Thomas Marent/Minden Pictures; 326(c) Paul Sawer
Fotolia.com 21(tl) Paul Heasman, (cr) Dariusz Kopestynski; 22(tl) & 111(b) & 123(tl) & 134(t), (c), (b) & 135 (tl), (br) & 188(tc) & 278–279(bg) Sharpshot; 29(b) photlook; 64(tl) MalDix; 65(tr), (tl), (cl), (br) Alexey Khromushin; 100(bl) Rafa Irusta; 172(bl) D. aniel; 221(b) sharply_done; 223(br) Chris Fourie; 237(br) Jetpics-Fotolia.com; 238(bl) IL-Fotolia.com; 296(c) & 297(bl) Kirsty Pargeter 309(cr), (br) & 322(bg) & 323(bg) & 324 (tr), (bl), (br) & 325 (tl), (bl), (cr) Alexey Khromushin; 345(cl) chrisharvey; 347(cl) Alexander Yakovlev; 365(cr) Andres Rodriguez;
Getty Images 60(bg) Will & Deni McIntyre; 68(tl) Mark Ralston, (c) Barcroft Media/Contributor; 76(tr) Gaston Melingue; 194–195(bg) SSPL; 195(br) & 206(b) & 280(cl) Time & Life Pictures; 258–259(bg) Andy Newman/Florida Keys News Bureau; 264(tr); 265(tr); 267(bg) Barcroft Media; 271(tl) Carsten Peter; 268–269(tr) & 277(b) & 278(tr) & 282(tr) AFP; 274–275(bg) Dennis O'Clair, 281(bg) National Geographic; 285(b); 329(b) Ariadne Van Zandbergen
iStockphoto.com 24–25(bg) Kevin Smith; 104–105(bg) Sander Kamp; 113(br) Duncan Walker; 122(b) HultonArchive; 124(tl) hohos, (bl) james steidl; 186(tr) Jan Rysavy; 227(tr) pawelb; 228(bl) egdigital; 232(bl) kickers; 249(br) itjoestheim; 313(tr) Jouke van der Meer; 337(b) ideabug
NASA 1(c) & 134–135(bg) & 166(cl) & 187(tl), (bl), (cr), (br) NASA/JPL; 44(c) NASA/JPL-Caltech/University of Arizona; 44–45(bg) Adam Block, Mt. Lemmon SkyCenter, U. Arizona/NASA; 84(c) ASA/JPL/California Institute of Technology; 85(bg) & 88(bg) & 137(c) &173(br) & 178(c) NASA/JPL-Caltech; 132(t), (c); 133(tr); 146(c) National Science Foundation/NASA; 149(tr) NASA Goddard Space Flight Center (NASA-GSFC), (br) Greatest Images of NASA (NASA-HQ-GRIN); 151(br) NASA, J.J. Hester Arizona State University, Greatest Images of NASA (NASA-HQ-GRIN); 152(bg) NASA/JPL-Caltech/ESA/Harvard-Smithsonian CfA; 153(c) NASA/STScI; 154(bl) NASA/STScI; ESO WFI; Magellan/U.Arizona/D.Clowe et al.; 156(bl) NASA/George Shelton; 156–157(bc); 157(bg) NASA/Tony Gray & Robert Murray; 159(cr) Carissa Callini/NASA; 161(tr); 177(br); 178(tl) NASA Langley Research Center (NASA-LaRC); 178–179(bc) NASA or National Aeronautics and Space Administration; 182(br); 182–183(tc) NASA/Johns Hopkins University Applied Physics Laboratory/Southwest Research Institute; 184(c) NASA/JPL/University of Arizona; 186(c); 187(tl), (c), (cl); 188–189(bg) NASA/STEREO; 188–189(c); 191(bl), (br); 194(bl) NASA/JPL/Cornell; 196(bl) NASA/Goddard Space Flight Center Scientific Visualization Studio; 196–197(bg) NASA/JPL/Cornell; 196–197 (l–r starting tl) 1.NASA, 2.NASA, (cr) NASA/Russian Space Research Institute (IKI), 4. NASA, 5.NASA, 6.NASA, 7.ESA/D.Ducros, 8.NASA/JPL/UA/Lockheed Martin/SPL, 9.NASA/JPL, 10. NASA; 198–199(bg); 203(br), (b); 205(cr), (br); 207(tl) ESA/NASA/JPL/University of Arizona, (tr) NASA/JPL/Space Science Institute; 208(b) NASA/Johns Hopkins University Applied Physics; Laboratory/Southwest Research Institute; 209(bc); 210–211(bg) NASA/JPL-Caltech/T. Pyle (SSC); 255(b) Nick Galante/PMRF/NASA; 292–293(bl) NASA Kennedy Space Center (NASA-KSC)
Nature Picture Library 9(b) Andy Rouse; 266(cl) Robin Chittenden; 301(b)
Newscom 301(tl) Album/Prisma
NHPA 306(c) Gerard Lacz; 308(cl) Theodore Clutter
Photolibrary 45(b) Laguna Design; 300(bg) Flirt Collection/Jim Zuckerman/Getty; 328(b) Spencer Grant/Getty
Photoshot 268–269(bg) UPPA
Reuters 173(tr) Kimimasa Mayama
Rex Features 87(cr) Jason Rasgon; 121(c); 191(tl); 199(br) NASA; 210(tl) Everett Collection; 210–211(c) Paramount/Everett; 211(b) KeystoneUSA-ZUMA; 264–265(c) Sipa Press; 270(bl) Ashley Cooper/SpecialistStock/SplashdownDirect; 275(tl) Claire Leimbach/Robert Harding; 282–283(bg) Charles M. Ommanney; 283(t) Curventa; 288–289(bg); 292–293(c) Everett Collection; 298–299(c); 299(b) Sipa Press; 309(tr) KeystoneUSA-ZUMA

383

ACKNOWLEDGEMENTS

Shutterstock.com 5(tl) qingqing, (br) takasu; 6(tr) Steve Bower, (bl) Gino Santa Maria; 7(br) Dja65; 8(bl) Triff, (tr) iurii; 9(cr) Richard Peterson, (br) Fedorov Oleksiy; 10(tr) Svetlana Foote, (bl) Dmitry Yashkin; 11(tr) Catmando; 12(bg) Alexander Raths; 14–15(bg) ssguy; 16–17(c) Sergey Lavrentev; 17(tr) Ljupco Smokovski; 18(tr) Vakhrushev Pavel, (bl) Ivonne Wierink; 18–19(bg) Deymos; 19(t) w shane dougherty; 20(tr) yuyangc; 22(bg) yxm2008; 23(b) Tatiana Makotra; 28(bg) asharkyu, (cr) Eimantas Buzas; 30–31(bg) vadim kozlovsky; 32(bc) Smileus; 32–33(bg) Gunnar Pippel; 33(cl) Ray Hub; 34(c) Sebastian Crocker; 35(br) Hywit Dimyadi; 36–37(bg) Archibald, (c) ifong; 39(tl), (cl), (bl), (br) Annette Shaff; 40(bg) Jaggat; 41(t) michael rubin; 42(bl) Jaochainoi; 48(tl) Kurhan, (br) Tamara Kulikova; 49(t) Alexander Raths, (bc) Kirsty Pargeter; 51(tr) wim claes, (b) indiangypsy; 52(bg) beerkoff; 55(tr) Morgan Lane Photography, (b) ssuaphotos; 56(bg) ktsdesign; 59(b) Cameramannz, (cr), (r), (br) kanate; 63(tr) happydancing, (br) Maridav; 64(tr); 65(tr) Janaka Dharmasena, (bl) Suzan Oschmann; 66(bg) basel101658, (tr) D. Kucharski & K. Kucharska, (cr) Jubal Harshaw, (br) happydancing; 67(bg) argus; 68(bg) Chepko Danil Vitalevich, (bl) testing; 69(bl), (tr) koya979; 70(b) & 71(bl) happydancing; 70–71(b) beboy; 71(tr) thoron; 72(bg) JonMilnes; 73(tl) Arturo Limon, (tc), (tr) bonchan, (t) Denis Selivanov, (bg) omer cicek, (br) fzd.it; 74–75(bg) Gunnar Pippel; 77(bg) Fotocrisis; 78(t), (b) argus; 79(t), (b) nuttakit; 86(bl) Lisa F. Young; 87(t) Andrey Yurlov, (bl) Linda Z Ryan; 90(bg) archibald, (c) Julien Tromeur; 96(tc) Marijus Auruskevicius; 97(tr) Maksym Gorpenyuk; 99(tl) Bernd Juergens, (br) Michael Stokes; 101(b) Orientaly; 103(br) Julija Sapic; 105(c) Oleg-F, (r) Kjersti Joergensen; 107(br) Darren Baker; 108(tl) lrafael; 109(tr) Thirteen; 110(cl) Alex Staroseltsev; 113(bl) K.L.Kohn; 114(bl) Geoffrey Kuchera; 115(t) Alexandru Chiriac; 116(tl) marekuliasz; 117(bl) Lim Yong Hian; 118(tl) alexnika; 119(cr); 120–121(c) Milan Vasicek, (bc) HitToon.Com; 121(br) Stephen Meese; 122(bl) Ew Chee Guan, (cr) Barry Barnes, (b) Pakhnyushcha; 123(br) Alexandr Kolupayev; 125(cl) Gordan, (bl) drfelice; 127(t) Maksym Bondarchuk, (bl) steamroller_blues, (br) Slaven; 128–129(bg) iurii; 136(tr) Andrea Danti; 141(tr) Shawn Hine; 166(c) Elisei Shafer; 166(cr) Incredible Arctic, (bc) javarman; 174(bg) Phase4Photography; 177–178(bg) surabky; 182–183(bg) & 186–187(bg) plavusa87; 183(cl) jamie cross; 188(bc) Shawn Hine; 204–205(bg); 212(c) McCarthy's PhotoWorks; 256(bg) LevanteMedia; 260(b) papkin; 261(c) Max Earey, (cr) JetKat; 262(l) nuttakit; 262–263(bg) Brian Weed, (c) somchaij; 263(br) Picsfive; 264(cl) Garsya, (bl) Edgaras Kurauskas; 265(tr) piyato; 266(br) Linali; 269(c) Ahmad Faizal Yahya; 271(bg) exclusive studio; 272(cl), (tr) Kraska; 273(c) Kraska, (br) Cathy Keifer; 274(cl) vesna cvorovic; 276(br) Andrey Yurlov; 277(tl) alexkar08; 278(bl) Ralf Siemieniec; 281(tr) Graham Bloomfield, (tl) Piyato; 283(c) Picsfive; 284(tl) Germanskydiver, (cr) Péter Gudella, (bg) MustafaNC, (b) sabri deniz kizil; 285(tr) dicogm, (tl) Pavel Kapish; 288(tl) Andrei Marincas; 289(c) somchaij; 293(tr) bedecs, (bg) argus; 294(bg) Benjamin Albiach Galan; 298(tr), (br) Andy Lidstone; 298–299(bg) Mark Carrel, (c) MalDix; 299(br) Andy Lidstone, (cr) donatas1205; 300(br) Brandelet; 301(bg) Ragnarock; 302(bg) kanate, (t–b) Rostislav Ageev, Christopher Elwell, FAUP, NatalieJean, Philip Lange, (bl) donatas1205; 303(bg) Mark Carrel, (caption bg) sharpner, (tiger, lion, caracal, cat, cheetah, fox, sea lion, gorilla, koala, frog) Eric Isselée, (weasel) Ronnie Howard, (wolf) Maxim Kulko, (bat) Kirsanov, (whale) Computer Earth, (rabbit) Stefan Petru Andronache, (polar bear) Ilya Akinshin, (hummingbird) Steffen Foerster Photography, (sailfish) holbox, (crocodile) fivespots, (dragonfly) Subbotina Anna, (frog) Arek Rainczuk, (snail) Sailorr, (eagle) Steve Collender, (starfish) Mircea Bezergheanu, (jellyfish) Khoroshunova Olga, (shark) Rich Carey, (snake) fivespots; 304(cr) Uryadnikov Sergey, (c) Mark Bridger, (bl) Paul Broadbent, (b), (cr) U.P.images_vector; 305(map) AridOcean, (globe) Anton Balazh, (bl) Stubblefield Photography; 305(tr) & 308(bl) & 316(bl) & 319(bl) & 323(tr) donatas1205; 307(bl) Anton Balazh; 311(cr) illustrart; 316–317(bg) Andre Mueller; 318–319(bg) Pakhnyushcha; 320(bg) Lucy Baldwin, (tr) FloridaStock; 323(bl), (b), (cr) sharpner; 324–325(bg) Mark Carrel, (c) saiko3p; 327(b) Dudarev Mikhail; 329(tl) Pasi Koskela; 330–331(bg) Pete Saloutos; 332–333(bg) jan kranendonk, (tl), (br) Fotoluminate LLC; 334–335(bg) casejustin; 337(tl) Kozlovskaya Ksenia; 338(bl) Lilya Espinosa; 339(bl) Stanislav Fridkin; 340(cr) Jeanne Hatch, (c) Felix Mizioznikov, (br) wong sze yuen; 341(cl) Steven Chiang, (br) Carmen Steiner; 344(cr) konmesa; 348(bl) Taranova; 348–349(bg) PILart; 349(tr) Jaren Jai Wicklund; 350(cr) JonMilnes; 352(cr) Lawrence Wee; 354(bc) Yuri Arcurs; 354–355(c) Elena Schweitzer; 360–361(bg) Sebastian Kaulitzki; 363(cl) beerkoff; 365(cl) Paul Matthew Photography; 367(tl) Elena Elisseeva; 371(tr) Patricia Marroquin

Science Photo Library 58–59(bg) Anakao Press/Look at Sciences; 75(bl) Peter Menzel; 80–81(bg) U.S. Navy; 83(bg) Mikkel Juul Jensen, (bl) Lawrence Livermore; 84(tr) Harvard College Observatory; 86–87(c) Jacopin; 89(t) Thomas Deerinck, NCMIR, (b) David Parker; 170(b) ESA, D. Ducros; 175(br) NASA; 181(tr) David Ducros; 183(r) David Parker; 191(tr) NASA; 192(bg) Detlev Van Ravensowaay; 194–195(c) NASA/JPL/UA/Lockheed Martin; 197(tr), (bg) NASA/JPL-Caltech; 200(t) SOHO/ESA/NASA; 201(tl) NASA; 202(cl) Chris Butler; 205(tr) NASA/JPL; 261(tr) NASA; 267(tr) David Parker; 279(br) NASA; 286–287(br) NASA; 287(cr) Peter Menzel; 296–297(bg) Mark Garlick; 298–299(cr); 310–311(bg) & 328(cl) Jose Antonio Peñas; 312(bg) & 316(tr)Christian Jegou Publiphoto Diffusion; 314(bl) Alan Sirulnikoff; 321(b) Jaime Chirinos; 322(cr) Christian Darkin; 324–325(c) Philippe Plailly/Eurelios; 327(cl) Philippe Psaila

Topfoto.co.uk 66(bl) & 69(bg) & 74(tr) The Granger Collection; 77(bl) The British Library/HIP; 79(t) World History Archive; 216(b) Roger-Viollet; 239(tc) Star Images; 243(tr) ImageWorks; 250–251(c); 254(b) keystone; 282(bl) UPP;

All other photographs are from:
Corel, digitalSTOCK, digitalvision, ImageState, John Foxx, PhotoAlto, PhotoDisc, PhotoEssentials, PhotoPro, Stockbyte

Every effort has been made to acknowledge the source and copyright holder of each picture.
Miles Kelly Publishing apologises for any unintentional errors or omissions.